Insiders 11-14

Ins  ce

LONGMAN

Contents

Biology

Introduction

What Inside Science does

- This book is a companion to the Science you will do at Key Stage 3 from Year 7 to Year 9. It breaks the course down into all the topic areas you will cover in school and explains all the most important ideas you need to understand..

- Each double-page spread covers one Science topic. Each spread is organised in the same way. The information on each spread will give you a clear guide to that topic.

- The format guide on pages vi and vii will show you how each topic works.

- Each spread starts with an introduction to the topic and finishes with a summary of the key points.

- At the end of every topic there is a question section. The A questions are quick questions which you can use to check your understanding of the topic. The B questions need more detailed answers and will help you with all aspects of that topic. You can use the C questions to take your understanding further and to help you find out more about that topic.

How Inside Science can help you

- The book will help you with your Science homework by providing all the essential information on every Science topic for you to refer to and to help you understand the work.

- You can also use the book to help you with your classwork. When you cover a topic in school you can use the book to help you with any problems and to give you a better understanding of that topic. It can also help you with any work that you miss.

- The book will help you with revision for tests by providing all the key information you will need to learn. The summaries on every spread will remind you of the key points you need to know and you can use the questions in Sections A and B to check that you understand these key ideas.

Inside Science and the National Curriculum

Science in the National Curriculum

The National Curriculum describes the Science you will learn in school. Science is split up into four 'Attainment Targets'. These four attainment targets are:

Sc1 Experimental and Investigative Science

This attainment target is about practical work and investigations which you carry out at school. It aims to make sure that you learn how to plan and carry out experiments and analyse your results. This Attainment Target is not tested at the end of Year 9: you will be given a level for Sc1 by your teachers based on investigations you have carried out at school.

Sc2 Life Processes and Living Things

Some of the topics covered in Sc2 include the human body and how it works, cells, how plants grow and reproduce, how living things change from one generation to the next, and the environment.

Sc3 Materials and their Properties

This covers topics such as ways of describing and classifying materials, physical changes and different kinds of chemical reactions, acids and bases, and how rocks are formed and changed.

Sc4 Physical Processes

These topics include electricity and magnetism, forces and motion, light and sound, the Solar System, and energy resources and energy transfer.

This book covers Attainment Targets 2, 3 and 4. You can use it throughout Key Stage 3 to help you understand the course and to help you with your homework and your classwork.

Inside Science and the Key Stage 3 Tests

What are the Key Stage 3 Tests?

Science, Maths and English are the core subjects of the National Curriculum. The government tests all students in these subjects at the ages of 7, 11 and 14. You will sit these National Tests in May during Year 9. The tests for Science will cover all the work you have done for Attainment Targets 2, 3 and 4, described above.

When the tests are marked by external markers (not your teacher) you will be given a 'level' for your work. The levels you reach in the Key Stage 3 tests are sent to your parents and the overall results for each school are also published in the form of league tables.

What are Levels?

The National Curriculum gives teachers a way of measuring your achievement by describing eight different 'levels' for each attainment target. The levels describe the kind of knowledge and understanding you should have at each level. In Science you should be working at a level between 3 and 7 at the end of Key Stage 3, although some students might achieve Level 8 or even the ninth, 'Exceptional Performance' level.

What are Teacher Assessments?

Your teachers will measure your progress in Science towards the end of Year 9, and give you a level for the work and tests you have done in school. These teacher assessment levels are also put on the report that is sent to your parents.

How can I use this book for revision?

As well as helping you throughout Years 7, 8 and 9, you can use this book to help you with your revision for the tests.

Everybody has their own way of revising before tests and examinations, and you should revise in a way that suits you. You can use the summaries and quick Section A questions on every spread to check how much you are remembering and to quickly test your basic understanding of a topic.

You might also like to try these ideas:

● Cover up the summary on a spread and read the rest of the spread carefully, then try to write a short list of the important points on the spread. Check your list against the summary to see if you have come up with the same things.

● Go straight to the questions on a spread, and try to answer as many as possible of the Section A and Section B questions without looking at the rest of the spread. When you have answered as many as possible look at the spread and check your answers yourself before looking at the answers in the back of the book.

How this book works

Refraction

These pages are about bending light and making coloured light.

intro

Light normally travels in straight lines.
You can make light bend by using a piece of glass.

Refraction

When light bends like this it is called **refraction**.

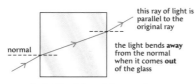

this ray of light is parallel to the original ray

the light bends **away** from the normal when it comes **out** of the glass

normal

the light bends **towards** the normal when it goes **into** the glass

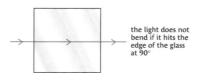

the light does not bend if it hits the edge of the glass at 90°

The same thing happens when light goes into clear plastic or into water. You can see this for yourself.

Using refraction

Lenses are pieces of glass or plastic which have been shaped so that they will bend light in a particular way.

Converging lenses make a beam of light converge to a point. Converging lenses are used in telescopes and binoculars to make distant things look bigger. They are also used in microscopes which make small things look bigger.

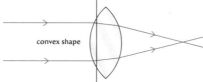

convex shape

Diverging lenses make a beam of light spread out

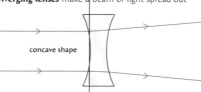

concave shape

Many people need spectacles or contact lenses to help them to see clearly. Some people need diverging lenses and other people need converging lenses. The kind of lens they need depends on what is wrong with their eyes.

Making coloured light

The normal light that comes from the Sun or from light bulbs is called **white light**. White light is really a mixture of different colours of light. When all the colours of light go into your eyes at once your brain tells you that the colour is white.

There are seven colours in the **spectrum** th makes up white light. The colours are red, o yellow, green, blue, indigo and violet.

Prisms are triangular blocks of glass. A prism be used to help you to see the colours in wh

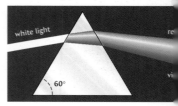

white light

re

vi

60°

This 60 degree prism is being used to split of light so you can see the colours of the sp This happens because the prism bends the colours by different amounts.

You can also see the spectrum by looking at playing side of a CD.

Rainbows are formed when there are tiny c of water in the air. Sunlight is split up into colours by the drops of water.

You can remember lists of things by making their initial letters into a sentence. The first letters of the wo in this sentence are the same as th letters of the colours in the spectru

Richard Of York Gave Battle In Vai Some people prefer to remember t colours using the name **ROY G BIV**

120

For more information about colour see pages 12

Introduction
This gives you a starting-point for the topic and some of the ideas that you will want to think about first.

Learning objectives
This box tells you what part of your course is covered in this topic. It is your quick guide to the content of the two pages.

Cross-references
This box provides you with links to other pages where you can find out more about ideas contained in this topic. This box is not used in all topics.

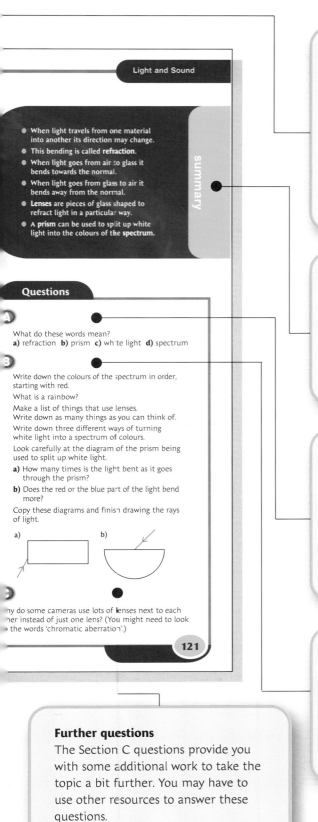

Light and Sound

summary

- When light travels from one material into another its direction may change.
- This bending is called **refraction**.
- When light goes from air to glass it bends towards the normal.
- When light goes from glass to air it bends away from the normal.
- **Lenses** are pieces of glass shaped to refract light in a particular way.
- A **prism** can be used to split up white light into the colours of the **spectrum**.

Questions

A

What do these words mean?
a) refraction b) prism c) white light d) spectrum

B

Write down the colours of the spectrum in order, starting with red.

What is a rainbow?

Make a list of things that use lenses. Write down as many things as you can think of.

Write down three different ways of turning white light into a spectrum of colours.

Look carefully at the diagram of the prism being used to split up white light.

a) How many times is the light bent as it goes through the prism?

b) Does the red or the blue part of the light bend more?

Copy these diagrams and finish drawing the rays of light.

a)   b)

C

Why do some cameras use lots of lenses next to each other instead of just one lens? (You might need to look up the words 'chromatic aberration'.)

121

Interesting Facts and Helpful Hints

This box is a Helpful Hint box. It gives you a special tip or some extra ideas to help you with the topic.

Another box you will see from time to time is the Interesting Fact box. It has a symbol which looks like this:

Summary

The Summary gives you a checklist of all the key points on the topic. You can use it while you are working on the topic to check that you have understood the work, or you can use it when you revise as a guide to the main points.

Quick questions

The questions in Section A are quick questions. You can use them to quickly test that you understand the topic either when you cover it during your course or when you revise. The first question always asks you about the meaning of certain key words.

Main questions

The Section B questions are your main question resource. These questions cover the different areas of the topic and allow you to check that you can answer questions about all these different areas.

Further questions

The Section C questions provide you with some additional work to take the topic a bit further. You may have to use other resources to answer these questions.

Inside Science

Cells in Animals and Plants

All living things, or **organisms**, are made up of **cells**. Some tiny organisms, like bacteria, consist of only one cell. Your body is made of millions of cells, and these cells all work together to keep you alive.

These pages are about cells and how they work together.

Animal cells

cytoplasm – where chemical changes happen, the 'factory' of the cell

cell membrane – controls substances passing in and out; keeps the cell in shape

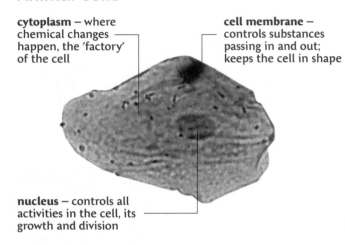

nucleus – controls all activities in the cell, its growth and division

This photo shows a cell taken from the inside of a person's mouth.

The cheek cell is an example of an **animal cell**. There are lots of different kinds of cell in your body, but nearly all of them have a **nucleus**, a **membrane** and **cytoplasm**.

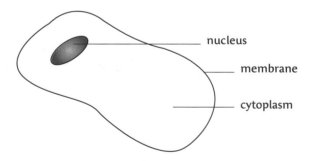

nucleus

membrane

cytoplasm

The nucleus controls what happens in the cell.

The membrane is like a thin skin around the outside of the cell. It holds the cytoplasm together, and it controls chemicals going into or out of the cell.

The cytoplasm is a liquid containing chemicals and **organelles**. Organelles are small particles that do particular jobs in the cell (like the nucleus). The chemical reactions that keep the cell alive and doing its job all happen in the cytoplasm.

Plant cells

Most **plant cells** have a nucleus, a membrane and cytoplasm, but they also have a **cell wall**, a **vacuole** and **chloroplasts**.

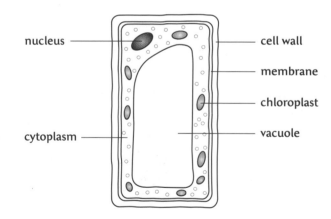

nucleus

cell wall

membrane

chloroplast

cytoplasm

vacuole

The cell wall is made of **cellulose**, which is a non-living substance. It is stiff and hard, and helps to protect and support the cell. The cell membrane is usually pressed against the inside of the cell wall.

Chloroplasts are organelles containing a green chemical called **chlorophyll**, which makes food for the plant using energy from sunlight.

The vacuole is a space in the middle of the cell filled with a watery liquid. The cell can store chemicals in the vacuole. Water pressure inside the vacuole helps to keep plant stems stiff.

Most animal cells are about 100 micrometres across. This means that ten cells end to end would only measure one millimetre. Some cells in your body are very long. For instance a nerve cell that stretches from your brain to your stomach could be nearly a metre long.

Tissues, organs and systems

Groups of cells work together. A group of similar cells is called a **tissue**. For instance, a group of muscle cells forms muscle tissue, and a group of skin cells forms skin tissue.

Different kinds of tissue make up **organs**. Your heart is an organ that is made of muscle and nerve tissue, and pumps blood around your body. Some of the other organs in your body are your brain, your stomach, your eyes and your lungs.

Some organs work together as part of a **system**. Your mouth, stomach, and intestines work together to digest your food. This group of organs is called your **digestive system**. Your **circulatory system** transports blood around your body, and your **excretory system** gets rid of waste.

summary

- All living **organisms** are made of **cells**.
- Cells contain smaller structures called **organelles**.
- **Animal cells** usually have a **nucleus**, a **membrane** and **cytoplasm**.
- **Plant cells** usually have a **cell wall**, **chloroplasts** and a **vacuole** as well as a nucleus, membrane and cytoplasm.
- A group of similar cells is called a **tissue**.
- Different tissues make up **organs**.
- Organs work together as part of a **system**.

Questions

 A

1 What do these words mean?
   a) organism
   b) cell
   c) organelle
   d) tissue
   e) organ
   f) system
2 Which three things do most animal cells have?
3 Which three things do most plant cells have that animal cells do not have?

 B

1 What do these parts of an animal cell do?
   a) nucleus
   b) membrane
   c) cytoplasm
2 What do these parts of a plant cell do?
   a) cell wall
   b) chloroplasts
   c) vacuole
3 Why do plants go limp when they are short of water?

 C

Find out how nerve cells are specialised to do their job.

For more information about how plants make food see pages 28-29

Leaves and their Cells

intro

Green leaves make food for plants. They collect energy from sunlight and use it to make food by **photosynthesis**. Leaves are often exposed to strong sunshine and dry winds.

These pages are about the leaves and their part in photosynthesis.

Leaves

Leaves are arranged on the stems of plants in such a way that they can catch the sunlight. Some of this light is **reflected** from the leaf surface. Some passes through the leaf and some is trapped by it.

On any leaf you can see lines making a pattern. These lines are the **veins** which take food away from the leaf into the body of the plant and also bring large amounts of water to the leaf from the roots.

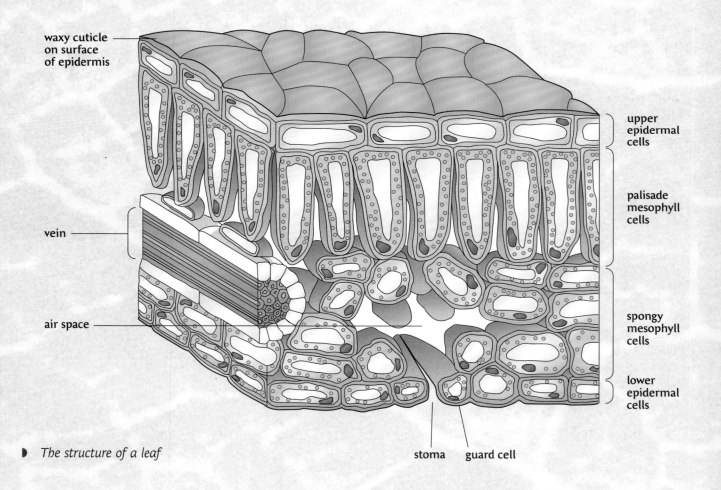

waxy cuticle on surface of epidermis

vein

air space

upper epidermal cells

palisade mesophyll cells

spongy mesophyll cells

lower epidermal cells

stoma   guard cell

▶ *The structure of a leaf*

The surface of a leaf may look shiny. This is because there is a waxy layer on the surface, called the **cuticle**. This stops the leaf drying out in the sun. **Water vapour** and other gases can get in and out of a leaf through tiny holes which can be opened and closed. The holes are called **stomata** (the singular of stomata is **stoma**). Each one leads into a space inside the leaf. These holes can be opened or closed by two **guard cells** around each stoma.

All parts of the plant are made of cells. The leaf cells vary in size and shape. The diagram shows the cells inside a leaf. The cells on the edges are called **epidermal** cells. Inside are the **mesophyll** cells. Some of these are shaped like columns and are closely packed together (**palisade mesophyll** cells), while others have lots of air spaces around them so that they look like a sponge. These are **spongy mesophyll** cells.

Leaves are green in colour because of a chemical called **chlorophyll**. This is held in organelles called **chloroplasts**. Chlorophyll traps sunlight. Most chloroplasts are found in the cells near the top of the leaf so these are the cells where most photosynthesis takes place. Chloroplasts move from place to place inside the cell. When the light is dim, the chloroplasts move towards the tops of the cells.

How do you think climbing plants manage to climb up fences or trellises? They use **tendrils** to do this.

A tendril is a long, thin leaf that reaches out, wraps around any solid object it touches and then coils up like a spring so that it holds on tight. This helps the plant to climb up a support like a fence.

- Plants make food using energy from the Sun. This process is called **photosynthesis**.
- Most photosynthesis happens in the leaves of plants.
- Leaf cells have lots of **chloroplasts**, which contain a green chemical called chlorophyll.
- Water vapour and gases get into and out of leaves through small holes called **stomata**.
- **Veins** bring water to the leaf and take food away to the rest of the plant.

summary

Questions

 A

1. What do these words mean?
   a) mesophyll b) cuticle
   c) stomata d) chlorophyll
   e) tendril f) epidermis
   g) reflection

 B

1. What are the jobs of the leaf veins?
2. What is the difference between chlorophyll and chloroplast?
3. How do gases get into and out of leaves?
4. In a leaf where does most photosynthesis take place?

 C

Look at some plants and their leaves.
a) Draw the shapes of the leaves and the pattern of their veins.
b) Find how scientists describe the shapes, patterns and edges of leaves.

For more information see pages 6–7, 28–29, 30–31, 118–119, and 122–123

Chemicals in Living Things

intro

The cells of all **organisms** are made from **elements**. These elements are linked together to form different **compounds** which can be divided into seven groups. These seven groups are **water**, **proteins**, **carbohydrates**, **lipids**, **minerals**, **vitamins** and **nucleic acids**.

These pages are about the chemicals in living things and the way we use them.

Element	Chemical symbol	% of body weight
oxygen	O	65.0
carbon	C	18.0
hydrogen	H	10.0
nitrogen	N	3.0
calcium	Ca	1.5
phosphorous	P	1.0
others	–	1.5

Compounds in living things

meat 65% water

potato 80% water

cabbage 95% water

Water is used to carry dissolved chemicals around inside the body of an animal or plant. Water also helps to keep land animals and plants cool and carry out life processes.

The living tissues of animals and plants are made from **protein**, so protein is needed for the growth and repair of the cells. Without proteins, animals and plants cannot grow and would die. Proteins form **enzymes** (see page 11).

Carbohydrates are packed with energy. Animals and plants use the energy stored in carbohydrates as fuel for their cells. Sugar and starch are both forms of carbohydrate.

Lipids are used in many ways. **Fats** and **oils** are lipids which store energy. They are stored inside animals to help to keep them warm. **Waxes** are lipids that make waterproof coatings on the outside of organisms.

Vitamins and **minerals** are needed to control body processes. Animals get most of the vitamins and minerals they need from their food. Plants can make vitamins and also take in minerals from the soil or water around them.

Nucleic acids, like DNA and RNA, are found in the cell nucleus.

Plants can make their own proteins, lipids and carbohydrates using chemicals from the air and the soil.

The chemicals needed by animals and people come from the food they eat. Some animals (**herbivores**) eat only plants, others (**carnivores**) eat only other animals, and there are some who eat a mixed diet (**omnivores**). Most people are omnivores.

Did you know that if all the water was removed from a man who weighs 76 kg, his dried body would weigh 19 kg? This is because most of every cell is water. Even a peanut is one-tenth water.

If you want to know more about all the different vitamins and minerals you need to take in each day, have a look at the nutritional information on a packet of breakfast cereal.

Using plants

Because plants are a source of food, people **cultivate** (grow) them as crops. Today many crops are **cereals** which are grain-bearing plants like wheat and rice. The grains (seeds) are processed. Wheat grains are ground into flour which can be made into bread, cakes, spaghetti and breakfast cereal. Other parts of the grain are used to make bran and animal food. Grass is also used for animal food. Some specially made animal foods are mixed from soya beans, cotton seeds and linseed oil which are all produced by plants.

People use plants in many other ways. Chemicals from plants can be used to make drugs, dyes and other products such as soap. Fibres from cotton and flax plants can be woven into cloth. Wood from trees can be made into paper, furniture and planks used in building or burned as fuel. Rubber is made from latex (sap) from rubber trees.
Coal and oil were once plants too!

Most of the cells in your body have a nucleus containing DNA. There are about 2.5 metres of DNA in each cell! A DNA molecule has a spiral shape called a double helix.

- Living organisms contain chemicals which can be sorted into seven groups.
- Plants can make all the compounds they need except minerals.
- Animals get most of the compounds they need from their food.
- People use the chemicals found in plants in many different ways.

summary

Questions

 A

1 What do these words mean?
   a) herbivore
   b) carnivore
   c) omnivore

2 Name the seven groups of compounds found in living things.

3 Name three different kinds of lipid.

 B

1 **a)** Why are proteins needed by living things?
   b) What do plants and animals use carbohydrates for?
   c) Describe two ways that lipids are used by living things.
   d) Why are vitamins and minerals needed?

2 **a)** Where do animals get vitamins and minerals from?
   b) Where do plants get their vitamins and minerals from?

3 How are cereals used?

4 List as many ways that humans use plants as you can think of.

 C

A cucumber is thought to be 90% water. If you were given a number of fresh cucumber slices, how would you find out if this was true?

For more information see pages 8–9 and 58–59

Nutrients, Vitamins and Minerals

Nutrition means getting the right sorts of foods to stay healthy and keep cells growing. All animals eat food to stay alive. People eat food that comes from other animals (meat, fish, eggs) and from plants (vegetables, cereals and fruits). The range of foods you eat is your **diet**. We have an **omnivorous** diet.

These pages are about the chemical nutrients in your food and the effects some of them have on your body.

Food

A food is something which does one or more of these things:

- it gives your body energy
- it supplies materials that can be used in the growth and repair of your body
- it supplies certain chemicals that help to control important life activities in your body.

Nutrients

Scientists study foods to find out how they are used. They sort the foods into groups. The best way to group foods is by the **chemicals** they have in them. These chemicals are **nutrients** and your body needs about 45 of them. These nutrients are put into six groups, **proteins, carbohydrates, lipids, water, minerals** and **vitamins**. No matter how much food is eaten, a person will only stay alive if the right amounts of these nutrients are eaten regularly. If you eat the wrong amounts of nutrients, you will become **malnourished**. If you eat too much energy-giving food, you may become overweight or **obese**. In the developing world many people do not get enough food and they become **under-nourished**.

Minerals and vitamins

If you burn food, you are left with a dark grey ash. There are many elements in this ash. Some of them are metals and some are non-metals but they are grouped together as inorganic **minerals**. They are used to help to build up parts of the body and to keep the way it works under control. People need some minerals in large amounts. A 12-year-old boy needs 700 milligrams (mg) of calcium and 13 mg of iron each day for healthy growth. Other minerals, called **trace elements**, are only needed in very tiny amounts.

	Use in body	Adult daily requirement
Mineral		
Calcium	hardens bones and teeth, needed for muscles, helps blood to clot	about 700 mg
Fluorine	hardens bones and teeth	0.7 parts per million in water
Iron	helps the blood to transport oxygen	13–16 mg
Magnesium	bone structure, control of nerve and muscle action	about 13 mg
Potassium	needed for muscles and nerves	1–2 mg
Sodium	needed for nerves to work, controls the amount of water in cells and blood	about 6 g
Vitamin		
A (carotene)	keeps skin healthy and helps sight	5000 international units (IU)
B (thiamine)	needed so the body can use energy from food	1.5 mg
C (ascorbic acid)	needed for healthy flesh, teeth and bones	75 mg
D_3 (calciferol)	needed for strong bones	400 IU
E (tocopherol)	helps blood clotting	not known
K (naphthoquinone)	blood clotting	not known

intro

Vitamins are also needed in small amounts. They help to control chemical processes in the body.

If someone's **diet** is lacking in one of the main groups of nutrients, they will suffer from a **deficiency disease**. Someone suffering from **scurvy** will be very weak, will bleed inside their body and at the gums and hair roots, and any wound will take a long time to heal. If scurvy is not treated, the sufferer will die.

We know that citrus fruit, like oranges and limes, contains the vitamins needed to prevent scurvy. If this vitamin is missing from your diet, you will develop scurvy. This vitamin is **ascorbic acid** or **vitamin C**

summary

- Foods give the body energy, supply the materials needed for growth and repair and help to control the body's activities.
- Foods are grouped by the **nutrients** they contain.
- A person is **malnourished** if they have too little or too much food or eat the wrong kinds of food.
- A shortage of any mineral or vitamin causes a **deficiency disease**.

Food source	Effect of too little
dairy products, eggs, fish, soya-beans, leaves of sweet potato, cocoyam	weak or brittle bones
milk, toothpaste	tooth decay
liver, eggs, red meat, beans, groundnuts, plantain, raisins, cocoa	anaemia
green vegetables, milk, meat	muscles do not work properly
all foods, expecially meats, vegetables, milk	heart and other muscles may not work properly
most foods, table salt	dehydration, muscle cramps, kidney failure
egg yolk, green or yellow vegetables, e.g. sweet potatoes; fruits, e.g. mango, liver, butter, palm oil	night blindness, skin sores
brain, liver, kidney, heart, whole grains, yeast, eggs, spinach, beans, groundnuts	various diseases, including heart failure
fresh fruits, raw vegetables, tomatoes, sweet potatoes	scurvy
fish oils, liver, milk; formed beneath the skin in sunlight	rickets (soft bones)
green leafy vegetables, whole grains, cottonseed oil	fewer red blood cells and anaemia
liver, leafy vegetables; made by intestinal bacteria	blood may not clot

For more information on chemicals see pages 6–7 and 58–59

Questions

1 What do these words mean?
a) nutrition b) omnivorous c) diet
d) deficiency disease e) vitamin f) food
g) malnourishment h) mineral i) obese

1 What happens to the body if the diet contains:
a) no vitamin A b) no calcium c) no iron?

2 Name one food source of:
a) vitamin A and magnesium
b) vitamin K and potassium.

3 List the vitamins and minerals contained in:
a) eggs b) fish

4 Why are people living in hot, sunny countries unlikely to suffer from a shortage of vitamin D in their diet?

Find out about:
a) how your body uses proteins, lipids and carbohydrates
b) the effect on the human body if the diet contains very little protein.

Guts and Food

intro

All animals must eat food so that they can survive.
The nutrients in food must be soluble so that they can move
from the gut into the blood and be carried around the body.
To dissolve nutrients, the body has to break down the large nutrient
molecules into smaller ones. This is **digestion**.

These pages are about what happens to food after you swallow it.

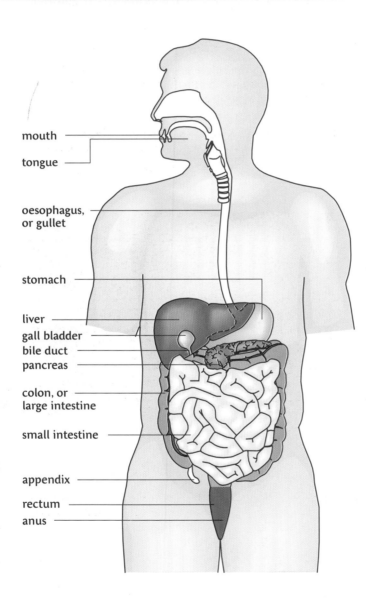

mouth

tongue

oesophagus, or gullet

stomach

liver
gall bladder
bile duct
pancreas

colon, or large intestine

small intestine

appendix

rectum

anus

How are big molecules broken up?

Big molecules are broken into smaller ones by special proteins called **enzymes**, found in **digestive juices**. Digestive juices are made by **glands**, and pass along tubes called **ducts** into the space inside the gut.

The story of a sandwich

The first part of digestion happens in your **mouth**. Your teeth chop up food into small pieces, and it is mixed with **saliva**. Your sandwich is now a soft, sticky ball. The saliva contains enzymes that start to break up large starch molecules.

The balls of food travel down your **oesophagus** into your **stomach**. Cells in the wall of your stomach produce **hydrochloric acid** and enzymes, which are churned up with the food. Your sandwich is now an acidic, watery liquid.

More enzymes get added to the food in the small intestine. The liver produces a green fluid called **bile** which helps to break up fats. The **pancreas** produces more enzymes which are added to the food. As it travels through the small intestine, small molecules made from the large molecules in the food are absorbed through the wall of the intestine and go into the blood. Your sandwich is now just the indigestible fibre and water.

This liquid passes through the **colon**, or **large intestine**, where the water in it is absorbed back into the body. All that is left now is the solid waste that passes through the **rectum** and out of the **anus**. This waste material is called **faeces**.

Enzymes

Enzymes are grouped according to the type of nutrient they help to digest. The nutrient that an enzyme works on is the **substrate**. The smaller, soluble, food molecules that are made are the **products**. There are three main groups of digestive enzymes. Their substrates and products are shown in the table. (The names of most enzymes end in '**ase**'.) Cellulase digests cellulose.

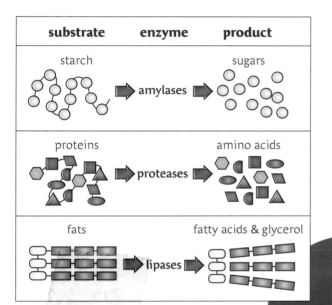

substrate	enzyme	product
starch	amylases	sugars
proteins	proteases	amino acids
fats	lipases	fatty acids & glycerol

When you eat a slice of bread you put a lot of starch into your gut. **Amylases** start breaking up the starch into sugar. After a short time all the starch has gone because it has been broken down into sugar. At first there was no sugar in the gut. At the end of the reaction there is a lot of sugar.

All enzymes are made from **proteins** and proteins can be damaged easily. If an enzyme is damaged it will not work. Enzymes are affected by heat. They work best and quickest at 37°C (body temperature). This is the **optimum** or best temperature. At cooler temperatures they work more slowly. If enzymes are heated to 60°C or above they do not work at all.

All enzymes are damaged by **acids** and **alkalis**. Each enzyme is designed to work at a certain level of acidity. If the acidity level changes, an enzyme will work more slowly.

- Food must be digested before the nutrients can move from the gut into the blood.
- Large molecules are broken down into smaller ones by proteins called enzymes.
- Food passes through the mouth, oesophagus, stomach and small intestine.
- Waste material passes through the colon, rectum and the anus.
- Enzymes act on a substrate and make products.
- Enzymes work best at their optimum temperature, and at a particular level of acidity.

summary

Questions

A

1 What do these words mean?
a) enzymes b) digestion
c) gland d) duct
e) substrate f) product
g) optimum temperature

2 What do these parts of the digestive system do?
a) mouth b) stomach
c) small intestine
d) large intestine

B

1 Many vitamins and minerals dissolve in water. Explain why these nutrients do not need to be digested.

2 Some diseases such as cholera force food to 'run' through your gut very quickly. Why do people with cholera often suffer from dehydration?

3 Plan an experiment to show that amylase in your saliva breaks down starch to sugars best at 37°C.

(*Hint* – starch solution turns blue-black when you add iodine; sugar solution does not.)

C

Find out which parts of the digestive system produce these enzymes:
a) amylases
b) lipases
c) proteases

For more information about foods see pages 6–7

The Skeleton, Muscles and Movement

Bones give a framework to your body, but the **muscles** which cover the bones give your body its final shape. You have about 650 muscles and they make up about four tenths of your weight. Every movement you make is controlled by different muscles working together.

These pages are about muscles and the way they move the joints of the skeleton.

intro

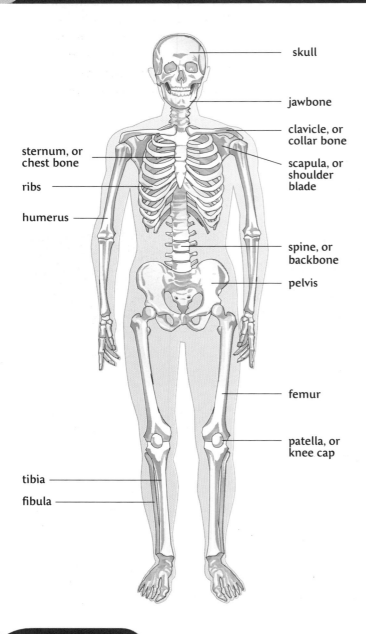

- skull
- jawbone
- clavicle, or collar bone
- scapula, or shoulder blade
- sternum, or chest bone
- ribs
- humerus
- spine, or backbone
- pelvis
- femur
- patella, or knee cap
- tibia
- fibula

The skeleton

You have 206 bones in your body. Each one is joined to another one and, together, they make up your skeleton. The skeleton not only gives your body its shape, it also supports you and protects organs such as your heart, lungs and brain. You can only bend or move your body at **joints**, the places where two or more bones meet.

Muscles

Muscles are made of cylindrical cells called **muscle fibres**. These cells can be several centimetres long. Muscles can **contract** (shorten). A single muscle often contains lots of fibres and these give the muscle its strength. Muscle fibres get the energy they need to contract from **respiration**. Most muscle fibres contract when they are triggered by **nerves**.

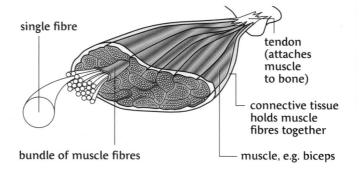

single fibre

tendon (attaches muscle to bone)

connective tissue holds muscle fibres together

bundle of muscle fibres

muscle, e.g. biceps

Muscles can pull but they cannot push. Even when you push against a wall or push open a door, your muscles are working by **pulling**. To be able to work only by pulling, muscles have to be arranged in pairs. As one muscle contracts, gets shorter and pulls on a bone, another muscle **relaxes** or returns to its normal length.

Moving your arm

Your **biceps** muscle contracts to bend your arm while the **triceps** muscle at the back of your arm relaxes. If you simply relax the biceps, your arm will stay bent. To straighten it again, you have to contract the triceps. This pulls the bone the other way. The action of one muscle is opposed to the other. They work together as an **antagonistic pair**.

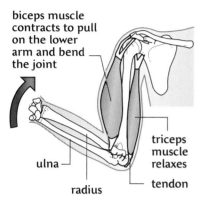

biceps muscle contracts to pull on the lower arm and bend the joint

ulna

radius

triceps muscle relaxes

tendon

antagonistic pair of muscles

biceps muscle relaxes

triceps muscle contracts to pull on the lower arm and straighten the joint

 The muscles that bend your arm

If you don't work a muscle often enough, it becomes thin and weak. Astronauts working in space are weightless. Their muscles only have to do a little work to move their bodies. When astronaut Michael Foale returned to Earth in October 1997, after three months in space, his muscles were so weak that he couldn't walk! His first journey back on Earth was in a wheelchair.

- Muscles are made of cells, called **fibres**, which can **contract**.
- Muscles move **joints** by pulling on a bone on one side of the joint.
- Muscles can only pull, so movement is caused when a pair of muscles (an **antagonistic pair**) work in opposition to each other.

summary

Questions

A

1 What do these words mean?
a) muscle b) contract
c) skeleton d) joint
e) tendon f) antagonistic muscles

2 Copy out the following sentences and fill the gaps.
When the forearm is _____, the radius and ulna move upwards towards the shoulder. They are pulled in this direction when the biceps _____. At the same time, the triceps _____. Muscles that work in this way are called _____.

B

1 a) How is muscle connected to bone?
b) What surrounds the bundles of fibres in a muscle?

2 Where do muscles get the energy they need to work?

3 Move each of these parts of your body:
- your arm at the shoulder
- your arm at the elbow
- your first finger.

a) How is the movement of the shoulder different from the elbow?

b) How is the movement of the first finger the same as the elbow?

C

1 Find a diagram of the skeleton. Draw and name the bones in your:
a) arm b) leg
c) chest and abdomen
d) head and neck.

2 Find out about fixed joints, ball and socket joints, and where they occur in your body.

For more information about muscle movement see pages 20–21

Blood and Circulation

Your **circulatory system** is a network of tubes which carries blood round and round your body and delivers it to the cells. The blood is pumped through the tubes by your heart. When it is in contact with air, human blood looks like a thick, red juice, but it is really a yellow liquid called **plasma** with different cells floating in it.

These pages are about blood and the way it is moved from one part of your body to another.

The **cells** in the **organs** and **tissues** of large animals cannot move to gather their own food and they cannot get rid of their waste easily. They rely on the blood circulating round the body to bring **nutrients** and **oxygen** to them and to take away waste. Blood also circulates heat throughout the body and helps to fight off **microbes** that may enter the body and cause disease.

The circulation of blood

In humans, the pumping action of the heart keeps blood circulating around the body in a network of branching tubes and in a **one-way system**. The heart is really two pumps working side by side. Each pump has an upper space called an **atrium**, which takes blood in, and a lower space, called the **ventricle,** which pumps blood out. The right side pumps blood to the lungs and the left side pumps **oxygenated** blood (blood containing oxygen) to the body.

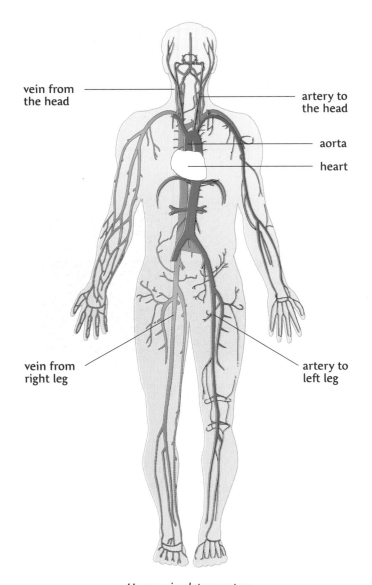

Human circulatory system
This diagram shows the major blood vessels in the human circulatory system. On the left side of the diagram the veins (blue) are shown, and on the right side of the diagram the arteries (red) are shown.

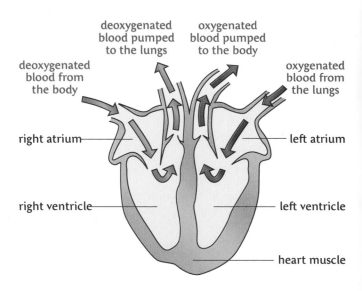

The tubes that carry the blood away from the ventricles are **arteries**. The tubes that bring blood to the atria are **veins.** An artery has a thick muscular wall which can stretch and contract with every heart beat, creating a **pulse**. You can feel your own pulse at your wrist or neck. An adult person's pulse (and therefore the heart) beats about 70 times every minute when the person is sitting quietly.

Capillaries

When an artery reaches an organ, it divides into finer and finer branches. The smallest branches are as fine as a human hair, and are called **capillaries**.

Capillaries have very thin walls. Substances can pass back and forward through the walls into and out of nearby cells. After flowing through the capillaries, blood enters the veins. The veins have thinner walls than the arteries and they also have **valves** to prevent blood flowing the wrong way.

All arteries take blood away from the heart.
All veins take blood back to the heart.

Your heart is about the size of a clenched fist. It pumps blood through 80 000 km of blood vessels every day. During your life, it will beat about 25 000 million times. Blood makes up about 10% of your body mass and an adult has between 4 and 6 litres of blood.

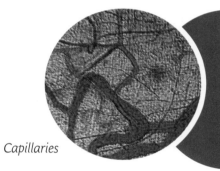

▶ *Capillaries*

summary

- Blood transports substances to and from the cells of the body.
- Blood is moved along **arteries** by the pumping of the heart.
- Blood flows along a **one-way route**.
- **Capillaries** carry blood through organs where substances are exchanged.
- Blood travels back to the heart along **veins**.
- The heart is two pumps. The right side of the heart pumps blood to the lungs. The left side pumps blood to the rest of the body.

Questions

1 What do these words mean?
   a) artery **b)** vein **c)** capillary
   d) heart **e)** atrium
   f) ventricle **g)** plasma

2 List the jobs that the blood does.

1 Copy and complete the table.

2 List the parts through which blood passes as it goes from the right atrium to the left ventricle.

3 If a pulse beats 70 times in a minute, how many times does the heart beat in that time?

1 By counting the number of beats in one minute, find out what happens to your pulse when you are seated, standing, lying down and after exercise.

2 Find out about:
   a) the names and jobs of the valves in the heart
   b) the sounds made by the heart when it beats
   c) blood pressure
   d) the valves in the veins.

	Artery	Vein	Capillary
Thickness of wall			
Direction of blood flow (e.g. away from heart)			

For more information about circulation see pages 20–21

Growing Up and Puberty

As boys and girls grow, their bodies increase in size and they get taller. Other changes also take place so that they will be able to **reproduce**. These changes are brought about by **hormones** which begin to be made inside the body at **puberty**.

These pages are about the way the body of a boy or a girl changes as they mature.

Puberty and adolescence

As you grow, parts of your body grow at different speeds. One time of fast growth is at **puberty**, which is when your body becomes sexually **mature**. This means that you are able to **reproduce** (have children). The physical changes that happen to your body during puberty are controlled by special chemicals called **hormones**. The way the levels of hormones change at puberty can mix up your emotions. During puberty and for a few years afterwards, a teenager's behaviour changes. This time is called **adolescence**.

Male puberty

For boys puberty usually starts at around 11 or 12 years of age. The following changes occur:

- Start to produce male **gametes** (sex cells), called **sperm**, and a hormone called **testosterone**, in the **testes**
- Penis grows larger and hair grows around the sex organs
- Voice becomes deeper
- Hair grows under the arms and on the chest and face.

Female puberty

For girls puberty usually starts at around 9 or 10 years of age. As for boys, puberty may start earlier or later without there being anything to worry about. The following changes occour:

- Start to release female gametes, called **ova** (or eggs) and hormones called **oestrogen** and **progesterone**, from the **ovaries**
- The nipples, breasts, hips and buttocks change
- Hair grows under the arms.

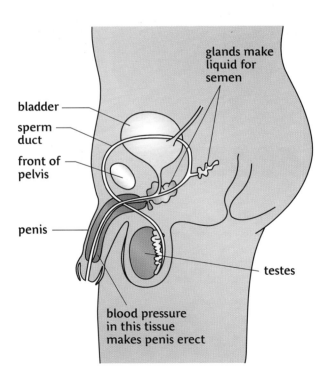

glands make liquid for semen

bladder

sperm duct

front of pelvis

penis

testes

blood pressure in this tissue makes penis erect

At puberty girls start their **periods**; this is part of the **menstrual cycle**. Oestrogen and progesterone control the release of one egg from the ovaries every 28 days; this is called **ovulation**. The egg travels along the **oviduct** to the **uterus** (or womb). Before ovulation the lining of the uterus thickens in preparation to receive a fertilised egg (see pages 18–19). If the egg is not fertilised the lining of the uterus breaks up and blood and dead cells pass out through the vagina during **menstruation**.

summary

- **Hormones** cause the changes at **puberty** that lead to sexual **maturity**.
- The monthly **menstrual cycle** in girls and women is linked to the release of an egg from the **ovary**.
- The ovaries release eggs until the **menopause**. Men can produce sperm throughout their adult life.

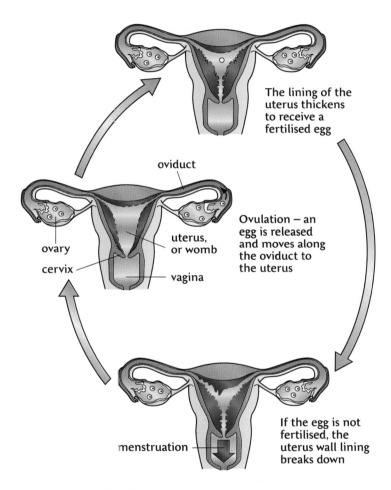

The lining of the uterus thickens to receive a fertilised egg

oviduct

ovary

uterus, or womb

cervix

vagina

Ovulation – an egg is released and moves along the oviduct to the uterus

menstruation

If the egg is not fertilised, the uterus wall lining breaks down

▶ *The menstrual cycle*

Questions

A

1. What do the following words mean?
   a) gamete   b) puberty
   c) testosterone d) oestrogen
   e) womb   f) menstruation
   g) testes   h) ovaries
2. List the changes that take place at puberty in the body of:
   a) a boy   b) a girl.

B

1. Explain why boys and girls may have mixed-up emotions at puberty.
2. List the events that happen in a girl's body during the menstrual cycle if the egg is not fertilised.

C

Find out:
a) the names of organs that prodcue hormones and where they are in the body
b) how the organs that produce hormones are different from those that produce digestive juices

For more information about reproduction see pages 18–19

Pregnancy

Like all **mammals**, humans reproduce by **sexual reproduction**. The process begins when the female ovum or egg is joined or **fertilised** by a male sperm. Once this has happened, a woman becomes pregnant as the baby begins to develop inside her womb or uterus. The time taken for the baby to develop is called the **gestation period**.

intro

These pages are about the way a fertilised human egg cell develops into a baby in nine months and how a woman's body protects and feeds the developing child inside her.

Intercourse and fertilisation

Because the eggs are in the ovary inside a woman's body and the baby will also develop and grow inside her body, an egg can only be fertilised when sperm are placed inside her body. This happens during **sexual intercourse** when a man's penis is inside a woman's **vagina**. The tip of the penis is sensitive and during intercourse, it will fill with blood and become stiff and erect. When the penis enters the vagina and moves up and down, **orgasm** may occur causing a milky-white liquid called **semen** containing sperm to be pumped or **ejaculated** out of the penis. Once they have been released from the penis the sperm swim towards the egg – if one is there. The sperm and egg usually meet in the **oviduct**.

Only one sperm will fertilise the egg. The **nucleus** in the head of the sperm passes through the egg **membrane**. The two nuclei join together (**fertilisation**). The egg membrane immediately changes and prevents other sperm from entering the egg. The fertilised egg takes about a week to pass down the oviduct and reach the uterus. The egg divides many times to make a ball of cells called the **embryo** which will sink into the soft lining of the uterus (**implantation**).

Life inside the womb

Once it is in the uterus wall the embryo begins to get nourishment from the mother. At first, food and oxygen come directly from the uterus wall but after a couple of weeks an organ starts growing from the tissues of the embryo and the mother. This is the **placenta.** It acts as a 'life support system'.

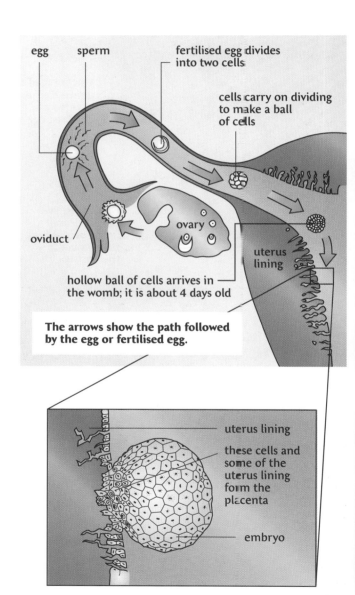

egg   sperm   fertilised egg divides into two cells

cells carry on dividing to make a ball of cells

oviduct

ovary

uterus lining

hollow ball of cells arrives in the womb; it is about 4 days old

The arrows show the path followed by the egg or fertilised egg.

uterus lining

these cells and some of the uterus lining form the placenta

embryo

At about three months, bone starts to develop in the embryo which is now called a **fetus**. In the placenta chemicals are exchanged between the mother's blood and the baby's blood. These chemicals can pass across from one to the other by **diffusion** across the **capillary** walls. The **umbilical cord** is the 'lifeline' that connects the baby to the placenta. It carries oxygen and food chemicals from the mother to the baby and carbon dioxide and other waste chemicals from the baby to the mother. The placenta acts as a barrier between the two blood supplies. The fetus grows inside a bag of watery liquid. This is **amniotic fluid** which protects the developing baby from knocks.

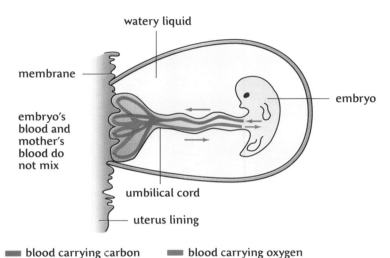

watery liquid

membrane

embryo's blood and mother's blood do not mix

umbilical cord

uterus lining

embryo

▬▬ blood carrying carbon dioxide and waste   ▬▬ blood carrying oxygen and food

- A human baby takes 38 weeks to develop inside its mother's body.
- The baby receives the materials needed for growth through blood flowing from the mother to the **placenta**.
- A baby is protected from knocks by the **amniotic fluid**.
- When the baby is born, the placenta is pushed out of the mother's womb as the **afterbirth**.

summary

About 38 weeks after fertilisation a baby is born weighing about 3–3.5 kg. During the last few days of pregnancy, the baby positions itself so that its head is near the opening of the uterus. The baby is pushed out of the mother's body by the action of the muscles of the womb. The process is called **labour**.

Life outside the womb

At birth, a baby comes from a dark, warm, wet, quiet world where it had a steady supply of food and oxygen. It is born into a world which is light, dry, cooler and noisier. The umbilical cord is cut. This separates the baby from the mother and now the baby has to change the way it breathes, feeds and gets rid of waste. It also has to start controlling its own temperature.

About 15 minutes after the baby has been born, the placenta, umbilical cord and membranes are pushed out of the mother's body. This is the **afterbirth**.

Questions

1   What is the meaning of these words?
    a) semen **b)** fertilisation
    c) implantation **d)** embryo
    e) placenta **f)** gestation period
    g) labour **h)** afterbirth

1   Describe the changes that take place between fertilisation and implantation.

2   What is the difference between an embryo and a fetus?

3   State two ways in which the developing baby is protected inside the womb.

4   Describe the changes in a baby's surroundings that take place at birth.

Pregnant women are advised not to smoke or drink alcohol. Why not?

For more information about reproduction see pages 16–17

Breathing and Respiration

All animals need to take **oxygen** from the air and get rid of carbon dioxide. Large animals have organs known as **lungs** where this **gas exchange** takes place. Lungs bring air and blood close together so that the gases can travel from one to the other.

These pages are about the way air is pulled into and pushed out of your body, and the changes made to the air.

intro

Breathing

Your **breathing system** begins in your nose (and mouth) and finishes in your lungs. Air enters the system through your nose or mouth. When you breathe in through your nose it does a most useful job. It warms and moistens the incoming air, filters out the dust and helps deal with the microbes that are drawn in with every breath. The air then passes down your **trachea** (windpipe) into your lungs.

Air has to be pumped into and out of your lungs so that you can get enough oxygen. Your lungs are inside your chest and this is separated from your lower body by the **diaphragm**.

You can see your chest moving gently when you are breathing. The muscles that move are between your ribs and around your diaphragm. These movements squash your lungs as you breathe out, then make your lungs bigger to make you breathe in.

Breathing in

When you breathe in, the **diaphragm** muscles pull the diaphragm downwards.

The ribs lift up and out.

This **increases** the volume of the chest, and air is sucked into the lungs.

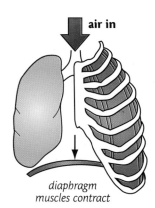

air in

diaphragm muscles contract

Breathing out

When you breathe out, the **diaphragm** and muscles connected to the ribs relax.

This **reduces** the volume of the chest, and forces air out of the lungs.

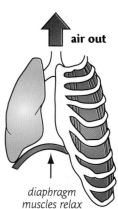

air out

diaphragm muscles relax

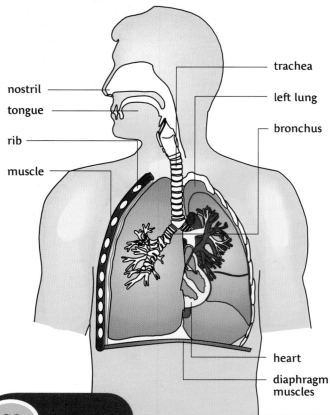

- nostril
- tongue
- rib
- muscle
- trachea
- left lung
- bronchus
- heart
- diaphragm muscles

The lungs are made up of millions of tiny **air sacs**, called **alveoli**. Each alveolus is surrounded by a network of **capillaries**. Gases can be transferred from the blood to the air in the air sacs.

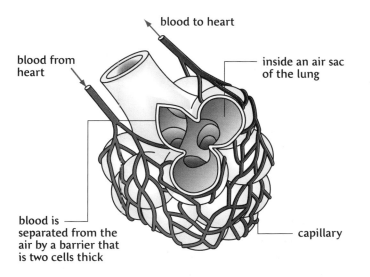

blood to heart

blood from heart

inside an air sac of the lung

blood is separated from the air by a barrier that is two cells thick

capillary

Respiration

Cells use oxygen to get the energy they need from food and produce carbon dioxide and water. This process is **respiration**. The food substance that the cells use is **glucose**, which is a kind of sugar.

glucose + oxygen → carbon dioxide + water + energy

Blood passing through the lungs collects oxygen from the breathed-in air and carries it to the cells.

Glucose is also carried to the cells by the blood. These substances pass through thin capillary walls into the cells.

The waste products of respiration (carbon dioxide and water) pass out of the cells into the blood, and are carried to the lungs. In the lungs the carbon dioxide and some of the water pass through the capillary walls into the air sacs and are breathed out. The rest of the waste water is lost as sweat or urine.

Changes made to the air

The air you breathe out has less oxygen, more carbon dioxide and more water vapour than the air you breathe in.

The air you breathe out still has oxygen in it, because your lungs do not absorb all the oxygen in the air.

- Air is pulled into and pushed out of the lungs by the action of muscles between the ribs and around the **diaphragm**.
- The thin walls of the lungs and **capillaries** allow gases to move across easily.
- Oxygen and glucose are used by cells for **respiration**. Carbon dioxide and water are waste products and energy is released.

summary

Questions

1 What do these words mean?
 a) lung **b)** diaphragm
 c) respiration **d)** breathing
 e) capillary

1 What happens to the **volume** or space inside your chest when you:
 a) breathe in
 b) breathe out?

2 What must happen to the **pressure** of the air inside your chest when you:
 a) breathe in
 b) breathe out?

3 Copy and complete the table.

4 Why is it better to breathe in through your nose than your mouth?

5 State **two** ways in which the lungs are suited to the job of gas exchange.

Measure the number of breaths you take when you are sitting. After exercise, what do you predict will happen to the size of each breath and the number of breaths taken in one minute? Why do you think this will happen?

Part of breathing system	What happens when you	
	breathe in?	breathe out?
muscles between ribs diaphragm muscles diaphragm lungs		

For more information about respiration see pages 30–31 and 74–75
For more information about pressure see pages 54–55 and 112–113

Health and Disease

There are many living things and substances in our surroundings that can cause disease. Children can also inherit diseases from their parents.

These pages are about some of the ways a person's health can be damaged.

Symptoms and diagnosis

When you have a cold, you do not feel well. You are suffering from a **disease**. The word 'disease' means 'not at ease'. When a person has a disease, there are signs or **symptoms** that a doctor can see. These include things like a high temperature, a skin rash or the wrong chemicals in the urine. By studying the symptoms, a doctor can identify the disease. The doctor then makes a **diagnosis**.

Microbes

There are many different kinds of disease. Some diseases are caused by **microbes.** These diseases can be **transmitted** (passed on) from one person to another. Other diseases cannot be transmitted from one person to another. These include diseases linked with a poor diet, chemicals in the surrounding environment or growing old. Some diseases may be inherited from parents.

A microbe which causes disease is called a **pathogen**. There are two main types of pathogen: **bacteria** and **viruses**.

Disease	Type of pathogen	Transmission
Cold	Virus	In air (sneezing)
Polio	Virus	In air, food or water
Cholera	Bacteria	Contaminated food or water
Typhoid	Bacteria	Contaminated food or water

Bacteria

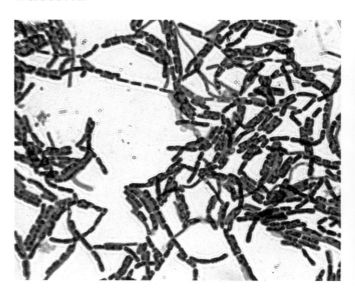

Bacteria are very small cells. They take many different shapes. Some are round, others spiral or rod shaped, and some have threads to help them to move.

Bacteria are found in large numbers in warm, damp places on the body, like in the armpits and between the toes. Harmful bacteria cause disease either by destroying your cells or by making poisons called **toxins**.

Bacteria reproduce by splitting in two. In the right conditions some can divide every 20 minutes. So in one day a single **bacterium** could make 1000 million, million, million offspring! There are more bacteria on your body than there are people on the Earth, yet they could all be packed into a soup tin!

Viruses

Viruses are so small they can only be seen with the help of an electron microscope (a very powerful microscope). Viruses can only live inside another living cell.

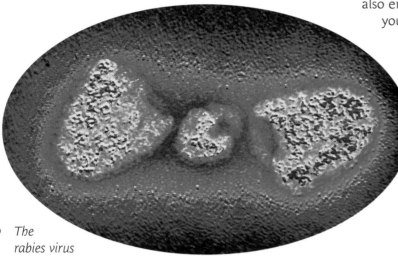

 The rabies virus

Harmful substances

Many substances can affect your body. Cigarette smoke contains dozens of chemicals. The main ones are **nicotine** and **tar**. Nicotine may stop the cleaning cells in your breathing tubes from working. It may also enter your blood through your lungs and affect your nervous system. Tar irritates and damages the breathing tubes.

Alcohol affects the nervous system. Taken in small quantities alcohol is a **stimulant** which helps the body and nerves to become more active, but if taken in larger amounts it becomes a **sedative** and slows things down. Your liver will be badly damaged if you drink large amounts of alcohol regularly.

- **Microbes**, like **bacteria** and **viruses**, which cause disease are **pathogens**.
- Diseases caused by microbes can be passed from one person to another in many ways.
- Different diseases have different **symptoms**.
- Substances like cigarette smoke and alcohol may cause disease.

summary

Questions

 A

1 What do these words mean?
   a) pathogen
   b) disease
   c) diagnosis
   d) symptom
   e) toxin
   f) bacteria
   g) virus
   h) stimulant
   i) sedative

 B

1 How could the transmission of the following diseases be prevented?
   a) cold
   b) cholera

2 Name three ways that cigarette smoke can harm your body.

3 **a)** Why is it dangerous if a person drives a car after they have been drinking?
   b) What damage is caused if a person drinks a lot of alcohol regularly?

 C

1 Cigarette smoke contains many chemicals. Find out what they are and what their effects are on the human body.

2 Different amounts of alcohol have different effects on the body. Find out what they are.

For more information on health see pages 8–9 and 24–25

Protection from Disease

Your body is always 'under attack' from microbes but it has ways of keeping microbes out and of dealing with them if they do get in.

These pages are about the ways your body is protected from disease.

measles virus

polio, cholera and food poisoning microbes

pimple and boil bacteria

malaria microbe in a mosquito bite

AIDS and sexually transmitted disease microbes

rabies microbe in a bite

athlete's foot fungus

▶ *Where microbes attack your body*

Your body's defences

Your body uses your skin, your breathing tubes and your stomach to help to defend itself against invasion by bacteria and viruses.

The dead, outer layer of your skin is kept moist by an oily fluid called **sebum**. This is an **antiseptic**, a substance which does not kill microbes but stops them multiplying. Sebum is made by glands found next to each hair on your body.

Another gland by your eyes produces tears which contain an **enzyme** that can destroy some types of bacteria.

If you breathe in dust or microbes from the air, they will be trapped in the sticky **mucus** which lines your breathing tubes. Tiny hairs, called **cilia**, move the dirty mucus towards your throat where the dirt and slime are swallowed. These microbes, as well as any you eat in your food, will enter your stomach. Here they will be killed by the **hydrochloric acid** and digestive juices made by your stomach cells.

Defences in the blood

If your skin is broken or cut, the blood vessels may be damaged and microbes may get into your body at the site of the wound. When a blood vessel is cut and becomes open to the air, a series of chemical reactions is triggered off to defend the body. The proteins in your blood form a sticky net which becomes plugged with blood cells. A blood **clot** forms at the wound. When the plug of blood dries out it forms a scab over the damaged area. New skin will grow underneath this.

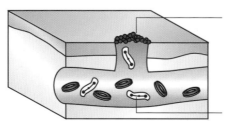

blood cells trapped in the net formed from blood proteins

white blood cells trap invading microbes

If any microbes do get into the blood, they are attacked by **white blood cells** called **phagocytes.** These destroy microbes. The phagocytes are produced in the **marrow** of your bones and in the **lymph nodes**. Sometimes these nodes swell up while they are working to make phagocytes to fight an infection.

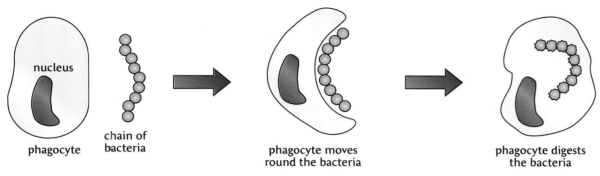

nucleus

phagocyte

chain of bacteria

phagocyte moves round the bacteria

phagocyte digests the bacteria

A wound may feel hot and have yellow pus around the scab. **Inflammation** (heat) is caused when more blood comes to the wound to help it to heal. Phagocytes leave the **capillary** and work to overcome the microbes. More and more cells form the **pus**. Because these cells are working hard, heat is produced. This picture shows a leg wound.

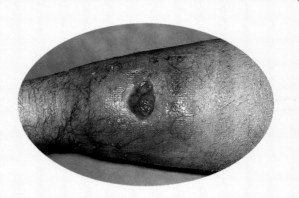

summary

- Your body is protected from microbes by its skin, tears, breathing tubes and stomach acid.
- A scab is formed when a blood vessel is damaged and this stops blood loss and the entry of microbes.
- If microbes enter the blood, blood cells called **phagocytes** attack them.

Questions

1 What do these words mean?
   a) antiseptic **b)** cilia **c)** mucus
   d) scab **e)** phagocyte

1 Explain why the temperature may increase in the skin around an infected wound.

2 Explain how a scab is formed.

3 How does your body deal with bacteria in the food you eat?

4 Describe how phagocytes destroy microbes.

C

1 Find out how surgeons remove the microbes from their skin before an operation.

2 Find out how surgical instruments are **sterilised** (have any microbes on them killed).

Immunity

Cells and chemicals in your blood work together to overcome an attack by a particular **pathogen** (a microbe which causes disease). Doctors can help your body to resist attack.

These pages are about the ways in which your body deals with microbes if they overcome its defences.

Natural immunity

Some microbes can cause diseases in animals. One virus which attacks cattle causes a disease called foot and mouth disease. This virus cannot grow inside the cells of the human body. This means that people cannot catch this disease. We are **naturally immune** to it.

Other pathogens do cause disease in people. If a pathogen, such as the virus that causes measles, gets into your blood then you will catch the measles disease unless your immune system overcomes it.

Antigens and antibodies

All microbes have a coating of **proteins** that are not found in your body. These foreign proteins are called **antigens**. Some of the white blood cells in your body can recognise these antigens and make defence chemicals called **antibodies**.

Antibodies stop the microbes getting into the cells of your body by making it easier for the phagocytes in the blood to attack them.

Some pathogens produce **toxins** (poison) inside the body. Different white blood cells can make **antitoxins** which destroy this poison.

Antibodies and antitoxins help you to fight off a disease. They give you **immunity** to the disease.

The immune reaction

The type of antibody that your body makes matches the type of pathogen that is invading. An invading measles virus will make the body produce 'measles antibodies'. A chicken pox virus will make the body produce 'chicken pox antibodies' which are not the same as measles antibodies.

When a pathogen first gets into your body it starts to reproduce and causes **symptoms** of the disease. It can take some time for your body to make enough antibodies to fight the pathogens. Eventually there are enough antibodies to destroy all the pathogens and you recover from the disease.

If the same kind of pathogen attacks your body again, your white blood cells already know how to make the antibodies. This time your body can make lots of antibodies very quickly, and it can destroy all the pathogens before they can cause the disease. You have become **immune** to that pathogen.

Preventing disease

You do not have to have an illness before you can become immune to it. You may have had injections to immunise you against some common childhood diseases such as whooping cough and measles. If you were travelling to some of the hot countries of the world you might need injections to protect you from diseases like yellow fever.

One way of becoming immune to a disease is to have an injection of a small dose of weakened, living pathogens. Your body will make antibodies to fight the infection. Once your cells know how to make the antibodies they can fight off any further attacks by that pathogen and you are immune to the disease that the pathogen causes.

A doctor can also give you the antibodies directly. If you cut yourself badly a doctor might give you an anti-tetanus injection which contains anti-tetanus antibodies. This kind of immunity does not last for ever, as the antibodies will gradually disappear from your blood.

Antibiotics

If you are already ill, a doctor can help your body to fight off the disease by giving you **antibiotics**. Antibiotics are chemicals which destroy bacteria but do not destroy human cells.

How a child is protected against polio

At 6 months a baby is given a weak dose of polio virus.
The virus multiplies in the baby's cells. White blood cells make antibodies that stay in the blood.
Later, more virus is given to the child. The child makes more antibodies and is protected against polio.

Sometimes the immune system breaks down and the body starts to attack itself. In **rheumatoid arthritis**, the antibodies attack the joints and make them tender and stiff to move.

Questions

A

1 What do these words mean?
 a) antigen b) antibody
 c) antitoxin d) immunity

2 Describe two ways of helping your body become immune to a particular disease.

B

1 Explain the sequence of events that take place to make a child immune to polio.

2 What is an antibiotic?

C

Boys and girls have a 'Heaf test' at about the age of 13. Find out about the test and the disease it detects.

For more information on disease see pages 22–23 and 24–25

Photosynthesis

Plants can make their own food using energy from the Sun. The chlorophyll in green plants absorbs energy and uses it to change carbon dioxide and water into glucose. Energy is stored in the glucose.

These pages are about the way green plants absorb energy from the Sun and use this energy to make food.

Plant nutrition

Nutrition means finding the right sorts of food to keep a living plant or animal healthy and let it go on growing.

Unlike other living things, green plants can make their own food. The materials they use are carbon dioxide from the air and water from the soil.

Chlorophyll in the leaves absorbs energy from the Sun, and transforms the carbon dioxide and water into glucose and oxygen. This process is called **photosynthesis**.

$$\text{carbon dioxide} + \text{water} \xrightarrow[\text{energy}]{\text{chlorophyll}} \text{glucose} + \text{oxygen}$$

Glucose is a kind of sugar. The plant changes the glucose into starch for storage. When the plant needs energy it can use the energy stored in the starch.

Only plants can provide animals with food to eat and oxygen-rich air to breathe.

Sunlight is energy from the Sun. Its light is a mixture of different colours. In photosynthesis, plants use some colours more than others. All plants on land and in the sea capture about 1/1000 of the light energy that reaches the Earth.

Investigating photosynthesis

An experiment can be done to show that green plants need light to photosynthesise and make food. Before this experiment is done, the plant must be kept in the dark for 24 hours so that any starch (food) being stored in the leaves is used up. The plant is **de-starched**. This must be done so that you know that any starch you find in the leaves after the experiment was made during the experiment.

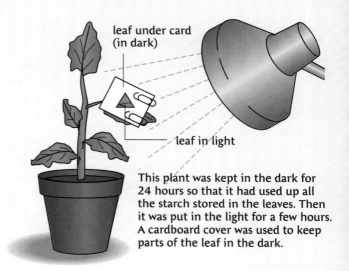

leaf under card (in dark)

leaf in light

This plant was kept in the dark for 24 hours so that it had used up all the starch stored in the leaves. Then it was put in the light for a few hours. A cardboard cover was used to keep parts of the leaf in the dark.

This leaf was not covered up. When iodine is put on it the whole leaf turns blue-black, showing that it contains starch. The leaf made the starch when the light was shining on it.

The parts of the leaf that were in the light have made starch.

This part of this leaf was covered up. It has not made any starch.

This shows that leaves only make starch when light is shining on them.

Measuring photosynthesis

The apparatus below can be set up in darkness and also in dim or bright light. It is used to measure the rate of photosynthesis.

The Canadian pondweed has large spaces in its stem. When the stem is cut and the plant is in light, big bubbles come from the cut end. The number of bubbles given off by the plant shows how quickly the plant is photosynthesising.

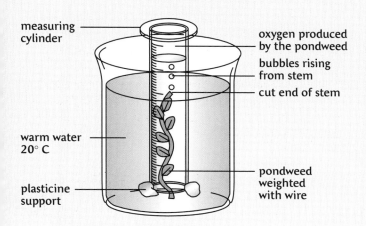

measuring cylinder

oxygen produced by the pondweed

bubbles rising from stem

cut end of stem

warm water 20° C

plasticine support

pondweed weighted with wire

The number of bubbles given off in a minute reaches a peak (at X on the graph). No matter how much brighter the light gets, the number of bubbles given off in a minute does not increase. This means that the process of photosynthesis is **limited**. This may happen because the temperature is too low or because there is not enough carbon dioxide available for photosynthesis.

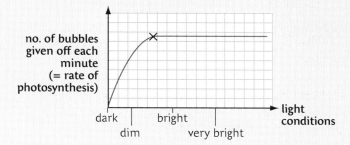

no. of bubbles given off each minute (= rate of photosynthesis)

dark   dim   bright   very bright

light conditions

Growers of greenhouse crops increase the amount of carbon dioxide in their greenhouses by using **methane** burners. These give off carbon dioxide so that the amount in the air is greater than normal. The air in the greenhouse is also warmer so the reaction of photosynthesis will happen quicker.

---

summary

- All living things need chemicals in order to grow.
- Plants make the food they need by **photosynthesis**.
- In photosynthesis, green plants trap light energy in **chlorophyll.**
- Photosynthesis uses carbon dioxide and water and produces glucose and oxygen.
- Gardeners and farmers can make plants grow more quickly by changing the conditions in their environment.

Questions

 A

1 What do these words mean?
   a) chlorophyll
   b) photosynthesis
   c) de-starched

2 Complete this word equation:
   carbon dioxide + _____
   →_____ + _____

3 Why do animals and plants need food?

 B

1 Why must plants be de-starched before they are used in a photosynthesis experiment?

2 Why is Canadian pondweed a useful plant for such experiments?

 C

1 The speed at which a plant photosynthesises may be limited. Explain what this means.

2 If a tomato grower wanted to get his crops to market before other growers are ready to sell their crops, he may grow his tomatoes in heated greenhouses. List the things he should consider if he wants to make the biggest profit possible.

Gas Exchange and Respiration in Plants

intro

All animals and plants use oxygen from the air to get energy from food. This energy is needed to keep animals and plants alive.

These pages are about the way plants breathe and use oxygen in respiration.

Lenticels

Air can get into a plant through tiny holes, called **lenticels,** in the stem and roots. Roots need air and there is usually lots of air in the spaces among soil particles. Roots in trodden down or waterlogged soil will die quickly because there is no air in between the soil particles and the roots cannot get the oxygen they need.

Stomata and air spaces

The surfaces of the leaves of plants have holes in them called **stomata**. These are usually on the lower side of the leaf's surface. Guard cells on either side of the stoma open and close the hole. Stomata are usually open during the day and closed at night.

When the stomata are open, air can go in and out of the leaf. The air moves into the spaces among the cells. When it reaches the cells inside the leaf, an **exchange of gases** takes place. The cells are loosely packed so there is a large area for gas exchange.

Most plant cells are alive and use oxygen for **respiration:**

oxygen + glucose ➤ carbon dioxide + water + energy

However, during daylight, the cells may use the carbon dioxide and water for **photosynthesis.**

Oxygen that is made during photosynthesis may also be used in respiration.

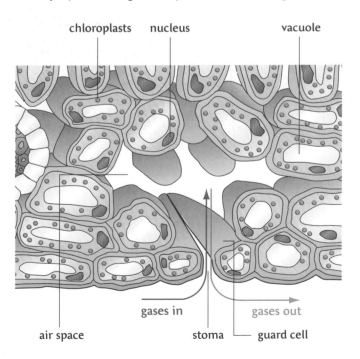

chloroplasts   nucleus   vacuole

gases in   gases out

air space   stoma   guard cell

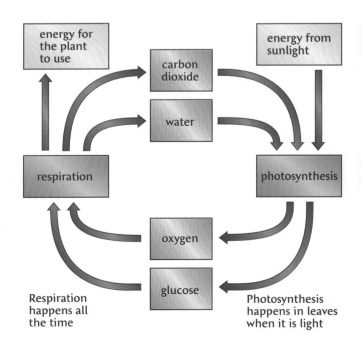

energy for the plant to use

energy from sunlight

carbon dioxide

water

respiration   photosynthesis

oxygen

glucose

Respiration happens all the time

Photosynthesis happens in leaves when it is light

Keeping the balance

All living animals and plants respire at all times. Plants photosynthesise in the light. Over the whole Earth, the balance between all the respiration and all the photosynthesis that is taking place helps to keep the amount of oxygen and carbon dioxide in the air steady (oxygen 20%; carbon dioxide 0.03%).

Because the Earth's forests are being cut down and people are producing more and more carbon dioxide from factories and by burning fossil fuels, the amount of carbon dioxide in the atmosphere is increasing. This has caused an increase in the Earth's average temperature, called global warming.

- Green plants **respire**, use oxygen and produce carbon dioxide at all times.
- Green plants use carbon dioxide for **photosynthesis** when it is light.
- Respiration in green plants can be shown using plants that have not grown green leaves.
- The increase in carbon dioxide in the atmosphere is the cause of **global warming**.

summary

Questions

A

1 What do these words mean?
  a) stomata
  b) lenticel
  c) respiration
  d) photosynthesis
  e) global warming

2 Complete these word equations:
  a) respiration
  glucose + _____ ⟶ _____
  _____ + _____ + energy

  b) photosynthesis

$$\_\_\_\_\_ + \_\_\_\_\_ \xrightarrow{\text{chlorophyll}} \text{glucose} + \_\_\_\_\_$$

B

1 Explain why plants do not grow well in heavily trampled soil like that found under footpaths.

2 Explain why stomata on a leaf are usually open during the day and closed at night.

C

1 Find out more about the 'greenhouse effect' and global warming.

2 Explain why a bottle garden can survive without being opened for months.

For more information see pages 84–85, 140–141 and 142–143

Plants, Water and Minerals

Soil particles are surrounded by water containing dissolved minerals. The minerals enter plants through their root **hairs**. The minerals are then **transported** (moved around) inside plants to where they are needed.

intro

These pages are about the way land plants get the water and minerals they need, and the way they use them.

Minerals in the soil

There can be many different minerals in the soil. What is there depends on the type of rock which formed the soil. Calcium, iron, magnesium, sodium, aluminium and potassium are some of the minerals found in soil that may be needed by plants for growth.

Some minerals are needed by plants in fairly large amounts. These are called the **major elements**.

Others are needed in very tiny amounts, so they are called **trace elements**. The elements required are usually combined with other elements in the soil. For example, the compound magnesium sulphate contains magnesium, sulphur and oxygen.

Behind the tip of every root are thousands of tiny root hairs. Each one is like a tube growing out from one cell. The hairs give the root a very big surface for taking in water and minerals.

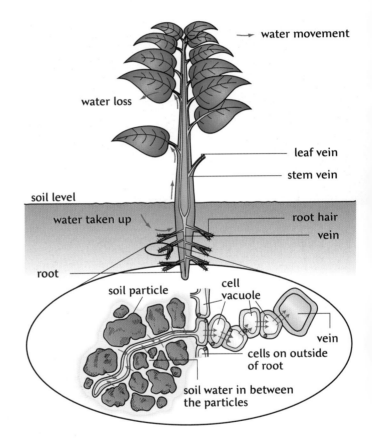

water movement

water loss

leaf vein

stem vein

soil level

water taken up

root hair

vein

root

soil particle

cell vacuole

vein

cells on outside of root

soil water in between the particles

How root hairs work

Each root hair is one cell. It has a **vacuole** inside it. Water and minerals in the soil can move into this vacuole and so get into the plant. Once inside the plant, water and minerals can move from that cell to another. Eventually they reach the vein in the root, and from there they will travel to the stem and leaves.

The uptake of minerals by root hairs is an active process which needs energy. If roots are starved of oxygen, they will not grow well as the cells cannot get the energy they need from respiration. The uptake of minerals by the root hairs is better when the oxygen supply is good.

The effect of minerals on growth

The effect of minerals on growth can be investigated by growing plant cuttings with their roots in solutions of different minerals. A cutting has no food store, so it has to make all the food it needs by photosynthesis. Anything else needed for healthy growth will be taken from the solution through the cut end of the stem. By changing the recipe of the solution or **culture**, the effect of the lack of any one mineral can be found. If the absence of one mineral makes the plant unhealthy, the plant has a **deficiency disease**.

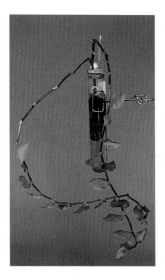 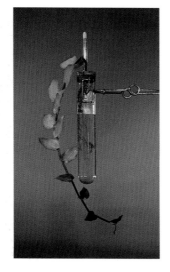

▶ *The plant on the left is healthy, the one on the right has a deficiency disease*

Adding fertiliser

When a farmer's crops grow well, the soil is said to be fertile. The growth of crops can be improved by adding things to the soil. Dung or manure from farm animals can be used. This is called a **natural fertiliser**. This improves the soil's texture by making it into a kind of sponge that will hold in moisture and minerals.

Many farmers add chemicals such as **ammonium sulphate** to the soil. These chemicals are **fertilisers**. They should be added to the soil in measured amounts. Farmers can choose a fertiliser to put right the shortage of minerals in the soil. Fertilisers increase the growth of the plant – the **biomass** increases.

Farmers say they have increased the **yield** of a crop. The yield is the amount of food produced by a crop that can be harvested and sold by the farmer. On some soils, fertilisers can increase the yield of a crop by about four times.

Ammonium sulphate is a widely used fertiliser. It is made in factories. The ammonium part adds **nitrogen** to the soil. Nitrogen is needed to make the proteins for cell growth and repair.

● Land plants get the water and minerals they need from the soil.
● Minerals are needed in different amounts.
● If a mineral is missing from the soil, a plant may suffer from a **deficiency disease**.
● Farmers can improve soil by adding manure and artificial **fertilisers** to it.

summary

Questions

1 What do these words mean?
a) root hair **b)** trace element
c) culture solution
d) deficiency disease
e) fertiliser **f)** biomass

1 Why is manure called a natural fertiliser?

2 Why do farmers add manure to soil?

3 Why do plants need nitrogen?

There are disadvantages involved in adding fertiliser to soil. Find out what they are.

For more information on fertilisers see pages 46–47

Pollination in Flowering Plants

A flowering plant carries out **sexual reproduction** by growing flowers that produce **seeds**. Before seeds can be made, **pollen** has to travel from the **male part** of a flower to the **female part**. This is called **pollination**. The seeds then develop inside a protective ovary.

These pages are about the way the sex cells of flowers are brought together to form a fertilised egg cell which will develop into a new young plant.

Flowering plants

Most of the plants we see around us are **flowering plants**. Some plants like roses or daffodils have flowers that are easy to see, but many flowering plants have very small, inconspicuous flowers. Trees such as oak, horse chestnut and sycamore are all flowering plants. Even grass is a flowering plant, but the flowers are very small and green. You hardly ever see grass flowers on lawns, because the grass is usually cut before the flowers have a chance to grow.

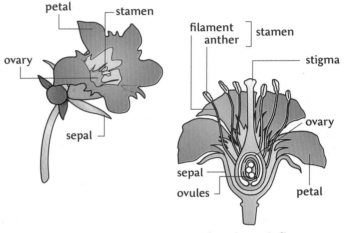

Section through flower

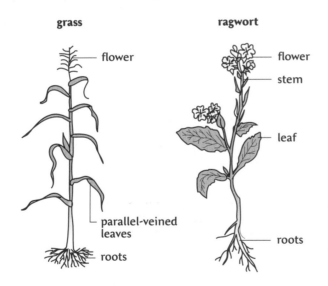

Parts of a flower

The **stamens** are the male parts of a flower.
The **anther** at the end of the stamen produces **pollen** grains, which are the male sex cells.

The **ovary** is the female part of a flower. It contains **ovules**, which are the female sex cells.
The **sepals** protect the flowerbud when it is growing.

When a flower is **pollinated** a pollen grain from one flower has to land on the **stigma** of another flower of the same species. The pollen can be carried by the wind, or by insects.

Insect pollination

Some flowers use insects to carry pollen from one flower to another. These **insect-pollinated** flowers usually have bright, colourful petals to attract insects. The flowers make a sugary liquid called **nectar**, and the insects visit the flower to feed on the nectar. Pollen gets rubbed off onto the bodies of the insects. When they later visit another flower of the same kind the pollen may be rubbed off onto the stigma of that flower.

Ragwort is an insect-pollinated flower.

▶ *Some flowers have patterns on their petals to attract insects.*
They can only be seen by humans in ultra violet light

Wind pollination

Plants that use wind to carry pollen from one flower to another are **wind-pollinated**. Wind-pollinated plants usually have very small flowers that are hard to see. The stamens hang out of the flower so that when they are moved by the wind, pollen gets into the air. This pollen is very light in weight and some grains will be carried through the air to the stigma of a female flower. The stigmas are large, feathery and sticky.

Grasses are wind-pollinated flowers.

This table compares wind- and insect-pollinated flowers.

Wind-pollinated flowers	Insect-pollinated flowers
Do not have brightly coloured petals.	Have brightly coloured and/or patterned petals. Flowers are perfumed and make nectar.
Stamens hang loosely outside the flower.	Stamens inside the flower.
Pollen is tiny and light so it can be carried by wind.	Pollen is sticky and has a rough surface so it sticks to the insect's body.
Stigmas have many fine branches to catch the pollen from the air.	Stigmas are small, sticky platforms.

For more information about plant fertilisation see pages 36–37

● Pollen must be moved from the **male parts** of a flower to the **female parts** before the plant can reproduce.

● The transfer of pollen is **pollination** and it is helped by wind or insects.

● **Wind-** and **insect-pollinated** flowers have different features.

summary

Questions

 A

1 What do these words mean?
   a) pollen **b)** ovule **c)** ovary
   d) pollination **e)** nectar

 B

1 Why do wind-pollinated flowers have large, feathery stigmas?

2 Why is pollen from insect-pollinated flowers sticky?

3 Name one job done by each of the following:
   a) petal **b)** sepal **c)** stamen

 C

Find out the names of two flowers that are pollinated by:
a) wind **b)** insects.

Fertilisation in Flowering Plants

When the **pollen** arrives at a flower's **stigma**, the male pollen **nucleus** is moved to the ovule nucleus. These two meet and the ovule is fertilised.

These pages are about what happens in the ovary of a flower after pollination.

Section through flower

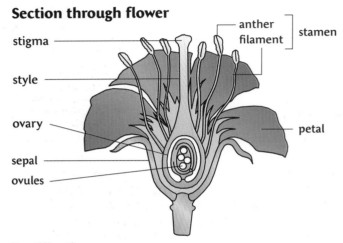

stigma
style
ovary
sepal
ovules

anther
filament — stamen

petal

Fertilisation

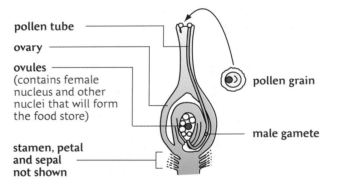

pollen tube
ovary
ovules
(contains female
nucleus and other
nuclei that will form
the food store)

stamen, petal
and sepal
not shown

pollen grain

male gamete

Flower after fertilisation

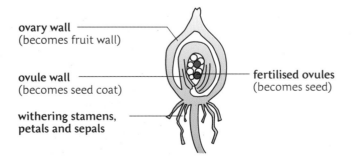

ovary wall
(becomes fruit wall)

ovule wall
(becomes seed coat)

withering stamens,
petals and sepals

fertilised ovules
(becomes seed)

Fertilisation

In all flowers, the **stigma** catches **pollen** that has been brought to the flower. When the right pollen arrives at the stigma, the coat of the pollen grain splits. A tube grows out. This grows down towards the ovule in the ovary. When the tube reaches the ovule, the male nucleus **gamete** (sex cell) passes down it. The nucleus of the male gamete **fuses** with the female. This is **fertilisation**. The fertilised ovule develops into the **embryo** plant.

The wall around the fertilised ovule changes. It becomes a hard protective cover called the **testa**. The testa, embryo and food store all together form a **seed**. The ovary wall changes too. It may become hard and leathery or soft and fleshy as in a gooseberry. This makes the **fruit.**

Cross- and self-fertilisation

An ovule is fertilised by a male gamete. If the pollen has been brought from another flower, this is called **cross-fertilisation**. Sometimes, however, pollen of the right kind does not get to the stigma and there are some flowers, for example, the flowers on a *Viola* plant, which can fertilise themselves. This is called **self-fertilisation**. Here the stigma gets pollen from the stamens in its own flower.

Fruits and seeds

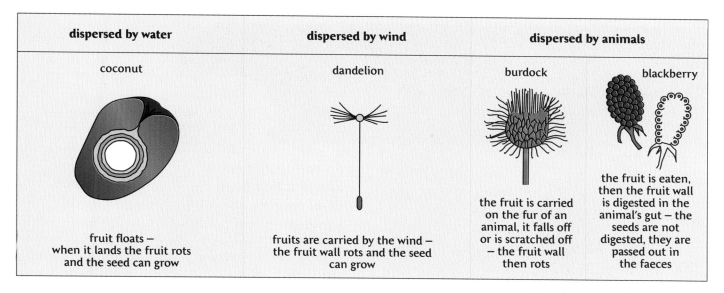

dispersed by water	dispersed by wind	dispersed by animals	
coconut	dandelion	burdock	blackberry
fruit floats – when it lands the fruit rots and the seed can grow	fruits are carried by the wind – the fruit wall rots and the seed can grow	the fruit is carried on the fur of an animal, it falls off or is scratched off – the fruit wall then rots	the fruit is eaten, then the fruit wall is digested in the animal's gut – the seeds are not digested, they are passed out in the faeces

Conkers, acorns, cucumbers, bananas, coconuts, peas and peaches are all kinds of fruit. They all contain one or more seeds. Each of these contains an embryo

plant. The seeds need to reach the ground at a distance from the parent plant. If they land too close to the parent plant, they may not be able to get enough light, water or minerals to grow. Seeds cannot move by themselves. They need to be **dispersed** (carried away) by wind, animals and water. Some fruits split and push their seeds out. Others open and shake out the seeds.

Some plants produce a fruit that contains one large seed, such as a peach. Some fruits, like pomegranates, contain lots of seeds. Other plants carry their seeds outside their fruits, like strawberries.

- After fertilisation, all parts of a flower change.
- The **ovary** may be leathery or fleshy and will have seeds inside or outside.
- Seeds contain the **embryo plants** formed when the ovule was fertilised by the **male nucleus**.

summary

Questions

1 What is the meaning of these words?
a) testa
b) fruit
c) self-fertilisation
d) cross-fertilisation
e) dispersal

1 What is the difference between pollination and fertilisation?
2 Describe what happens to each of the following parts of a flower after fertilisation:
a) petals
b) stamens
c) ovary

1 Look at the outside and then at a slice through each of the following: banana, tomato, orange. Work out which parts are:
a) the seeds
b) the remains of the flower
c) the join to the stem.
2 Find out about the features found on seeds and fruits which help them to be dispersed by wind, water or animals.

Animal and Plant Breeding

The natural differences among individuals of any type of animal or plant mean that some are more likely to survive if the surroundings change. People have used these differences to breed animals and plants with the sizes, colours, features and shapes that are most suited to our needs.

intro

These pages are about the way people have used selection to produce new forms of living things.

▶ *Polar bears' coats match their surroundings*

Selection

All living things vary. Some **variations** help living **organisms** to survive in their natural surroundings. These variations have **survival value**. For example, a light-coloured coat on the body of a predator in snow-covered land means that the animal can hide and hunt better than one with a dark coat. The light-coloured animal is more likely to survive longer and therefore to breed more. This process is called **natural selection**. When humans interfere in a breeding process it is called **artificial selection**.

Domestication

Wolves were the first animals to share people's homes. Ancient peoples may have raised wolf cubs whose parents had been killed for food or fur. If its parents were not around, a wolf cub would become attached to any animal which cared for it. The cub would obey and try to please the human in return for food and protection. The tamed wolf would help in hunting animals for food and would guard the camp. In this way the wolf was **domesticated**. By about 5000 BC a tame stock of wolves had been developed.

Selective breeding

Primitive people might have noticed that two of their domesticated wolves (dogs) protected sheep better than the others. When the owners mated these two animals, they found that the litter of puppies contained dogs that grew up to be protective too. When these dogs were mated with each other, their offspring would be better still. This **inbreeding** of closely related dogs eventually resulted in different types of dogs which looked quite different from wolves.

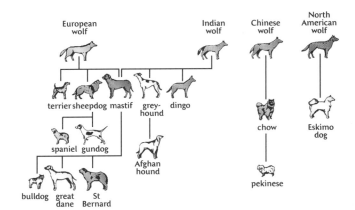

European wolf — terrier, sheepdog, mastif, grey-hound, dingo — spaniel, gundog — bulldog, great dane, St Bernard — Afghan hound

Indian wolf

Chinese wolf — chow — pekinese

North American wolf — Eskimo dog

Their jaw size, leg length and colour changed from generation to generation. Experts believe that all the different breeds of domestic dogs in the world originally came from four different wolf stocks.

In the wild only the fittest animals survive. The 'fittest' animals are those best suited to their surroundings. If a wild wolf pup was born with abnormalities, like an over-large head or short legs, these would weaken the animal. It would die before it was fully grown and able to mate so the abnormality would not be passed on.

Selective breeding can be harmful. Breeds of dogs produced by selective breeding may have faults in their breathing passages, jaws, eyes and nervous system. Wolves are carnivores with sharp teeth to tear open their prey. The German Shepherd Dog may look similar to a wolf, but its jaws are shorter and its teeth smaller and more crowded together. The jaws of the Pekinese have become so squashed that there is no room for all its teeth.

When animals are **bred selectively** (bred by people), use can be made of these abnormalities if people wish to keep them. Because the animals are fed by their owners and do not have to find their own food, they will survive. By careful selection, people have bred dogs to help them do a wide variety of tasks.

Crop breeding

Most of the crops we grow and eat have been bred by artificial selection. Scientists have selected parent plants which show **characteristics** that would be useful. For example, one type of cereal plant may produce lots of grains but its stalks may be too short for harvesting by machine. Another type may have stalks of the right length, but only produce a few grains. By **crossing** these two types of plant, the scientist hopes to produce cereal plants that have the right length of stalks and many grains.

- People can choose animals or plants with certain desirable characteristics and use them to produce animals or plants with combinations of characteristics that are useful to us.

summary

Questions

A

1 What do these words mean?
   a) survival value
   b) natural selection
   c) artificial selection
   d) domestication

2 Explain why camouflage helps animals to survive.

B

1 Sometimes an animal is born without any colour in its coat. It is an albino. If this animal was prey in woodland, why might it be hard for it to survive?

2 Using ideas about natural selection, explain:
   a) why giraffes have long necks
   b) why tigers have striped coats.

C

Find out how selective breeding has changed the appearance of:
   a) apples
   b) potatoes
   c) carp
   d) cattle.

Sorting Out Living Things

intro

All living things show seven characteristics. They all breathe, feed, excrete (get rid of waste), reproduce, respond to their surroundings, grow and move. There is a great variety of living things, from elephants to tiny bacteria. Scientists classify (group) them to make sense of the variety. The science of classifying is called **taxonomy**.

These pages are about the way scientists sort living things into five main groups and use keys to help to identify each one.

The five kingdoms

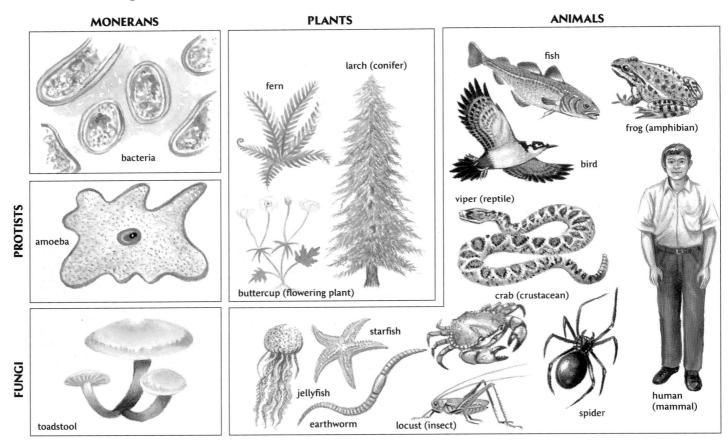

MONERANS

bacteria

PROTISTS

amoeba

FUNGI

toadstool

PLANTS

fern

larch (conifer)

buttercup (flowering plant)

ANIMALS

fish

bird

viper (reptile)

frog (amphibian)

crab (crustacean)

starfish

jellyfish

earthworm

locust (insect)

spider

human (mammal)

Scientists classify living things by looking at their **characteristics**. At first scientists said there were only two big groups, animals and plants. Later they had to add more groups to make room for the other living things that did not fit easily into these two groups. Today there are five big groups or **kingdoms: Monerans, Protists, Fungi, Plants** and **Animals.**

Monerans are single-celled organisms. The **cells** have no **nucleus** and can only be seen with a microscope. Bacteria are in this kingdom. There are about 4000 kinds of moneran.

The other four groups all have cells with a nucleus.

Protists are also single-celled organisms. Some have **chlorophyll** in them so they can make food. Others need ready-made food. Amoebas are in this kingdom. There are about 50 000 kinds of protist.

Fungi are made of many cells and get food from their surroundings. Some are brightly coloured, like the Fly Agaric; others have no colour. There are about 100 000 kinds of fungus.

Plants make their food by **photosynthesis**. The plant group is split into smaller groups: the **algae, mosses, ferns, conifers** and **flowering plants**. There are about 400 000 types of plant.

Animals live by eating food. Every animal can move at least part of its body. The animal group is split into two. The largest animals are the **vertebrates** which have a bony skeleton inside their body. There are five groups of vertebrates. The mammals are the only group that give birth to live young. All the other groups lay eggs.

Mammals are warm blooded and covered in hair or fur. They usually have four limbs.

Birds are warm blooded and covered in feathers. They have two legs and two wings.

Fish are cold blooded and covered in slimy scales. They have fins and use gills for breathing.

Reptiles are cold blooded and covered in dry scales. Most have legs.

Amphibians are cold blooded and covered in damp skin. Most have legs.

However, most animals do not have an inside skeleton. These are the **invertebrates**. There are over 2 million types of animal and 97% of these are invertebrates.

Scientists use **keys** to help them to identify living things. A key contains questions. Each question asks about one **characteristic.** The questions lead you through the key until you find out what the organism is.

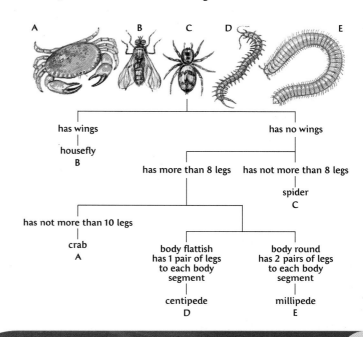

```
                          A          B        C       D                E

        has wings                                         has no wings
           |                                                   |
        housefly                                               |
           B                              has more than 8 legs   has not more than 8 legs
                                                   |                      |
                                                   |                    spider
                                                   |                      C
    has not more than 10 legs                      |
           |                                        |
          crab                          body flattish        body round
           A                            has 1 pair of legs    has 2 pairs of legs
                                        to each body          to each body
                                        segment               segment
                                            |                     |
                                        centipede             millipede
                                            D                     E
```

● All living things show the following seven characteristics: breathing, feeding, excreting, reproducing, reacting to their surroundings, growth and movement.
● Living organisms are sorted into **five kingdoms.**
● Each kingdom shares the same **characteristics.**
● **Organisms** can be identified with a **key.**

summary

Questions

1 What do these words mean?
  a) taxonomy
  b) moneran
  c) protist
  d) key
  e) plant
  f) animal

2 List the seven characteristics of living things.

1 A car can move, but it is not alive. How do you know it is not alive?

2 State one difference between each of the following:
  a) conifer and buttercup
  b) invertebrate and vertebrate.

3 Make a table that summarises some of the differences between the five vertebrate groups. Use these headings: Group, Warm/Cold Blood, Limbs, Covering, Breathing.

1 Find out which vertebrate groups the following animals belong to. Explain why they are unusual.
  a) bat **b)** penguin **c)** dolphin
  d) turtle **e)** snake

2 Find out about different ways that plants move and respond to their surroundings.

The Environments of Living Things

Living things are found in many different places.
All living things have **adaptations** or **features** that help them to survive.

These pages are about how living things are affected by their surroundings.

Habitats

Living things are found on land, in air and in water. These surroundings are their **environment**. There are many different places on land, in air and in water where animals and plants can live. Such places are called **habitats**. In each habitat there will be a **community** (a collection of living organisms). Some of the animals and plants in a rock pool community are shown above. There is one shore crab, three anemones and many shrimps. The number of one kind of organism in any habitat is the **population** of that organism. So, in this habitat, the population of anemones is three.

Biotic and physical factors

The non-living parts of a habitat – water, air or bits of rock – are called **physical factors**. The living organisms are **biotic factors**. All the living organisms and non-living things in a particular place make up an **ecosystem**. All ecosystems are always changing. When the tide is out, and if it is dry and hot, this rock pool may dry up. When it is really cold, it may freeze over. Conditions change from day to day and from season to season. Living organisms must survive these changes.

Water as a habitat

Water is a liquid. It is denser than air. Seawater contains many dissolved substances, such as salt. The living things found in water are called **aquatic** animals and plants. Those in seawater can also be called **marine** animals and plants. Marine animals include the cod fish, jellyfish and lobster.

The water in rivers, lakes, streams and ponds is fresh water. It is not pure. Fresh water contains substances that have been dissolved from the rocks or riverbeds over which the water flows. The living things found in fresh water are **freshwater organisms**. A stickleback is a freshwater animal. Canadian pond weed is a freshwater plant.

Where rivers flow into the sea, at an **estuary**, the water is a mixture of fresh and salt water. This is **brackish** water. **Estuarine organisms** live in brackish water.

In the sea, the water in the top 50 metres warms up or cools down depending on the weather. Between 50 and 400 metres deep the water takes longer to warm or cool and the temperature changes from season to season.

freshwater

brackish water

seawater

If you climb up a mountain, the higher you climb, the less oxygen there will be in the air around you. The temperature drops too, so the higher up the mountain you go, the colder the air will feel. The peak of a high mountain is very cold indeed.

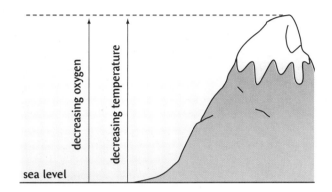

decreasing oxygen

decreasing temperature

sea level

The water of rivers, streams, ponds and lakes is not as deep as the sea. The temperature changes here too.

Land and air habitats

Air is a mixture of gases. The main gases are **nitrogen, oxygen** and **carbon dioxide**. There is also **water vapour** in the air. If a lot of water is present, the air is **humid**. The air in the jungles of hot countries is humid.

Plants such as oak trees, and animals such as cats and birds, which live on land and in air, are called **terrestrial organisms**.

F

The study of living things in the places where they live is called ecology. This word comes from two Greek words: *oikos,* which means 'house', and *logos,* which means 'study of'.

● **Living organisms live in communities within places called habitats.**
● **Any environment has a number of different habitats.**
● **Conditions in any habitat are always changing.**

summary

Questions

A

1 What do these words mean?
   a) adaptation
   b) population
   c) ecosystem
   d) marine
   e) estuarine
   f) terrestrial

B

1 List the physical factors in the rock pool habitat.

2 List the biotic factors in the rock pool habitat.

3 Say how the air at the top of a mountain is different from that at the bottom.

C

1 Find out how any one of the rock pool animals is adapted to the daily changes in its habitat.

2 Eels and salmon are fish which swim across oceans and through rivers during their lifetimes. Find out why they do this and how their bodies change.

Food Chains, Webs and Pyramids

Animals cannot make food. They get their food by eating plants and other animals. Green plants are **producers**, they make food from carbon dioxide and water in **photosynthesis**.

Nutrient chemicals and their **energy** are passed from one organism to another along a **food chain**.

intro

These pages are about the feeding relationships among organisms.

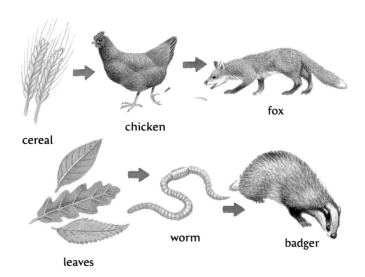

cereal

chicken

fox

leaves

worm

badger

Food chains

Herbivorous animals eat plants. Other animals feed on animal flesh. These animals are called **carnivores**.

green plant → herbivore → carnivore
food goes to   food goes to

As herbivores and carnivores both eat food, they are **consumers**. Herbivores are the first link in the chain, so they are **primary consumers**. Carnivores are the second link, so they are **secondary consumers**. If another carnivore ate the first carnivore, it would be a **tertiary consumer**.

Some animals are **omnivores**. They eat both plants and flesh. A badger is an omnivore.

What happens to the energy?

Every living thing in a food chain uses some energy from its food to live and stores some in its body. A herbivore uses up some of the energy stored in the plants it eats and stores the rest. This extra energy is stored in the chemicals that make up the herbivore's body. Only about 10% of the energy it eats is stored in its flesh for the next consumer. If a carnivore eats the herbivore, some of this stored energy can be used. Because of the energy losses in a food chain, it is very rare to find more than four organisms in any one chain.

As green plants are the only organisms in the food chain to trap energy from the Sun, they support all the other animals in the chain.

Food webs

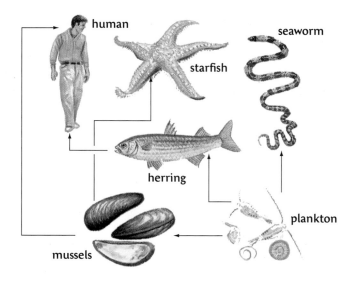

human

starfish

seaworm

herring

plankton

mussels

In nature most food chains are linked together. One animal may feed on different types of plants and another animal may eat a number of other, different animals. For example, an owl might eat mice, voles and even young rabbits. By having different animals in its diet, the owl will still survive when one of the food animals is not available. This means that the owl can live through the winter when food is in short supply. As any one animal or plant can have its place in several food chains, food chains are linked to form a **food web**.

Pyramids

In a food chain, there have to be more producers than consumers. This is because the producers must provide all the energy for themselves *and* the consumer. Look at this food chain:

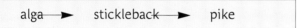

alga → stickleback → pike

If the number of each type of organism in a part of a pond is counted, there will be more alga plants than sticklebacks. There will also be more sticklebacks than pike. If the number is shown as a block, and the blocks are piled up, a **pyramid of numbers** is made.

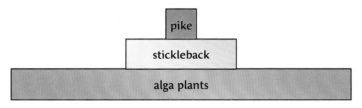

▶ *A pyramid of numbers*

Sometimes, instead of being a large number of tiny plants, a producer is just one plant, like an oak tree. A pyramid of numbers wouldn't make much sense in this case, so it is best to show the relationships of the organisms in this food chain using the mass of each organism. This is a **pyramid of biomass**.

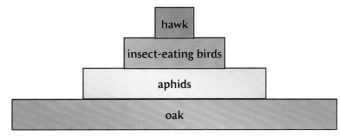

▶ *A pyramid of biomass*

For more information about food chains see pages 46–47

---

summary

- All living things depend on the Sun for energy.
- Green plants are the only living things that can trap energy.
- Animals feed on plants or other animals.
- Feeding links can be shown as **food chains** and **webs**.
- The numbers or mass of organisms in a chain can be shown as a **pyramid**.

Questions

1   What do these words mean?
    a) producer
    b) consumer
    c) food chain
    d) omnivore
    e) pyramid of numbers
    f) biomass

1   Explain why it is useful for the badger to be an omnivore.

2   Explain why there are usually only four organisms in a food chain.

3   Explain why it is better to use a pyramid of biomass than a pyramid of numbers.

4   Write out three different food chains shown in the food web.

Find out about other food chains that start with plankton.

Food Chains and Pollution

The numbers of animals and plants in food webs are kept in balance in nature. This balance makes sure that some organisms survive to produce offspring. However, the use of chemicals and other organisms to improve crops has caused damage to food webs and affected the lives of organisms.

These pages are about the way the activities of people can affect the survival of animals and plants.

Water pollution from farms

Farmers use **fertilisers** to make their crops grow better. Some fertiliser may drain into rivers and streams. Most fertilisers contain **nitrates**, which pollute the water.

Many farm animals are kept in sheds. They make a lot of waste which gets washed out of the shed and may get into rivers or streams. This waste contains a lot of nitrates and phosphates.

Nitrates in rivers can enter water supplies and might be drunk by people. This does little damage to adults, but it can harm babies by damaging their blood cells.

fertiliser left on soil

some chemicals are washed into the river

surface soil

lake

some chemicals pass through soil

water plants growing very fast

rock will not allow water to pass through

Nitrates and food chains

Plants need nitrates to make protein. If a stream has a lot of nitrates in it, it will encourage the growth of microscopic plants that live in the stream. The numbers of these plants will increase much faster than the animals higher up the food chain can eat them. If the plants are not eaten they die and fall to the bottom of the stream where they rot away. The bacteria that rot them use up all the oxygen in the water, and so fish and other aquatic animals die. The extra nitrate in the water has upset the balance of the food web in the stream.

Pesticides in food chains

Many crops are ruined when they are used as a food supply by other animals, fungi, bacteria and viruses. These organisms are called **pests** and the crops may be protected from pests if they are sprayed with chemicals called **pesticides**. These pesticides may also be washed into rivers and get into food chains.

The pesticide DDT was first used in the 1930s. DDT kills insects and it was sprayed in buildings and on people to kill and control fleas, lice and mosquitoes. DDT does not break down quickly; it remains harmful for a long time.

The osprey eats lots of pike. The DDT in the osprey is very concentrated, and it can poison the bird.

Each pike eats lots of roach.

Each roach eats lots of pond weed, so the DDT gets more concentrated.

Each pond weed plant only has a little DDT in it.

When the DDT reached the rivers, it got into plants there. These plants were eaten by other animals and fish so the chemical entered and stayed in their bodies. As a carnivore, like an osprey, may eat lots of fish containing DDT, quite soon the osprey would have a lot of DDT in its body. The osprey would be slowly poisoned.

In the 1960s, the numbers in the population of a carnivorous bird called the sparrowhawk were dropping. This bird was laying eggs with very thin shells, so that they cracked when the adult birds **incubated** them. The chicks did not hatch and so the number of adult sparrowhawks dropped. Scientists discovered that DDT was causing the problem, and soon its use was banned. Now that DDT cannot be used any more, the sparrowhawk population has recovered.

▶ *How a pesticide becomes more concentrated as it moves along a food chain*

summary

- **Fertiliser** and **pesticide** chemicals used on crops may get into rivers. Fertilisers in rivers can upset the balance of food chains by encouraging too many microscopic plants to grow.
- Chemicals in rivers may enter food chains.
- Chemicals passing through a food chain can affect the numbers in carnivore populations.

Questions

A

1 What do these words mean?
a) fertiliser
b) pesticide
c) pests

B

1 Explain why the body of a carnivore may be damaged by chemicals used on farmland.

2 Explain why nitrogen fertiliser is harmful to humans.

3 Explain why DDT is a dangerous pesticide.

C

Find out about the work of Rachel Carson (1907–1964) on pesticides in the environment.

For more information about numbers of animals and plants see pages 44–45

Death and Decay

All animals and plants eventually die. Their bodies contain stored chemical energy. This energy is not lost. There are many animals which feed on the bodies of other dead animals and plants.

Other living things or chemicals may be used to control organisms looked on as pests. Their use may affect the populations of organisms.

intro

These pages are about the importance of decay in a food web and the factors that affect the numbers in populations.

Death

Every living thing will die. However our surroundings are not littered with the corpses of animals and the remains of dead plants. Other organisms make use of these remains.

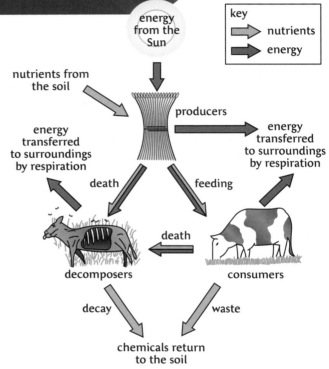

key
→ nutrients
→ energy

energy from the Sun

nutrients from the soil

producers

energy transferred to surroundings by respiration

energy transferred to surroundings by respiration

death

feeding

death

decomposers

consumers

decay

waste

chemicals return to the soil

Some animals, like vultures and hyenas, feed on the corpses of dead animals. Wood lice feed on fallen logs.

There are also microbes which get their energy by feeding on dead plants or animals. The feeding action of microbes causes the dead bodies or plants to rot or **decay**. Some of the chemicals from the decaying matter get into the soil, and can be used as nutrients or minerals by plants which take them in through their root hairs. Fungi, like toadstools and mushrooms, also feed on decaying remains and release chemicals for plants and animals to use again.

Some of the processes carried out by microbes and fungi also return carbon dioxide and water to the environment.

The carbon dioxide and water are used in photosynthesis. Fungi and microbes are called **decomposers**.

The balance of nature

The population of animals or plants in a particular area depends on how much food, water and space is available, and on how many individuals are killed by predators or diseases.

If one species in a food web is affected by a disease, the populations of other species can also change. Look at the food web on page 44. If a disease kills all the mussels, the population of starfish will also go down, because there is not enough food for them. If some predators moved into the habitat and ate most of the herring, the population of plankton might go up because there would be fewer herring to eat them.

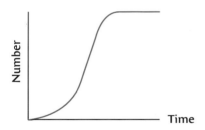

Living alone
In the absence of predators, a species quickly increases in numbers. Eventually, a shortage of resources forces the population to level out.

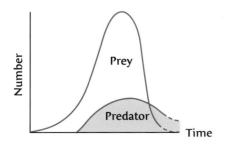

Living together
If a predator is introduced, the numbers of its prey fall. Both populations soon decrease, but in nature, the prey rarely dies out altogether.

Biological control

As scientists discovered the dangers of using chemical fertilisers and pesticides, they worked on new ways of controlling pests. **Biological control** is when other animals, plants, bacteria or viruses are used to kill off unwelcome pests.

Apple growers needed a way to get rid of a spider mite that damaged their apples. Ladybirds feed on mites. So the growers put large numbers of ladybirds in the apple trees. These ate the mites and the population of the pest dropped.

Trying to control nature sometimes has results that were not expected. About 40 years ago farmers killed off large numbers of rabbits by giving them a terrible disease called **myxomatosis**. There were no rabbits for owls or foxes to eat. The predators had to find other food. Many foxes raided chicken farms! This was the effect of upsetting the balance of nature.

summary

- The dead remains of animals and plants are rotted by **decomposers**.
- If the balance of organisms is changed, a community may be damaged.

Questions

A

1 What do these words mean?
   a) decomposer **b)** balance of nature
   c) biological control **d)** predator **e)** prey

B

1 Wood lice feed on fallen leaves and branches. Explain why this makes wood lice important animals in a woodland.
2 Explain why the disease myxomatosis upset chicken farmers.
3 Explain what happens to the population of a predator and its prey over a number of years.

C

Find out what problems have been caused by the following plant pests:
a) Spartina grass **b)** Japanese knot weed **c)** Rhododendrons.

Solids, Liquids and Gases

All materials that exist are classed as **solid** (such as rock), **liquid** (such as water) or **gas** (such as oxygen). Solid, liquid and gas are the three **states of matter**.

These pages are about the differences between solids, liquids and gases.

Solids

Movement
- A solid stays still and does not move.

Shape
- Its shape does not change. It is fixed.

Volume
- Its volume does not change. It is fixed.

Effect of pressure
- Even if a solid is pressed or squeezed it will not get much, if any, smaller because solids are not really compressible.

The bottom row of bricks in this house are not squashed even under the high pressure exerted by all the bricks above.

Liquids

Movement
- Liquids do not stay still. They move about and we say that liquids **flow**.

Shape
- Because they flow, liquids do not have a fixed shape. They take the shape of their container.

Volume
- As the liquid flows the amount of liquid does not change, and we say that liquids have a fixed volume.

Effect of pressure
- Liquids are very slightly compressible so they can be squeezed into a slightly smaller volume if pressure is applied to them.

Gases

Movement
- Like liquids, gases will flow and move about.

Shape
- Unlike liquids, gases will spread out and completely fill the container they are in. Gases, therefore, do not have a fixed shape.

Volume
- Gases do not have a fixed volume.

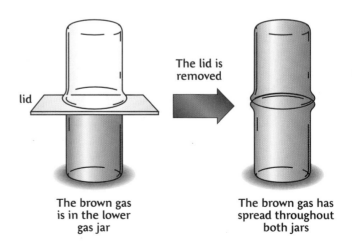

The brown gas is in the lower gas jar

The brown gas has spread throughout both jars

When the lid is taken away the brown gas spreads to fill both jars. The gas does not have a fixed shape or a fixed volume.

Effect of pressure

● Gases are very compressible and can be squashed into a much smaller volume if pressure is applied to them.

Density

Density is the amount of **matter** packed into a space.

● Solids have a lot of matter packed into them and have a high density.
● Liquids have less matter packed into them and have a lower density.
● Gases have very little matter packed into them and have a very low density.

Density is measured by finding the mass (in grams) of 1 cubic centimetre of the material.

$$\text{density (g/cm}^3) = \frac{\text{mass (g)}}{\text{volume (cm}^3)}$$

The table gives three examples of the density of a common material.

Material	State	Density in g/cm³
lead	solid	11
water	liquid	1
air	gas	0.0013

Solids, liquids and gases have properties which are different from each other. However, all solids have properties in common with each other, as do all liquids and all gases.

● Solids do not flow. They have a fixed volume and shape. They have a high density and are not compressible.
● Liquids flow. They have a fixed volume but take the shape of their container. They have lower densities than solids and can be compressed a little.
● Gases flow to fill their container completely. They do not have a fixed shape and do not have a fixed volume. They have very low densities and are highly compressible.

summary

Questions

 A

1 What do these words mean?
a) flow b) compressible
c) density d) volume

2 Solids, liquids and gases are the three states of matter. Which of these states:
a) keeps its shape
b) takes the shape of its container
c) does not flow
d) cannot be compressed
e) is very compressible
f) has no fixed volume
g) has the highest density
h) have fixed volume?

 B

1 Say whether each of these materials is a solid, liquid or gas:
a) sand b) oil c) ice
d) polythene bag e) air
f) fizzy drink g) apple
h) carbon dioxide
i) car exhaust fumes j) petrol

2 Name one property which solids and liquids have in common.

3 Name one property which liquids and gases have in common.

4 Name two properties which make solids different from gases.

5 'Solids are not compressible but gases are very compressible.' Explain what this statement means.

6 If you had 100 cm³ of lead and 100 cm³ of water, which would be heavier? Explain your answer.

 C

1 It is not always easy to decide the state of a particular material. Is mud a liquid or a solid, is it both, is it neither? Explain your answer.

2 What is the state of matter of butter and low-fat spreads? Explain your answer.

For more information on materials see pages 60–61, 62–63, 64–65 and 70–71

The Particles of Matter

All matter is made up of **particles**. The arrangement and movement of these particles are different in solids, liquids and gases. By looking at these differences you will understand the differences in appearance and behaviour of solids, liquids and gases.

These pages are about the arrangement and movement of particles in solids, liquids and gases

intro

The particles in a solid

The particles in a solid are packed tightly together. Strong **forces** hold them together. The particles stay in place in an orderly structure and move only by vibrating to and fro in the same place. This is why solids do not flow and have a fixed shape and volume.

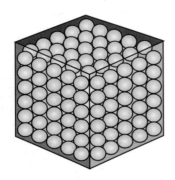

The particles in a liquid

The particles in a liquid are free to move from place to place. The movement is **random** (not in any fixed pattern) and the particles sometimes move past each other and sometimes bump into each other. There are forces holding them near to each other and keeping the volume of the liquid fixed, but these forces are weaker than the forces between the particles in a solid. The movement of the particles means that the liquid flows and does not have a fixed shape.

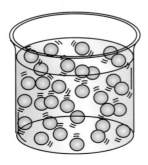

The particles in a gas

The particles in a gas move very fast and are spaced far apart from each other. There are hardly any forces at all holding them together and the movements are random and in all directions. This is why gases eventually spread to fill their container and have neither a fixed shape nor a fixed volume.

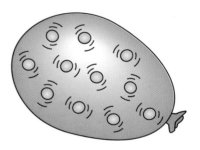

Changes of state

Materials can be changed from one **state** to another by heating or cooling. The most familiar example of this is that if it is heated enough, solid ice will turn into liquid water and then into **gaseous** steam.

By cooling the steam sufficiently you can reverse this process and turn the steam back into water then into ice again. Each **change of state** has its own name and all of these changes can be written as follows:

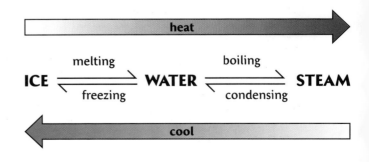

heat

melting   boiling

ICE ⇌ WATER ⇌ STEAM

freezing   condensing

cool

Particles and changes of state

By looking at the behaviour of the particles you will understand each of these changes of state.

Solid
particles in place
but vibrating

HEAT →

The particles gain energy and vibrate more and more. At first the solid expands as the particles move slightly apart then, eventually, the particles vibrate so much that they break away from the structure and move about. This is the melting point. The solid has become a liquid.

Liquid
particles
moving about

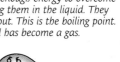

COOL

Further cooling slows the particles so much that the forces are able to hold them still in a structure. This is freezing and the liquid is now a solid again.

More and more energy makes the particles move faster and faster. Eventually the particles have enough energy to overcome the forces holding them in the liquid. They leave and spread out. This is the boiling point. The liquid has become a gas.

HEAT ↓

Cooling removes energy and slows the particles. Eventually the forces between particles suddenly come back into play and the particles are immediately pulled back together. The gas has condensed back into a liquid.

Liquid

COOL ←

Gas
particles are
free to spread

summary

- The **particles** in a solid are packed tightly together. They do not move from place to place but only vibrate in a fixed place. The forces between particles are strong.
- The particles in a liquid move from place to place randomly. They are quite close together and are held together by the forces between the particles.
- The particles in a gas move randomly and are spread throughout the container. They are spread far apart and the forces between them are weak.
- **Changes of state** can be brought about by changes in temperature. This gives energy to the particles or takes energy from the particles.

Questions

A

1   What do the following words mean?
    a) melting point **b)** boiling point
    c) condensing **d)** freezing

2   Here are some statements about particles. Say whether each one describes a solid, a liquid or a gas.
    a) The particles are packed closely together.
    b) The particles are moving in all directions at random.
    c) There are strong forces between the particles.
    d) The particles move from place to place but stay together in the same volume.

    e) There are some forces holding the particles together but the forces are not strong enough to hold the particles in place.
    f) The particles are in a pattern.
    g) There are hardly any forces between the particles.

B

1   'The particles in a solid are vibrating.' Explain what this statement means.

2   What does 'melting' mean? Explain what happens to the particles when materials melt.

3   What does 'condensing' mean? Explain what happens to the particles when materials condense.

4   Use the behaviour of the particles to explain why a solid cannot be compressed while a gas is very compressible.

5   Use the behaviour of the particles to explain what is happening when water boils and turns into steam.

C

Do you think liquids are more like solids or more like gases? Explain your answer.

For more information on changes of state see pages 64–65 and 68–69

Properties and Particles

The **properties** of a material depend entirely upon how its particles behave. Knowing what the particles in a material are doing will help you to explain its properties.

These pages are about how to explain the properties of materials by looking at the behaviour of particles.

Diffusion

If someone squirts air freshener from its can, the smell quickly spreads throughout the room. This is because the smell released from the can is actually made up of fast moving gaseous particles of a material that smells pleasant. These particles mix with the air particles and quickly spread through the room.

This movement of particles is called **diffusion**.

Diffusion also takes place in liquids, but here it is much slower than in gases because the particles in a liquid move much more slowly, and there are also stronger forces between the particles.

Gas pressure

When you blow up a balloon you breathe air into it. This air is made up of millions of fast moving gas particles. These particles hit the sides of the balloon and keep it inflated by exerting a pressure on it.

The particles are moving very fast and are exerting pressure on the walls of their container (in this case, the balloon).

Diffusion is taking place in your body all the time.

The oxygen you breathe in passes into your blood by diffusion.

The food you have eaten is broken down into very small particles which also pass into your blood by diffusion.

The food and oxygen can now produce the energy you need.

There is plenty of diffusion going on here!

If the gas in the container is heated, the particles will gain energy and hit the walls harder and more often. This means the gas pressure increases.

If the container of gas is squeezed to make it smaller, then the particles will be able to hit the walls more often. This means the gas pressure will increase.

These photographs show how gas pressure is important in our everyday lives.

 The drink is pushed up the straw by the pressure of the air particles pushing down on the surface of the drink in the glass.

 The tyres are kept inflated by the pressure of the air particles inside them.

- The properties of a material can be explained by looking at the behaviour of the particles in the material.
- The movement of particles through a space is called **diffusion**.
- Diffusion is fast in gases and slower in liquids.
- Gas **pressure** results from the particles of the gas hitting the walls of the container.
- Gas pressure is increased by raising temperature or lowering volume.

summary

Questions

A

1. What does 'diffusion' mean?
2. What is gas pressure?
3. What happens to gas pressure when the temperature of the gas is increased?
4. What happens to gas pressure when the volume of the gas is decreased?

B

1. Which would you smell first, hot cooked cheese or solid uncooked cheese? Explain your answer.
2. Explain why placing a sealed balloon of gas in a refrigerator will cause the volume of the balloon to decrease.
3. Explain why squeezing a sealed balloon of gas until it becomes smaller and smaller can eventually make the balloon burst.

C

Some air fresheners come in solid blocks which are left to stand in a room. Explain why they give off a smell and why they slowly reduce in size until eventually there is nothing left.

For more information about gas pressure see pages 70–71

Elements and Atoms

If a piece of bread is toasted in a high heat, it becomes covered in a black solid. This black solid is called **carbon** and no matter what you do to it you cannot break it down any further. Carbon is an **element**.

These pages are about elements and atoms and show that elements have symbols and can be arranged into a table called the Periodic Table.

An element is a single material that cannot be broken down into simpler materials.

There are 109 elements in total. 90 of them have been obtained naturally from the Earth's **crust** or its **atmosphere** and 19 of them have been made artificially by scientists.

There are millions of different materials on Earth and all of them are made up from combinations of one or more of the 90 **natural elements**. The proportions of the natural elements in the Universe, the Earth's crust and the human body are given below.

Universe	Earth's crust	Human body
hydrogen 90%	oxygen 48%	oxygen 65%
helium 9%	silicon 27%	carbon 18%
all others 1%	aluminium 8%	hydrogen 10%
	iron 4%	nitrogen 3%
	calcium 3%	calcium 1.5%
	sodium 2.5%	phosphorous 1.0%
	potassium 2.5%	all others 1.5%
	magnesium 2%	
	hydrogen 1%	
	all others 2%	

Symbols

All elements have a one- or two-letter **symbol**. If a symbol has two letters, the first one is written as a capital letter and the second is written as a small letter. If a symbol has only one letter then it is always written as a capital letter.

Element	Symbol	Element	Symbol
aluminium	Al	lead	Pb
calcium	Ca	magnesium	Mg
carbon	C	nitrogen	N
chlorine	Cl	oxygen	O
copper	Cu	potassium	K
helium	He	sodium	Na
hydrogen	H	sulphur	S
iron	Fe	zinc	Zn

The table above gives a list of the symbols of some of the more common elements. These symbols are taken from the names of the elements in various languages; for example, O for oxygen (English) and K for kalium (the arabic name for potassium).

Atoms

All elements are made up of tiny particles called **atoms**.

An atom is the smallest part of an element that can exist.

Atoms are very small. 100 000 000 (100 million) atoms laid side by side would make a line only **1 centimetre** long!

Different elements have different atoms. For instance, all magnesium atoms are identical but they are different from iron atoms.

Atoms themselves are made up of three kinds of particles called **protons**, **neutrons** and **electrons**. The protons and neutrons stay together in a small central **nucleus** and the electrons circle around the nucleus.

Protons have a positive charge, electrons have a negative charge and neutrons have no charge.

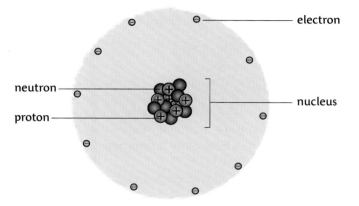

electron

neutron

proton

nucleus

While the number of neutrons can vary, all the atoms of an element have the same number of protons and electrons. Atoms of different elements have different numbers of protons and electrons.

The Periodic Table

This table arranges the elements in horizontal lines called **periods** and vertical columns called **groups.** The elements are placed in order of the number of protons their atoms contain. The Periodic Table for the first 20 elements looks like this.

this is group I	name symbol number of protons		Hydrogen H 1			this is group VII	Helium He 2
Lithium Li 3	Beryllium Be 4	Boron B 5	Carbon C 6	Nitrogen N 7	Oxygen O 8	Fluorine F 9	Neon Ne 10
Sodium Na 11	Magnesium Mg 12	Aluminium Al 13	Silicon Si 14	Phosphorus P 15	Sulphur S 16	Chlorine Cl 17	Argon Ar 18
Potassium K 19	Calcium Ca 20						

Groups are numbered with Roman numerals and each group contains elements which have similar properties to each other. Group I contains lithium, sodium and potassium which all have similar properties to each other. Group VII contains fluorine and chlorine which are also very similar to each other.

For more information about elements see pages 62–63

summary

- An **element** is a single material that cannot be broken down into simpler materials.
- Elements are made up of **atoms** of that element.
- Atoms are made up of **protons, neutrons** and **electrons**.
- All atoms of an element contain the same number of protons and electrons.
- Atoms of different elements have different numbers of protons and electrons.
- The **Periodic Table** contains all the elements arranged in the order of their number of protons.

Questions

1 What do the following words mean?
a) element **b)** atom

2 What is the symbol for each of the following elements?
a) copper **b)** hydrogen **c)** sodium **d)** zinc **e)** iron

3 What is the name of each of the following elements?
a) Pb **b)** N **c)** Mg **d)** S

1 What is the nucleus of an atom and what kinds of particles does it contain?

2 Atom A contains 6 protons and 7 neutrons. Atom B contains 6 protons and 6 neutrons. Are A and B atoms of the same element or atoms of different elements? Explain your answer.

3 Give the name and symbol of an element that you might expect to be similar to each of the following: **a)** sodium **b)** carbon **c)** chlorine **d)** calcium **e)** argon

Make a list of 25 elements with their symbols. Learn the name and symbol of each one. Get someone to test you.

Compounds

These pages are about how elements combine to make compounds and how atoms join to make molecules.

intro

If a piece of magnesium is burned in a Bunsen flame, a white powder is produced. This white powder is called magnesium oxide. It has been made by the magnesium **combining** (joining) with oxygen from the air. The magnesium oxide is a **compound** and it is a completely new material which is different from both the magnesium and the oxygen.

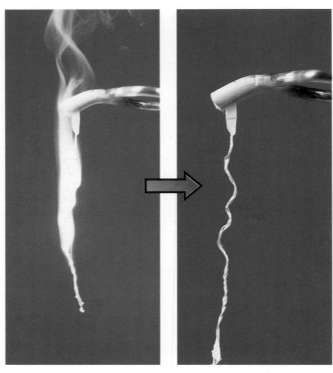

▶ *Magnesium burns in oxygen from the air.*

▶ *Magnesium oxide powder is produced.*

A compound is a pure material made up of two or more elements chemically combined.

Here are a few well-known compounds.

Compound	Elements in compound
water (hydrogen oxide)	hydrogen, oxygen
common salt (sodium chloride)	sodium, chlorine
carbon dioxide	carbon, oxygen
chalk (calcium carbonate)	calcium, carbon, oxygen
alcohol (ethanol)	carbon, hydrogen, oxygen

Molecules

When elements combine to form compounds, what actually happens, millions of times over, is that the atoms of one of the elements join up with the atoms of the other element. The larger particles formed when atoms combine are called **molecules**.

A molecule is the smallest part of a compound that can exist. It is made up of two or more atoms joined together.

Formulas

A compound is written as a **formula**. The formula is made up from the symbols of the elements in the compound.

Compound	Elements in compound
water	H_2O
sodium chloride (common salt)	NaCl
carbon dioxide	CO_2
calcium carbonate (chalk)	$CaCO_3$
ethanol (alcohol)	C_6H_6O

When two elements form a compound, the name of the compound usually ends in **-ide**.

magnesium + oxygen → magnesium oxide
sodium + chlorine → sodium chloride
hydrogen + oxygen → hydrogen oxide (water)

The definite composition of compounds

Some formulas have numbers in them. These numbers show how many of each kind of atom have joined together to make one molecule of the compound.

For example, water molecules are made from the combination of 2 hydrogen atoms with 1 oxygen atom. That is why the formula for water is H_2O.

The composition of water molecules is always the same: 2 atoms of hydrogen and 1 atom of oxygen in each molecule.

You can see from this that **all compounds have a fixed composition**. This is called the **law of constant composition**.

The weight of a magnesium atom is 1½ times the weight of an oxygen atom and the formula of magnesium oxide is MgO.

Therefore, the composition of magnesium oxide is constant at 1 atom of Mg : 1 atom of O.

Therefore, the composition **by weight** of magnesium oxide is constant at 1½ parts magnesium : 1 part oxygen (or 3 parts magnesium : 2 parts oxygen).

This means that 3 g of magnesium needs to combine with 2 g of oxygen to form 5 g of magnesium oxide. Or 6 g of magnesium need 4 g of oxygen to form 10 g of magnesium oxide.

- **Compounds** are made by the **chemical combination** of two or more elements.
- **Molecules** are made by the chemical combination of two or more atoms.
- **Compounds** are represented by a **formula**.
- **Molecules** are the smallest part of a compound that can exist.
- The **law of constant composition** says that the composition of all compounds is fixed.

summary

Questions

 A

1 What is a compound?

2 Give two statements that explain what a molecule is.

3 What is the formula of each of the following compounds?
a) water **b)** sodium chloride
c) carbon dioxide **d)** chalk

 B

Copy out and complete each of the following tables. The first example has been done for you in each case.

1

Name of compound	Elements in compound
copper oxide	copper, oxygen
	iron, oxygen
potassium chloride	
zinc sulphide	

2

Name of compound	Formula	Elements present
calcium oxide	CaO	calcium, oxygen
	MgS	
zinc oxide		

3

Formula	Name	Numbers of each type of atom
H_2O	water	2 hydrogen, 1 oxygen
Al_2O_3		
$MgCl_2$		
		2 iron, 3 oxygen

 C

The weights of some atoms relative to one hydrogen atom are:

H=1   C=12   O=16   S=32

a) If 32 g of sulphur always combine with 32 g of oxygen, what is the formula of the compound formed? Explain your answer.

b) What weight of oxygen is needed to combine with 6 g of carbon to form carbon dioxide?

For more information about the production of compounds see pages 74–79

Mixtures

These pages are about what a mixture is, how mixtures differ from compounds and how you can separate mixtures into their different parts.

Most of the things around you are not pure materials. They are **mixtures** of two or more pure materials. Each of these is a mixture: air, seawater, food, drinks, clothing, paper, ink, soap, soil. In a mixture the materials are jumbled up together but are **not** combined with each other. A mixture does not have a fixed composition and it can be made from any amounts of the materials it contains.

Mixtures and compounds

When elements combine they form a **compound** which is an entirely new material with new properties of its own. In a **mixture** the materials do not combine. They are still present in the mixture in their original form. This means that the mixture has the properties of its **constituents** (separate ingredients) and not new ones of its own. For example, salt in water tastes like salt and looks like water. The table below compares mixtures and compounds.

Mixtures	Compounds
The materials are not combined.	The elements are combined together.
No new material is formed.	A new material is formed.
The mixture has the properties of its individual materials.	The compound has entirely new properties of its own.
A mixture can be made using any proportions of the individual materials.	A compound always contains the same elements in the same fixed proportions.
A mixture can easily be separated.	It is very difficult to separate a compound into its original elements.

Separating mixtures

Materials you do want are almost always mixed with other materials that you do not want. Some of the simple ways of separating mixtures are described below.

Filtration – is used to separate a solid which has not **dissolved** (see page 64) from a liquid.

- Sand can be separated from water by pouring the mixture through a filter paper.

- The sand stays in the filter paper (the sand is called the **residue**) and the water passes through (the water is called the **filtrate**).

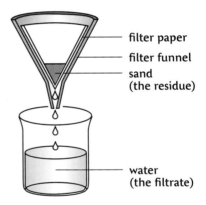

filter paper
filter funnel
sand
(the residue)

water
(the filtrate)

Evaporation – is used to get a dissolved solid back out of a liquid.

- Salt can be obtained from salt solution in this way.
- The clear solution is placed in an evaporating dish and heated until boiling.
- The liquid boils away leaving behind the solid that had been dissolved.

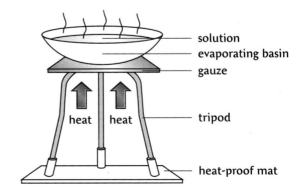

solution
evaporating basin
gauze

heat   heat   tripod

heat-proof mat

Solution and evaporation — are used to separate two solids, one which dissolves and one which does not dissolve. For example, water can be used to separate a salt/sand mixture.

● The mixture is stirred in water.

● The salt dissolves and the sand remains undissolved.

● The mixture is filtered to obtain the sand as a residue.

● The salt solution is evaporated to get the salt.

Distillation — is used to get the **solvent** (the pure liquid) from a solution. For example, distilled (pure) water can be made from salt solution this way.

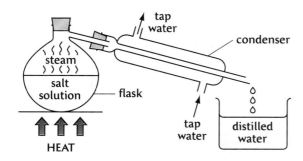

● As the solution is heated in the flask the steam rises and leaves the salt behind.

● The steam passes into the inner tube of the **condenser**, which is cold. This causes the steam to condense to pure water.

● The pure water collects in the beaker. It is called **distilled** water.

Chromatography — is used to separate mixtures of coloured liquids such as ink.

● A spot of the ink is placed in the middle of a filter paper resting on a Petri dish.

● When the drop has soaked in, a second drop is added. By continuing to add drops so that the water soaks to the edge of the paper, coloured rings will be left on the paper.

● The colours are the different materials in the ink.

● They separate out because they each dissolve to a different extent in water.

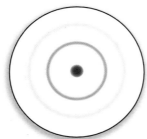

---

summary

● In a mixture the constituents are not combined together.

● A mixture is different from a compound in a number of ways.

● Mixtures are fairly easy to separate.

● Some methods of separation include: **filtration, evaporation, distillation, chromatography.**

Questions

1 What do these words mean?
a) evaporate **b)** chromatography
c) condense **d)** residue **e)** filtrate

2 What is a mixture?

3 Sort these materials into mixtures or pure compounds (non-mixtures):
a) steam **b)** air **c)** fizzy drink
d) sugar **e)** potato **f)** copper **g)** oxygen
h) seawater **i)** pizza **j)** petrol

4 List five differences between a compound and a mixture.

1 Describe an experiment to obtain each of the following:
a) pure water from ink
b) chalk from a mixture of chalk and water.

2 Describe how you would test whether some blue ink contained only one pure blue dye or a mixture of dyes.

3 Describe how you would obtain pure, dry salt from a piece of impure rock salt.

Sugar and salt both dissolve in water so water cannot be used to separate them. However, sugar dissolves in ethanol but salt does not. Describe how ethanol could be used to separate a mixture of sugar and salt. (**NB:** ethanol is highly flammable and must **NOT** be heated directly using a Bunsen burner.)

Metals and Non-metals

There are 109 elements. 88 of these are **metals** and 21 are **non-metals**. Many of the metals are very rare and hard to find. The 21 non-metals are more common and are therefore easier to find.

These pages are about how all elements are classified as either metals or non-metals, and the different properties of metals and non-metals.

intro

Metals

Most metals have properties in common.

These steel girders will not break under high loads.

This hot iron can be shaped by hitting it.

Metals

- are strong
- are **malleable** (can be beaten into shapes)
- are **ductile** (can be stretched into wires)
- are **sonorous** (make a ringing noise when struck)
- are shiny if polished
- are good **conductors** of heat
- are good conductors of electricity
- have high melting and boiling points
- have high **densities.**

Copper is used for electrical wiring.

This saucepan conducts heat quickly.

Gold melts at over 1000°C

There are some exceptions:
- Iron is **magnetic** while most other metals are not.
- Some metals, like sodium, potassium and lithium, are so soft that they can be cut with a knife.
- Mercury is the only metal that is a liquid at room temperature.
- Aluminium is very light but is still very strong.

Non-metals

The 21 non-metals are quite different from the metals.

Bromine is the only liquid non-metal.

Non-metals

- have very low melting and boiling points
  - bromine is the only liquid at room temperature
  - 11 (including hydrogen, oxygen and nitrogen) are gases
  - 9 (including carbon and sulphur) are solids
- are not strong – diamond, which is a form of carbon, is an exception and is the hardest natural substance known
- are not sonorous
- are not ductile
- are not malleable – when solid non-metals are hammered they break up because they are **brittle**
- are poor conductors of heat
- are poor conductors of electricity
  – graphite, which is a form of carbon, is an exception and is a good conductor of electricity
- are light because they have low densities.

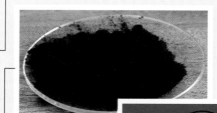

Solid carbon is easily powdered.

Sulphur is a solid non-metal.

Graphite is the only non-metal conductor of electricity.

- Elements can be classified as **metals** or **non-metals**.
- There are 88 metals and 21 non-metals.
- Metals have a lot of properties in common although there are some exceptions.
- Non-metals are very different to metals and have almost opposite properties.
- The properties of non-metals vary quite widely. They are not as like each other as metals.

summary

Questions

A

1. What do the following words mean? **a)** malleable **b)** brittle **c)** sonorous **d)** ductile

2. Name ten metals and five non-metals and give the symbol of each.

3. Name one liquid metal and one liquid non-metal.

4. Name a non-metal that conducts electricity.

5. Name a non-metal that is so hard it is used to cut metals.

6. Name a metal that is used to make:
   a) electrical wiring
   b) saucepans **c)** horseshoes
   d) girders

B

1. List five of the general properties of metals and, for each one, state how non-metals behave in contrast to metals.

2. Look at the four elements A, B, C and D in the table.

Element	Melting point (°C)	Does it conduct electricity?	Is it shiny?
A	1064	Yes	Yes
B	−101	No	No
C	119	No	No
D	317	Yes	Yes

Say whether each one is a non-metal or metal and explain your reasoning in each case.

3. For each of the following metals, give **two** properties it possesses that enable it to be used in the way stated:
   a) copper for electrical wiring
   b) aluminium for saucepans
   c) iron for wrought iron gates
   d) gold for jewellery
   e) iron for domestic central heating radiators.

C

Name two elements which you think are difficult to classify as either metal or non-metal. Explain why you think they are difficult to classify.

For more information about metals see pages 86–87 and 88–89

Physical Changes

When ice is heated it **changes** into water. If the water is heated enough, it **changes** again into steam. If the steam is cooled down sufficiently, it will change back to water and then to ice.

> These pages are about physical and chemical change, and how mass is conserved when a physical change takes place.

Changes of state

Throughout the changes described above the material involved does **not** change. It is always made up of the same particles, which are water molecules, and it always has the same formula, H_2O. What changes is the **physical state** of the material. The molecules themselves stay the same throughout.

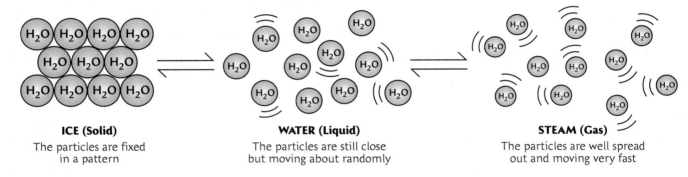

ICE (Solid)	**WATER (Liquid)**	**STEAM (Gas)**
The particles are fixed in a pattern	The particles are still close but moving about randomly	The particles are well spread out and moving very fast

This change is called a **physical change. A physical change is one which can be reversed by changing the conditions and in which no new substance is formed.**

All changes of state must be physical changes because the material involved does not change; the changes are confined to those between solid, liquid and gas.

Dissolving

Dissolving materials to form solutions (see pages 66–67) is a further example of a physical change.

When salt is dissolved in water the granules of salt are broken up by the water into individual salt particles. These are too small to be seen. No new substance has been formed and the process is easily reversible by boiling the solution until all the water has evaporated. The salt will then be left in its original form.

Conservation of mass

When a physical change takes place there is **no change of mass**. If 10 g of ice are melted, 10 g of water will be formed. This can be boiled to form 10 g of steam, which can be condensed back into 10 g of water, and so on.

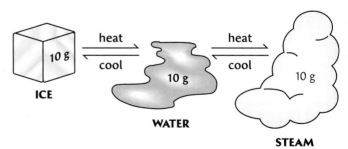

Similarly, if 20 g of salt are dissolved in 100 g of water then 120 g of salt solution will be formed. If the 120 g of solution are carefully evaporated so that no salt is lost by spitting out, then 20 g of salt will remain when the solution is completely dry.

Comparing physical changes to chemical changes

If a piece of paper is lit and left to burn, only flimsy black ashes remain. These ashes are a new substance and the ash cannot be changed back into paper.

 This cannot be turned back into paper.

If flour, butter, eggs and milk are mixed and heated in an oven, a cake is produced. The process cannot be reversed.

 You cannot 'unbake' this cake.

Changes like these, which make new materials and cannot be reversed, are called **chemical changes**. Burning and cooking are two examples. Food rotting and iron rusting are two other chemical changes that you can see around you.

Physical change	Chemical change
No new materials are formed.	One or more new materials are always formed.
The change is usually reversible by changing the conditions.	The change is usually difficult, and often impossible, to reverse.
Changes of state and making solutions are good examples.	Burning and cooking are good examples.

- Changes which do not produce new materials and are easy to reverse are called **physical changes**.
- Changes which do produce new materials and which are very difficult or impossible to reverse are called **chemical changes**.
- **Mass is always conserved in a physical change.**

summary

Questions

A

1 What is a physical change?
2 Give two examples of a physical change.
3 How do you know if a change is a chemical one?
4 Give two examples, other than burning paper and baking a cake, of chemical changes.

B

1 Say whether each of the changes listed is physical or chemical. In each case give reasons for your answer.

a) gas burning in a Bunsen burner
b) someone painting a door
c) the wick in a candle burning
d) the wax in a candle melting
e) your breakfast being digested
f) nails going rusty
g) someone frying an egg
h) someone folding a piece of paper
i) milk going sour
j) the tar on the road melting on a hot summer day.

2 What weight of steam could be obtained from 15 g of ice? Explain your answer.

3 Describe how you would make 130 g of salt solution starting with 20 g of salt.

A mixture of iron filings and sulphur can easily be separated by using a magnet. However, if the mixture is heated strongly first then the magnet has no effect. Explain these facts.

For more information on changes see pages 52–53, 66–67 and 74–75

Solutions and Solubility

intro

When salt is added to water and the mixture is stirred the salt seems to disappear. Tasting the mixture proves the salt is still there even if it cannot be seen. The salt is said to have **dissolved** in the water.

These pages are about materials that dissolve in other materials to produce solutions.

Solutions

The salt does this because it is **soluble** in water. The clear salt and water mixture that is produced is called a **solution**.

To make a solution you need a **solute** (the material that dissolves) and a **solvent** (the material it dissolves in). In salt solution the salt is the solute and the water is the solvent.

A solution with not much solute in it is a **dilute** solution. A solution with a lot of solute in it is a **concentrated** solution.

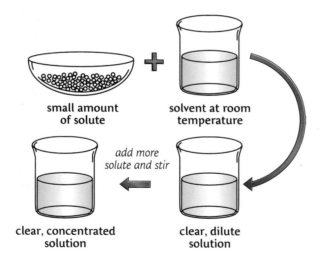

small amount of solute

solvent at room temperature

add more solute and stir

clear, concentrated solution

clear, dilute solution

Some materials, for example, sand and chalk, do not dissolve in water at all. They are said to be **insoluble** in water.

If you keep on stirring salt into the water to make the solution more and more concentrated, a point will be reached when no more salt will dissolve. This is now a **saturated** solution.

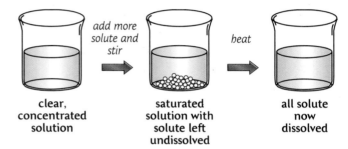

add more solute and stir

heat

clear, concentrated solution

saturated solution with solute left undissolved

all solute now dissolved

If the solution is heated, the excess salt will begin to dissolve. This is because salt is more soluble in water as the temperature increases. In other words, its **solubility increases with temperature.**

A **saturated solution** is one that cannot contain any more solute at that temperature.

The **solubility** of a solute in water at a particular temperature is the maximum amount of the solute in grams that will dissolve in 100 g of water at that temperature.

Different materials have different solubilities. The table shows the solubilities of some materials in water at 25°C.

Material	Solubility (g/100g)
common salt (sodium chloride)	30
potassium chloride	35
sugar	230
copper sulphate	22

Other solvents

Water is the most important solvent of all because there is a lot of it, it is readily available, it is cheap and safe to use and it will dissolve many materials. However, many materials, such as ball-point ink, nail varnish, oil, fat and paint, will not dissolve in water.

The table shows some solvents and the solutes they will dissolve.

Solvent	Can be used to remove
ethanol	grass, ball-point ink
paraffin	chewing gum, tar, grease
petrol	oil, grease
white spirit	paint, tar
acetone	nail varnish, ball-point ink
trichloroethane	tar, gum, grease

Dry cleaning means cleaning without using water. The clothes are cleaned in washing machines using a solvent such as perchloroethylene instead of water.

summary

● A **solution** is formed when a **solute** dissolves in a **solvent**.
● Materials which do not dissolve in a **solvent** are insoluble in that solvent.
● A **saturated** solution can hold no more solute.

Questions

 A

1. What do these words mean?
   a) solute b) solvent c) solution d) soluble e) insoluble f) saturated solution g) the solubility of a solute in water
2. Name three solvents other than water and one solute that each of them dissolves.
3. What is meant by 'dry' cleaning?

 B

1. Explain how you could make a dilute solution into a concentrated one.
2. Explain how you could make a concentrated solution into a dilute one.
3. Why is water the most important solvent?
4. What would you expect to happen if you left a hot, saturated solution to cool?

 C

Explain why water cannot be used to remove grease spots from clothing.

For more information about dissolving see pages 64–65

Energy and Changes of State

intro

When any liquid is heated its temperature rises until the liquid boils. The temperature at which this occurs is the **boiling point** of the liquid. If you keep on heating the liquid, it will continue to boil but its temperature will stay the same. But what is happening to the heat that is being put into the liquid if it isn't being used to raise the temperature of the liquid?

These pages are about the energy changes associated with changes of state, and how different materials change state at different temperatures.

The behaviour of particles

To answer the question above you must remind yourself of the behaviour of the **particles** in a liquid as it boils to a **vapour**.

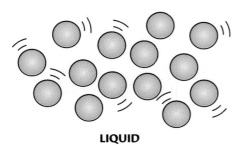

LIQUID
particles are close but moving randomly around

Heat gives the particles enough energy to overcome the forces holding them together

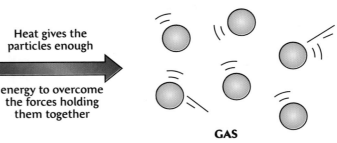

GAS
particles are spread and moving randomly and fast

Heating a liquid

Once the liquid has reached its boiling point the particles need energy to break away from the forces holding them in the liquid. They get this **energy** from the heat. So the heat is no longer being used to raise the temperature which now remains constant.

A graph of temperature against time as the liquid is heated shows how this happens. This graph is called a **heating curve**.

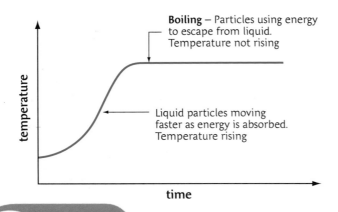

Boiling – Particles using energy to escape from liquid. Temperature not rising

Liquid particles moving faster as energy is absorbed. Temperature rising

Heating a solid

A similar effect is seen when a solid is heated. The temperature of the solid rises until the melting point is reached. The temperature now stays constant until melting is complete and all the particles have overcome the forces that were holding them in a rigid pattern. When the material is completely liquid the temperature starts to go up again.

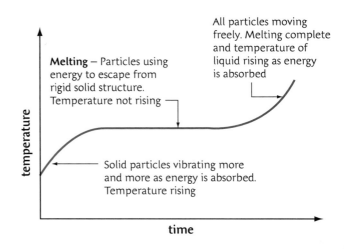

All particles moving freely. Melting complete and temperature of liquid rising as energy is absorbed

Melting – Particles using energy to escape from rigid solid structure. Temperature not rising

Solid particles vibrating more and more as energy is absorbed. Temperature rising

During the reverse process of cooling, bursts of energy will be released at the point of **condensation** and again at the point of **freezing** when the temperature stays constant for a short time.

Melting points and boiling points

The temperature at which a change of state occurs depends on the particles and the strength of the forces of attraction between them. This means that different materials change state at different temperatures. In general, the stronger the forces are and the heavier the particles are then the higher the temperature will be at which a change of state takes place.

The melting points and boiling points of some common materials are shown in the table.

Material	Melting point (°C)	Boiling point (°C)
water	0	100
iron	1540	2760
ethanoic acid (in vinegar)	17	118
aluminium	660	2350
sodium	98	900
ethanol (alcohol)	−114	78
sodium chloride (common salt)	808	1465
oxygen	−219	−183
diamond	3550	4827

summary

- When materials melt and boil, **energy is needed to separate the particles.**
- The energy is obtained from the heat being supplied. For this reason the temperature does not rise until the **particle separation** is complete.
- When the process is reversed the material gives out heat at the point of condensation and again at the point of freezing.
- Different materials change state at different temperatures; that is, they have different melting and boiling points.

Questions

1 In each of these processes say whether the material involved gains energy (absorbs heat) or loses energy (releases heat):
a) melting **b)** freezing
c) condensation **d)** boiling

1 Explain why the temperature of boiling water does not increase beyond 100°C even when heating continues.

2 When molten (melted) iron solidifies, does the iron lose or gain heat? Explain your answer.

3 When ice melts, do the water molecules lose or gain heat? Explain your answer.

4 Material A has a melting point of 84°C. Material B has a melting point of 207°C. Suggest a reason why these two materials have different melting points.

5 Explain why the back of your hand feels cold when nail varnish remover is placed on it.

6 Explain why people sweat in hot weather.

A piece of ice at −10°C is heated until it becomes boiling water. Sketch the heating curve you would expect to see and label the important parts and temperatures on it.

For more information about changes of state see pages 52–53 and 64–65

Expansion and Contraction

When a piece of iron is heated it **expands** (gets bigger) and when it is cooled it **contracts** (gets smaller) until it is back at its original size.

These pages are about how materials expand and contract when the temperature changes, and how the forces resulting from this are very great.

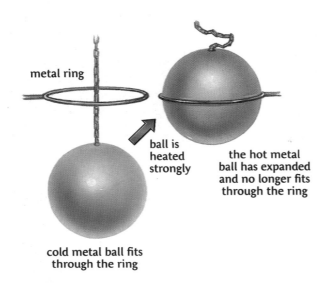

metal ring

ball is heated strongly

the hot metal ball has expanded and no longer fits through the ring

cold metal ball fits through the ring

All materials expand when they are heated and contract when they are cooled.

What is happening to the particles?

In a solid the particles are vibrating in a fixed place. When the solid is heated the particles get more energy and vibrate more. This causes them to push apart slightly and the solid expands.

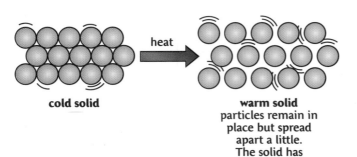

cold solid

heat

warm solid
particles remain in place but spread apart a little. The solid has expanded

The effect is the same when the particles of a liquid or a gas are heated.

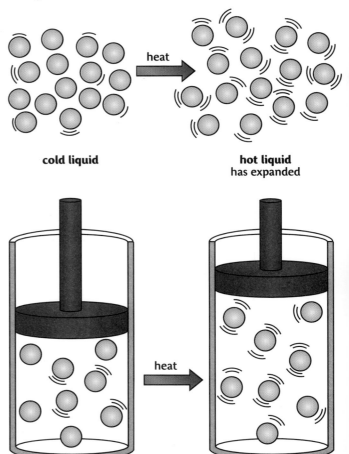

cold liquid

heat

hot liquid
has expanded

cold gas
in a container with a plunger

heat

hot gas
has expanded and the plunger has moved out

You can see, however, that the expansion is much greater in gases than it is in liquids, and that it is greater in liquids than it is in solids.

The forces of expansion and contraction

When a solid is heated and expands, the force of the expansion is very great indeed and almost impossible to hold back. If there is no space for a piece of hot metal to expand, the metal will bend and buckle.

Allowance is made for this force when railway tracks are laid. A gap is left between the ends of the lengths of line so that the metal can expand in hot weather without the line buckling.

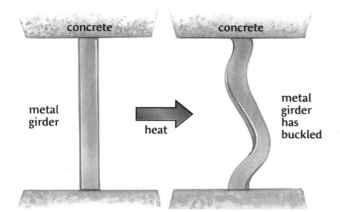

concrete — concrete — heat — metal girder — metal girder has buckled

● When materials are heated they **expand**, and when they are cooled they **contract**.
● This happens because the more energy the particles have, the more they spread out.
● The particles behave in the opposite way when they lose energy because they are being cooled.
● Expansion is greater in gases than in liquids and greater in liquids than in solids.
● The forces of expansion and contraction are great and they are often strong enough to cause damage.

summary

Questions

A

1 What does the word 'expand' mean?

2 How can you make a material expand?

3 What does the word 'contract' mean?

4 How can you make a material contract?

B

1 By describing the behaviour of the particles, explain why:
a) a solid expands when it is heated
b) a gas contracts when it is cooled
c) liquids expand more than solids when they are heated by the same amount.

2 Explain why railway lines that have been laid end to end, without gaps between the lengths of line, will buckle in hot weather.

3 Explain why a metal screw top that is stuck tight on a glass bottle can be loosened by running hot water over it.

4 Explain what happens to a syringe containing gas when the gas is warmed. Draw diagrams to help your explanation.

C

1 Give a full explanation, with diagrams, of how and why a thermometer containing mercury can be used to measure the rise and fall of temperature.

2 When a blacksmith puts the metal rim around the outside of a wooden cartwheel, he puts it on when the rim is very hot. Using diagrams, give an explanation for this.

For more information about expansion and contraction see pages 52–53 and 54–55

Rocks and the Rock Cycle

The Earth is made up of three main layers. On the outside is a thin, solid layer of rock called the **crust**. At the centre is a very hot, melted part called the **core**. In between the core and the crust is a layer called the **mantle**. The rocks in the Earth's crust were **formed** (made) in one of three ways and rocks are called **igneous**, **sedimentary** or **metamorphic** depending on which way they were formed. The materials in a rock are called **minerals**. The minerals contained in a rock depend on how it was formed.

intro

These pages are about the formation and cycling of igneous, sedimentary and metamorphic rocks, and about rock weathering.

Igneous rocks

Some parts of the Earth's crust are quite weak and sometimes **molten** (melted) rock called **magma** breaks through from the mantle and comes to the surface. This is what happens in a **volcano** and the molten rock which pours out is called **lava**. When the lava cools it becomes solid rock. This is **igneous rock**.

Igneous rock is made up of **crystals**. If the lava cools quickly, the crystals will be small. This happens when the lava is on the Earth's surface and it can take place within days. **Basalt** is an example of this type of igneous rock.

If the lava cools below the Earth's surface, it can cool so slowly that it takes hundreds of years to become solid. This produces large crystals. **Granite** is an example of this type of igneous rock.

▶ _Granite_

Sedimentary rocks

Bits of broken rocks, dust, soil, plants and dead animals can be moved from place to place on the Earth's surface by wind, water, ice or gravity. This material is then **deposited** (dropped) somewhere else. Material deposited like this is called **sediment**. One layer of sediment settles on another layer, with the youngest or newest layer always on the top. Gradually, the weight of the top layers causes the lowest layers to be **compacted** (pressed together) into **sedimentary rock**.

Limestone and chalk, which are made mainly from the shells of sea animals, are examples of sedimentary rock. Mudstone, shale and sandstone are also sedimentary rocks.

Metamorphic rocks

Rocks which lie deep below the surface of the Earth are under great pressure and are also very hot. This heat and pressure can change them permanently. Rock which has been formed in this way is called **metamorphic rock**. Both igneous and sedimentary rocks can undergo this change but it happens mostly to sedimentary rocks which usually lie deeper in the Earth than igneous rocks.

Both marble and slate are metamorphic rocks. Marble is formed from limestone.

▶ _Shale – a sedimentary rock, with fossils of ammonites_

▶ _Slate – a layered metamorphic rock_

The rock cycle

Over millions of years rocks change from one type to another constantly. This is called the **rock cycle**.

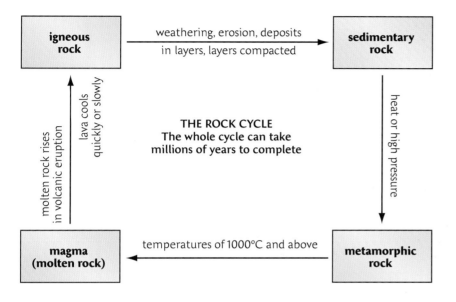

igneous rock → weathering, erosion, deposits in layers, layers compacted → sedimentary rock

molten rock rises in volcanic eruption / lava cools quickly or slowly

magma (molten rock) ← temperatures of 1000°C and above ← metamorphic rock

heat or high pressure

THE ROCK CYCLE
The whole cycle can take millions of years to complete

Weathering

Rocks are being broken up all the time. Because they are continually expanding when hot and contracting when cold, cracks can appear in the rocks. Rain and stream water fill up these cracks. When this water freezes, it expands. Because the ice has a bigger volume than the water, the cracks are forced apart. Eventually pieces break off the rock. Broken pieces such as these collect at the bottom of cliffs and are called **scree**. This type of weathering is called **physical weathering**. Rocks can also be weathered by the acids in rain-water. This is called **chemical weathering**. If rocks are broken by plants rooting in them or animals walking on them, this is called **biological weathering.**

---

summary

- The three types of rock found in the Earth are **igneous**, **sedimentary** and **metamorphic**.
- **Igneous rock** is **formed** when **molten lava** cools.
- Sedimentary rocks are formed when deposited layers are compacted under the weight of higher layers.
- Metamorphic rocks are formed when either igneous or sedimentary rocks are subjected to high pressures and temperatures.

- The **rock cycle** shows how, over millions of years, rocks can change from one form to another.
- **Weathering** is the process by which rocks are attacked and broken up in **physical**, **chemical** or **biological** ways.

Questions

1 What are: **a)** igneous rocks **b)** metamorphic rocks **c)** sedimentary rocks?

2 What do these words mean? **a)** weathering **b)** scree **c)** lava **d)** magma

1 Describe three ways in which sediment could be moved from place to place.

2 Explain how the sea could weather and erode rocks.

3 A particle of a rock material is erupted (thrown out) from a volcano. Describe and explain what might happen to that particle before it can be recycled to erupt again.

4 When the Earth was first formed only one form of rock was present. Which form do you think that was? Explain your answer.

The main mineral in limestone and chalk is calcium carbonate. Do some research to find the names of the main minerals in each of the following: **a)** basalt **b)** granite **c)** slate **d)** marble

---

For more information about the processes of weathering see pages 70–71, 94–95 and 96–97

Chemical Changes

You have seen that when materials burn or when food is cooked, new materials are made and that this change cannot be reversed. This type of change is called a **chemical change**.

> These pages are about the chemical reactions that are all around you, even inside living matter, and how mass is conserved during a chemical change.

Chemical change

A chemical change is brought about by a **chemical reaction**. The simplest form of chemical reaction is when two elements react together to form a **compound**. The compound formed is an entirely new substance and has new properties of its own which are different from the properties of the **elements** it is made up of.

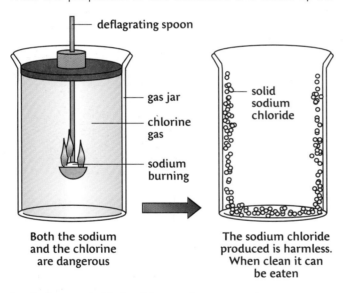

- deflagrating spoon
- gas jar
- chlorine gas
- sodium burning
- solid sodium chloride

Both the sodium and the chlorine are dangerous

The sodium chloride produced is harmless. When clean it can be eaten

> *Sodium and chlorine (elements) react together to form sodium chloride (compound)*

All materials are made through chemical reactions. Some of the chemical reactions which are important in our lives are:

- petrol burning as fuel in car engines
- making soap and soap powders by heating oils and fats with steam and sodium hydroxide
- making fertilisers from nitrogen and hydrogen
- making plastics from simple gases such as ethane and propane
- the corrosion of metals and the prevention of corrosion.

Chemical reactions in living systems

All living things are kept alive by a series of chemical reactions.

Respiration

All living things need to get energy from food. This is done by **respiration**. Respiration is a chemical reaction.

The food you eat reacts with the oxygen in the air you breathe in. From this reaction energy is produced. Carbon dioxide and water are also produced and they are found in the mixture of gases you breathe out.

air

carbon dioxide and water vapour

food + oxygen ⟶ energy

Digestion

In order to take part in respiration, the food you eat has to get into your blood where it can come into contact with the oxygen. To do this it must be **digested**.

Digestion is a chemical reaction during which **enzymes** in your body break down large food **molecules**, which cannot pass into your blood, into small molecules which can enter your bloodstream.

Conservation of mass

The law of 'conservation of mass' states that matter is neither created nor destroyed in a chemical reaction.

This means that the total mass of all the materials produced in a chemical reaction (the **products**) must equal the total mass of all the material that reacted together to make the reaction (the **reactants**).

Therefore, in any chemical reaction:
total mass of reactants = total mass of products

Copper carbonate is a green powder. When it is heated strongly, black copper oxide powder is left and carbon dioxide gas is given off into the air. The copper carbonate is the reactant and the copper oxide and carbon dioxide are the products.

Therefore, if 12.4 g of copper carbonate were heated until the reaction was complete and 8.0 g of copper oxide were left, you would know that, although they have been lost, 4.4 g of carbon dioxide were produced:

that is, 12.4 = 8.0 + 4.4

- A **chemical change** occurs when a **chemical reaction** takes place.
- A chemical reaction produces new substances which have new properties of their own.
- All materials are produced by chemical reactions.
- All living things are kept alive by chemical reactions taking place within their various systems.
- In any chemical change the total mass of products must equal the total mass of reactants.

summary

Questions

1 What do each of the following words or phrases mean?
a) reactants b) products
c) chemical change
d) chemical reaction
e) conservation of mass

1 When a marble chip is heated strongly, lime is left and carbon dioxide gas is given off. If 50 g of marble chips are heated until there is no further change, 22 g of carbon dioxide are given off.

What weight of lime remains?

2 What weight of oxygen is needed to make 40 g of magnesium oxide if 24 g of magnesium are burned in oxygen?

3 Explain two ways you can know that a chemical change has taken place.

4 Explain why, when copper carbonate is heated, the mass of the product appears to be less than the mass of the reactant.

5 Explain why respiration is a chemical change.

6 Explain why digestion is a chemical change.

1 Design an experiment you could do in your school laboratory to prove the law of conservation of mass. Include some sample results in your answer.

2 Find out in detail what chemical changes are involved in the making of normal, clear, window glass.

For more information about chemical changes see pages 10–11, 20–21 and 78–79

Word Equations

It is possible to write a **word equation** for any chemical reaction. The word equation is much shorter than writing whole sentences and paragraphs but it still tells us quite clearly what has happened.

> These pages are about how all chemical reactions can be represented by word equations.

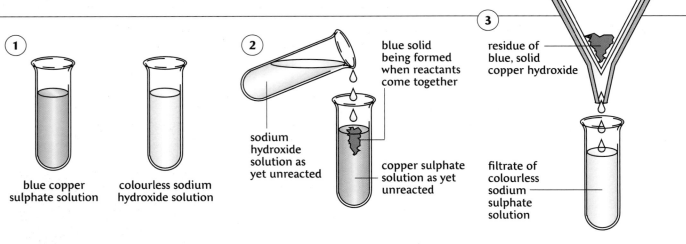

① blue copper sulphate solution   colourless sodium hydroxide solution

② sodium hydroxide solution as yet unreacted   blue solid being formed when reactants come together   copper sulphate solution as yet unreacted

③ residue of blue, solid copper hydroxide   filtrate of colourless sodium sulphate solution

Blue copper sulphate solution is in one test tube and colourless sodium hydroxide is in another. They are going to be put together. A **chemical reaction** will occur. The copper sulphate and the sodium hydroxide are the **reactants**.

The two solutions are put together. The reaction takes place.

The mixture produced is **filtered**. There is a blue solid residue in the filter paper. The filtrate is colourless sodium sulphate solution. The blue solid and the sodium sulphate solution are the **products**.

You can see that we have used three paragraphs of words to explain this chemical reaction but the explanation can also be written as a word equation:

> copper sulphate + sodium hydroxide → copper hydroxide + sodium sulphate

The word equation can also be used to describe the appearance of all the materials:

> copper sulphate + sodium hydroxide → copper hydroxide + sodium sulphate
> (blue solution)   (colourless solution)   (blue solid)   (colourless solution)

Two other very simple chemical reactions which could be done in a school laboratory are described below.

1   If small pieces of zinc are put into dilute hydrochloric acid, bubbles of hydrogen gas are produced and the pieces of zinc disappear to become colourless zinc chloride solution.

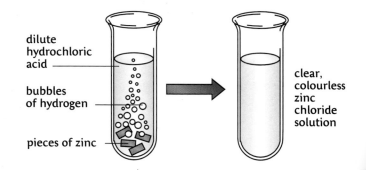

dilute hydrochloric acid

bubbles of hydrogen

pieces of zinc

clear, colourless zinc chloride solution

The word equation is

> zinc + hydrochloric acid → zinc chloride + hydrogen

The descriptive word equation is

zinc	+	hydrochloric acid	→	zinc chloride	+	hydrogen
(metallic pieces)		(colourless solution)		(colourless solution)		(bubbles of colourless gas)

2 If small pieces of iron are put into blue copper sulphate solution, the iron becomes coated with red copper and the blue copper sulphate solution becomes greenish iron sulphate solution.

The descriptive word equation is

iron	+	copper sulphate	→	iron sulphate	+	copper
(metallic pieces)		(blue solution)		(greenish solution)		(red/brown powder)

summary

● All **chemical reactions** can be represented by a **word equation**.
● The word equation is a short way of describing what happens in the reaction.
● The **reactants** are written to the left of the arrow and the **products** are written to the right of the arrow.
● Descriptions of the appearance of the materials can be included in brackets under the names.

Questions

1 What do each of the following words or phrases mean?
a) reactants **b)** products
c) word equation

2 Copy and complete the following word equations:
a) magnesium + oxygen →
b) sodium + chlorine →
c) iron + ... → .... + copper
d) zinc + hydrochloric acid →
.... + ...

1 What does a word equation tell us about a chemical reaction?

2 Copy and complete the following word equations:
a) magnesium sulphate + potassium hydroxide → ....
+ potassium sulphate
b) copper chloride + ... →
copper hydroxide +
sodium chloride
c) magnesium + sulphuric acid →
.... + hydrogen

3 Calcium hydroxide can be made from water and calcium oxide. Write a word equation for this reaction.

4 When pieces of calcium are added to water, bubbles of hydrogen are seen and calcium hydroxide solution is left.

a) Which materials are the reactants?
b) Which materials are the products?
c) Write a word equation for the reaction.

Look at pages 74–75, entitled 'Chemical Changes'.

1 Write a word equation for respiration.

2 Write a descriptive word equation for the action of heat on copper carbonate powder.

For more information about reactions see pages 78–79, 88–89 and 94–95

Types of Reaction

These pages are about some of the types of reaction that are used to classify chemical change.

intro

There are many millions of different chemical changes and it would be impossible to learn about or discuss them all. However, many chemical reactions fit into similar patterns or types. Scientists use the idea of **types of reaction** to discuss chemical changes in general. If you know what type of reaction a particular chemical change is, you can understand it and learn about it much more easily.

Oxidation

When a material gains oxygen in a chemical change, the change is an **oxidation** reaction. Oxidation is perhaps the most common chemical change of all.

Burning
Burning is an oxidation reaction.

magnesium	+	oxygen	→	magnesium oxide
(burning)		(from the air)		

Burning is more correctly called **combustion**.

Rusting
Rusting is an oxidation reaction.

iron	+	water	+ oxygen	→	iron oxide
(left out		(from the air)			(rust)
in the air)					

Sometimes oxidation takes place but the oxygen does not come from the air. If steam is passed on to heated zinc powder, zinc oxide and hydrogen are formed.

zinc	+ water	→	zinc oxide	+ hydrogen
(powdered)	(steam)		(white powder	(gas)
			when cold)	

The zinc has gained oxygen and has therefore been oxidised even though the oxygen has come from the steam and not the air.

Thermal decomposition

Some materials are broken down into 'pieces' when they are heated. There is only one reactant but there might be two or three (or more) products depending upon how many 'pieces' are formed. This type of reaction is called **thermal decomposition**. The word 'thermal' means heat and 'decomposition' means breaking down.

If green copper carbonate powder is heated it **decomposes** into black copper oxide powder and carbon dioxide gas.

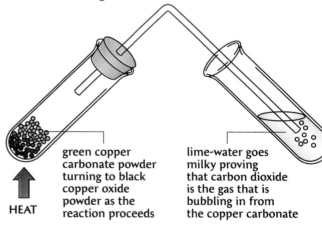

HEAT — green copper carbonate powder turning to black copper oxide powder as the reaction proceeds

lime-water goes milky proving that carbon dioxide is the gas that is bubbling in from the copper carbonate

$\xrightarrow{\text{heat}}$
copper carbonate → copper oxide + carbon dioxide

Thermal decomposition takes place when any metal carbonate is heated:

metal carbonate → metal oxide + carbon dioxide

There are many other examples of thermal decomposition.

● If lead nitrate is heated, it decomposes into three products:

$$\text{lead nitrate} \xrightarrow{\text{heat}} \text{lead oxide} + \text{nitrogen dioxide} + \text{oxygen}$$

● Potassium chlorate decomposes on heating to give potassium chloride and oxygen:

$$\text{potassium chlorate} \xrightarrow{\text{heat}} \text{potassium chloride} + \text{oxygen}$$

Precipitation

In the reaction between copper sulphate and sodium hydroxide (see page 76), you can see that the reaction happens because both compounds split in half and recombine with new 'partners':

$$\text{copper sulphate} + \text{sodium hydroxide} \rightarrow \text{copper hydroxide} + \text{sodium sulphate}$$

The copper hydroxide is a solid **precipitate** which has separated from the solution.

There are hundreds of examples of precipitation. Two are given below:

$$\text{silver nitrate} + \text{sodium chloride} \rightarrow \text{silver chloride} + \text{sodium nitrate}$$
$$\text{zinc sulphate} + \text{potassium hydroxide} \rightarrow \text{zinc hydroxide} + \text{sodium sulphate}$$

Other types of reaction are **neutralisation** (see page 95) and **displacement** (see page 88).

For more information about reactions see pages 90–91 and 94–95

---

summary

● Many chemical changes can be classified as a particular type of reaction.
● There are many different types of reaction.
● One type is **oxidation** in which oxygen is added to a material.
● **Thermal decomposition** is a type of reaction in which a single reactant is broken up by heat.
● A **precipitate** is produced when an insoluble substance separates from a solution as solid particles.

Questions

1 What do the following words mean?
  a) oxidation
  b) combustion
  c) decomposition
2 What is thermal decomposition?
3 What is precipitation?

1 Write word equations for:
  a) the thermal decomposition of magnesium carbonate
  b) the combustion of calcium in air
  c) the oxidation of magnesium by steam
  d) the reaction between solutions of calcium chloride and sodium sulphate
2 Explain why respiration is an oxidation reaction.

3 Do you think that food going bad is an example of thermal decomposition? Explain your answer.

1 Find out what happens when blue copper sulphate crystals are heated. What type of reaction is this? Explain your answer.
2 Find out what 'synthesis' is and give two examples of this type of reaction.

Everyday Materials

These pages are about how the materials you use in your everyday life are made by chemical reactions.

The clothes people wear, the buildings they live and work in, the cars and bikes they use and the articles they use for work and leisure, are all made by **chemical reactions**. Some of the chemical reactions we use are simple and easy, others are complex and difficult. Often the cost of something is determined by how easy or difficult it is to do the chemical reactions that make it.

Most of the things you see around you are made from materials which come from one of five types: **metals, fibres, plastics, glass,** and **ceramics**.

The production of metals

Metals are obtained from rocks in the Earth's crust called **ores**. The method used for **extracting** (taking) the metal from its ore depends upon the **reactivity** of the metal (see page 90). Metals which react very easily are difficult to extract from their ores.

There are four main ways of getting metals from ores.

Roasting the ore in air

By this method copper can be extracted from an ore called copper pyrites which contains copper sulphide:

> copper + oxygen $\xrightarrow[\text{strongly}]{\text{heat}}$ copper + sulphur dioxide
> sulphide (from
> (from   the air)
> the ore)

Heating the ore with carbon

By this method zinc can be obtained from zinc oxide by heating the ore with blocks of carbon:

> zinc oxide + carbon $\xrightarrow[\text{strongly}]{\text{heat}}$ zinc + carbon
> (from   (solid block)   monoxide
> the ore)

Heating the ore with carbon monoxide gas

By this method iron is extracted from an iron oxide ore called haematite in the **blast furnace process:**

> iron + carbon   heat to   iron + carbon
> oxide   monoxide   600°C   dioxide
> (in the $\rightarrow$
>   in a blast
> haematite)   furnace

Electrolysis

By this method sodium can be produced by passing electricity through melted sodium chloride:

> sodium chloride $\xrightarrow{\text{electricity}}$ sodium + chlorine
> (molten)

Electrolysis is an expensive process so it is used mainly to produce reactive metals which are difficult to extract from their ores by easier methods.

The production of plastics

There are a number of different plastics which can be made into many different articles.

Plastic	Uses
polythene	bags, cling film, buckets, washing-up bowls, wiring insulation
PVC	waterproof clothing, car seats, shopping bags, wallpaper
polystyrene	packing, tiles, plastic cups
nylon	clothing, ropes, tights, carpets, cupboard hinges, curtain rails

You will see that a number of plastics have names beginning with poly-. This is because plastics are made by a type of chemical reaction called **polymerisation**. In polymerisation small, single molecules (**monomers**) are joined together in chains to make very long molecules called **polymers**.

The production of fibres

Like plastics, fibres are long polymer molecules made by the polymerisation processes. Nylon can be made into fibres for use in clothing. Another example of clothing fibre is polyester.

 Items made from fibres, ceramics and glass

The production of ceramics

The most important use of ceramics is for making pottery but bricks and cement are also ceramics. Ceramics are made by heating clay to 1000°C. Clay contains aluminium, silicon and oxygen, and ceramics are complicated molecules made from these three elements.

The production of glass

Glass is a complex compound made by heating sand, limestone and sodium carbonate together at 1400°C.

$$\text{sand} + \text{limestone} + \text{sodium} \xrightarrow{1400°C} \text{glass}$$
(silicon   (calcium   carbonate
dioxide)   carbonate)

The glass produced is **molten** (melted) and can be made into different types of glass by adding in different materials.

- All the materials people use are produced by chemical reactions.
- Most materials come from one of five types: metals, plastics, fibres, ceramics, glass.
- Metals are **extracted** from **ores** that are found in the Earth's crust.
- Many other materials are made up of long chain molecules called **polymers**.

summary

Questions

A

1 What do the following words mean? **a)** ore **b)** extraction **c)** polymer **d)** monomer

2 Name the five main types of material from which most things are made.

3 Name four plastics and give two uses for each one.

B

1 Describe how copper can be extracted from its ore.

2 Name the ore of iron that is used in the blast furnace process and explain how iron is obtained from it.

3 Sodium is extracted from its ore by electrolysis. Explain what happens and say why we have to use this expensive method to get sodium.

C

1 Find out how aluminium is extracted from its ore. Name the method and the ore and give the word equation.

2 PVC is a polymer. Find out what the letters PVC stand for and name the monomer it is made from.

For more information see pages 74–75 and 90–91

Unwelcome Chemical Reactions

Some materials undergo chemical changes when they are left out in the air. These reactions occur quite naturally so if you do not want them to happen you have to do something to stop them. Iron going rusty and food going bad are two examples of chemical changes people try to prevent.

These pages are about chemical reactions which cause problems.

The corrosion of metals

When a metal is attacked by chemicals in the air we say the metal has **corroded**. Some of the materials in the air which can cause corrosion are oxygen, water vapour, acid rain and industrial waste gases and smoke. The more **reactive** a metal is the more easily it corrodes.

▶ *Sodium is very reactive and corrodes quickly. The freshly cut surface shows how shiny it is before corroding.*

▶ *Gold is very unreactive and never corrodes.*

Rusting

The corrosion of iron is called **rusting**. A simple experiment, in which three test tubes are set up, can be used to demonstrate that both air and water must be present for iron to rust.

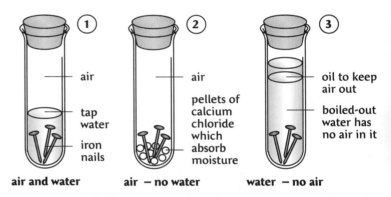

① air — tap water — iron nails — **air and water**

② air — pellets of calcium chloride which absorb moisture — **air – no water**

③ oil to keep air out — boiled-out water has no air in it — **water – no air**

The nails in tubes 2 and 3 do not go rusty.

The nails in tube 1 do go rusty.

Both air and water are necessary for rusting to occur. Rust can be prevented by keeping air and water away from the iron. The methods used to do this include:

Painting — as long as the paint is not scratched or peeled off it will keep air and moisture away from the iron.

Greasing — used mainly in machines and engines.

Coating with another metal — zinc plating (**galvanising**), tin plating and chromium plating are all effective. This means that the plating corrodes instead of the iron it is covering.

Coating with plastic — is used in many household articles such as dishwasher racks, cycle baskets, garden furniture.

Alloying — mixtures of metals are called **alloys**. Stainless steel is an alloy of iron, chromium, manganese and nickel. It does not rust but it is expensive.

The decay of food

Most foods eventually go bad if they come into contact with chemicals or bacteria in the air. For some foods decay happens quickly while for other foods it takes some time.

In food decay, chemical reactions change the food into new materials which are usually harmful to human health if eaten.

Food decay can be prevented by:

- Keeping food cool in a refrigerator for a few days.
- Putting food in a freezer where its temperature can become so low that it will keep for weeks or months.
- Killing bacteria or **organisms** in the food – this is done, for example, in pasteurised or sterilised milk.
- Removing water from food – this is done, for example, in dried peas and gravy granules.
- Adding a material such as salt to bacon, or sugar to jam.
- Vacuum wrapping – this means putting the food, for example bacon or cheese, in plastic wrapping and then sucking all the air out from inside the wrapping.
- Sealing food inside plasticised paper wrappers – this is done, for example, with cereals and crisps.
- Putting foods such as meat, fish or fruit into sealed tins.

Most foods are sold with a 'Sell by' date on their packaging. This date tells you whether food is safe to eat or not.

- Chemical reactions such as the **corrosion** of metals and **decay** of food occur naturally and are changes we do not want.
- The most common example of metal corrosion is the rusting of iron.
- Iron goes rusty when it is in contact with both air and water.
- Rusting can be prevented by keeping out air and water.
- Food goes bad in air and warmth, and through contact with **bacteria.**
- Preventing food from decaying means keeping out air and bacteria or keeping food cold.

summary

Questions

 A

1 What do the following words and phrases mean?
   a) corrosion **b)** rusting
   c) alloying **d)** galvanising
   e) vacuum wrapping
   g) refrigerating

2 How do painting and greasing metals prevent rusting?

3 How does metal plating prevent rusting?

 B

1 Which method of preventing rusting does *not* involve covering the iron with another material? What is the main problem with this method?

2 Describe, with diagrams, an experiment to find out what materials need to be present for iron to rust.

3 Describe four methods of preventing food decay and give two examples of each method being used.

4 Explain why a peeled apple goes brown quickly while an unpeeled apple does not.

5 Explain why iron gate posts often rust from the bottom upwards.

 C

1 Plan an investigation to find out whether iron nails go rusty quicker in distilled water or seawater.

2 Aluminium can be 'anodised'. Find out what this means and write an explanation of it.

Energy from Chemical Reactions

intro

Chemical reactions involve **transfers of energy**. Sometimes the energy goes from the materials to their surroundings and sometimes from the surroundings to the materials.

These pages are about how energy is given out and taken in during chemical reactions and how these reactions can affect the environment.

Transferring energy

If you hold a test tube of dilute hydrochloric acid in your hand and add a few pieces of magnesium ribbon to the acid, a reaction will take place which gives out heat. Your hand will feel warm because it receives the heat.

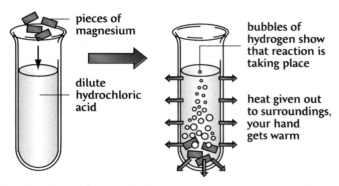

pieces of magnesium

dilute hydrochloric acid

bubbles of hydrogen show that reaction is taking place

heat given out to surroundings, your hand gets warm

A reaction like this, in which energy is given **out,** is called an **exothermic reaction**.

If you hold a test tube of water in your hand and add some ammonium nitrate crystals to it, the ammonium nitrate will dissolve. It will take in heat from the surroundings, including your hand, to help it to dissolve. Your hand will feel cold because it feels the loss of heat. A reaction like this, in which energy is taken **in,** is called an **endothermic reaction**.

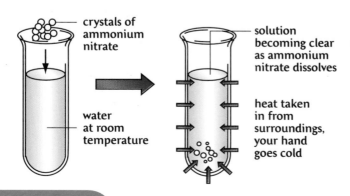

crystals of ammonium nitrate

water at room temperature

solution becoming clear as ammonium nitrate dissolves

heat taken in from surroundings, your hand goes cold

Burning of fuels

Most of the energy people use for warmth, travel and cooking comes from burning a fuel. Fuels give out energy when they burn in air or oxygen. Most fuels contain carbon and hydrogen, so when they burn the products are carbon dioxide and water:

$$\text{fuel} + \text{oxygen} \rightarrow \text{carbon dioxide} + \text{water} + \textbf{heat energy}$$

If you throw a match into a beaker of petrol, the petrol will burn so quickly that it **explodes**. The explosion is a result of all the energy being released at once. This uncontrolled release of energy is of no use. But if you control the burning then the energy is released in a safe and useful way.

The table lists some fuels which release useful energy from controlled **combustion**.

Fuel	Used in
natural gas	homes, school laboratories
propane	camping and calor gas
diesel oil	buses, lorries
petrol	cars
kerosene	aircraft
coke	domestic solid/smokeless fuel

Fossil fuels and the environment

Fossil fuels were formed from decaying plant and animal remains millions of years ago. They are found in the Earth. Coal, gas and oil are all fossil fuels. Like all fuels, fossil fuels produce carbon dioxide, water and heat when they burn:

coal, oil, gas + oxygen → carbon dioxide + water + heat out

Unfortunately, the nations of the world are burning fossil fuels in increasing amounts. This means that the amount of carbon dioxide in the Earth's **atmosphere** is increasing rapidly. Carbon dioxide is a heavy gas which remains in the atmosphere and keeps heat in. This means that the temperature of the Earth is very slowly rising.

This is called the **greenhouse effect** and carbon dioxide is a **greenhouse gas**.

- As well as carbon and hydrogen, most fossil fuels contain small amounts of sulphur and nitrogen.
- When sulphur burns, sulphur dioxide is produced. This forms an acid in water and causes **acid rain**.
- When nitrogen burns, nitrogen oxides are produced. These are both acid gases and greenhouse gases.

The table lists gases that contribute to the greenhouse effect.

Gas	% of greenhouse gases	% in the atmosphere
carbon dioxide	57	increasing
methane	14	increasing
nitrogen oxides	5	increasing
ozone	10	decreasing
CFCs	14	increasing

- Some reactions give out energy and others take in energy.
- **Controlled combustion** of fuels produces useful heat and energy.
- Combustion of **fossil fuels** is producing **pollutants** and **greenhouse gases**.

summary

Questions

 A

1 What do the following words and phrases mean?
a) fuel b) fossil fuel
c) greenhouse effect
d) greenhouse gas

 B

1 What is acid rain and how is it caused?

2 Around the world people are cutting down more and more forests. Explain how this might increase the greenhouse effect.

3 Methane is released into the atmosphere from rotting waste and sewage. Explain why the amount of methane in the atmosphere is steadily increasing.

4 Describe three ways in which air pollution in cities could be reduced.

C

1 Explain some of the problems governments face in introducing steps to reduce air pollution.

2 Find out what the letters CFC stand for, where CFCs are used, and how they affect the atmosphere.

For more information see pages 78–79, 96–97 and 140–141

Metals in Oxygen and Water

Most metals take part in chemical reactions. However, there are large differences in how easy the reactions are. Some metals react violently and dangerously while other metals react slowly or not at all.

These pages are about the reactions of metals with oxygen and with water, and the differences in each of the reactions.

Metals and oxygen

When a metal burns in air it combines with oxygen to form an **oxide**:

metal + oxygen → metal oxide

The reaction is always fiercer if the metal is burnt in pure oxygen.

If a piece of sodium is put on a combustion spoon and heated in a Bunsen flame, it burns easily, with a yellow flame. If the spoon is placed in a jar of pure oxygen while it is burning, the reaction becomes violent and an extremely bright yellow flame is seen.

sodium + oxygen → sodium oxide

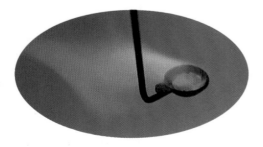

Repeating this experiment with a series of metals shows that the **vigour** (fierceness) of the reaction varies from violent to no reaction at all. The table shows this.

Metal	Description of the reaction
copper	The foil does not burn even in pure oxygen, but the surface becomes coated with a black powder.
gold	No reaction takes place in either air or oxygen.
iron	The filings glow red in air but very brightly, with sparks, in oxygen. They do not catch fire.
magnesium	Burns easily and brightly in air and even more so in oxygen.
potassium	Reacts like sodium but even more vigorously.
zinc	The powder needs a lot of heat to make it burn in air but it does burn in oxygen.

Metals and water

Some metals will react with cold water. The products are hydrogen gas, which is given off into the air, and a solution of the hydroxide of the metal:

metal + water → metal hydroxide + hydrogen

If a piece of potassium is dropped into water, a violent reaction takes place immediately. The potassium melts to shiny drops and the heat given out in the reaction is enough to set fire to the hydrogen. A lilac flame is seen.

potassium + water → potassium hydroxide + hydrogen

- The reactivity of metals varies. Some metals react vigorously while others do not react at all.
- When metals react with cold water, the metal hydroxide and hydrogen are produced:
  metal + water → metal hydroxide + hydrogen
- When metals burn in oxygen the metal oxide is produced: metal + oxygen → metal oxide
- When metals react with steam the metal oxide and hydrogen are produced:
  metal + water (steam) → metal oxide + hydrogen

Some metals do not react with cold water but do react if the metal is heated in steam. The products are hydrogen and the oxide of the metal.

metal + water (steam) → metal oxide + hydrogen

If a dish of powdered zinc is heated in steam, the reaction takes place quite slowly. Zinc oxide is left in the dish and hydrogen is given off.

zinc + steam → zinc oxide + hydrogen

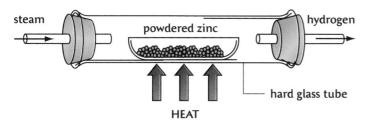

The table describes the reactions of some other metals with water and steam.

Metal	Description of the reaction
calcium	Reacts in cold water. Sinks to the bottom and reacts slowly. Bubbles of hydrogen are seen coming from the pieces of calcium.
copper	No reaction in water or steam.
magnesium	Reacts very slowly in cold water. Small bubbles of hydrogen are eventually seen on the magnesium. Reacts very quickly and glows brightly in steam.
sodium	Reacts immediately with cold water. The sodium melts to tiny drops which move about the surface of the water.

For more information about metals see pages 62–63
For more information about reactions see pages 78–79

Questions

 A

1. Write word equations for:
   a) a metal burning in oxygen
   b) a metal reacting with steam
   c) a metal reacting with cold water
   d zinc reacting with oxygen
   e) sodium reacting with cold water
   f) magnesium reacting with steam.

 B

1. Which is more reactive, sodium or potassium? Explain your answer.

2. Which is more reactive, zinc or iron? Explain your answer.

3. Which is more reactive, copper or gold? Explain your answer.

4. Metal X is not as reactive as magnesium but is more reactive than zinc. Describe the reactions of X with water and steam.

5. a) When copper is heated in oxygen the copper becomes coated with a black powder. What is this black powder? Explain how it is formed. Give a word equation.

   b) If the black powder is scraped off and the copper reheated in oxygen, what will happen? Explain your answer.

 C

1. Plan a series of experiments to find out which reacts more easily, a block of zinc or powdered zinc. Draw diagrams and give word equations. Make a prediction of what the result will be and explain your prediction.

2. Find out how the following metals react with water:
   a) lithium b) silver c) lead d) aluminium

Metals in Acids and Salts

Metals react with acids more easily than they react with water but similar differences in the vigour of the reactions can be seen.

These pages are about the reactions of metals with acids and with solutions of the salts of other metals.

Metals and acids

If small pieces of magnesium are added to dilute hydrochloric acid there is a vigorous reaction. Hydrogen bubbles are rapidly given off and the reaction does not stop until all the magnesium has gone. The clear solution left is magnesium chloride.

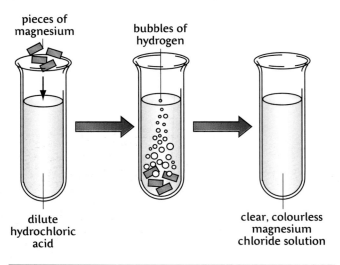

pieces of magnesium

bubbles of hydrogen

dilute hydrochloric acid

clear, colourless magnesium chloride solution

magnesium + hydrochloric acid
→ magnesium chloride + hydrogen

All acids contain hydrogen and the magnesium chloride is formed because the magnesium **displaces** (pushes out) the hydrogen from the hydrochloric acid and takes its place (see page 94). Magnesium chloride is a **salt**.

A salt is a compound formed when the hydrogen of an acid is replaced by a metal.

Whenever a dilute acid reacts with a metal, the same reaction takes place:

acid + metal → salt + hydrogen

The table describes the reactions of some metals with dilute acids.

Metal	Description of reaction
copper	No reaction at all.
gold	No reaction at all.
iron	Slow reaction eventually producing bubbles of hydrogen.
lead	Very slow reaction. A few bubbles of hydrogen can eventually be seen on the lead.
sodium	It would be far too dangerous even to try to do the reaction.
potassium	
zinc	Steady reaction which soon begins to produce a stream of hydrogen bubbles.

Displacement reactions

When a strip of zinc is put into a blue solution of copper sulphate (a salt of copper) the zinc gradually becomes coated with a red-brown powder. The blue of the solution fades to colourless.

The red-brown powder is copper and the final colourless solution is zinc sulphate (a salt of zinc).

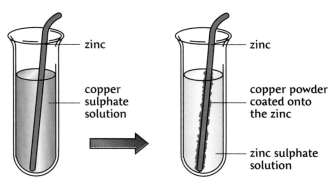

zinc

copper sulphate solution

zinc

copper powder coated onto the zinc

zinc sulphate solution

The zinc has displaced the copper.

zinc + copper sulphate → zinc sulphate + copper

Similarly, if pieces of iron are put into lead nitrate solution then displacement also occurs.

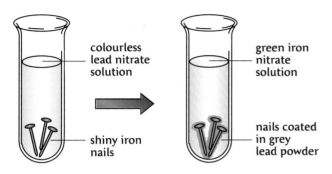

- colourless lead nitrate solution
- shiny iron nails
- green iron nitrate solution
- nails coated in grey lead powder

iron + lead nitrate → iron nitrate + lead

For displacement to happen, the displacing metal must be more **reactive** (powerful) than the metal being displaced. The examples show that zinc is more reactive than copper and that iron is more reactive than lead.

If pieces of iron are placed in zinc sulphate solution, no reaction takes place:

iron + zinc sulphate → no reaction

This shows that iron is *less* reactive than zinc and will not displace it from its salts.

A metal will displace a less reactive metal from a solution of a salt of the less reactive metal.

- When metals react with dilute acids the metal **displaces** the hydrogen in the acid. The products are the salt and hydrogen:
  acid + metal → salt + hydrogen
- A **salt** is a compound made by replacing the hydrogen in an acid by a metal.
- A reactive metal will displace a less reactive metal from solutions of its salts.

summary

Questions

A

1 What do the following words mean?
a) salt b) displace c) vigorous

2 Give the name of a metal that:
a) reacts with both steam and acid but not cold water
b) does not react with dilute acid
c) displaces copper from copper sulphate solution
d) will not displace iron from iron chloride solution.

B

1 Write word equations for each of the following reactions:
a) magnesium and dilute sulphuric acid
b) zinc and dilute sulphuric acid
c) magnesium and zinc sulphate solution
d) lead and copper chloride solution.

2 Name the salt formed from:
a) zinc and sulphuric acid
b) iron and nitric acid
c) magnesium and hydrochloric acid.

3 Describe what you would see when small pieces of lead are added to dilute nitric acid. Write a word equation for the reaction.

C

Given samples of three metals, X, Y and Z, plan a series of experiments to find out their order of reactivity and a second series of experiments to back up your results. Give diagrams in your answer.

For more information see pages 76–77 and 94–95

The Reactivity Series

Metals can be arranged into an order of **reactivity**. This list is called the **Reactivity Series**.

Below is part of the Reactivity Series with a summary of the reactions you have already looked at.

These pages are about the Reactivity Series of metals and how it can be used to make predictions about the reactions of metals.

	Metal	Symbol	Reactions with oxygen	Reactions with water	Reactions with dilute acids	Displacement
most reactive ↑	potassium	K		React in cold water to give hydroxide and hydrogen	Explosive reaction	Each metal displaces lower metals from salts in solution or from oxides
	sodium	Na				
	lithium	Li	Burn in air to give oxide			
	calcium	Ca			React with dilute acids to displace hydrogen	
	magnesium	Mg	Reactions more vigorous in pure oxygen			
	aluminium	Al		React with steam to give oxide and hydrogen		
	zinc	Zn				
	iron	Fe				
	lead	Pb	Do not burn but converted to oxide on heating in air		Very slow reaction only if acid warmed	
	copper	Cu		No reaction at all	No reaction at all	
least reactive ↓	silver	Ag	No reaction at all with air or oxygen			
	gold	Au				

The reactions of metals

Metals which react easily are found in the Earth's crust as **ores**, having already reacted with other materials around them.

Only copper, silver and gold are found as pure metals in the Earth's crust.

The more reactive a metal is, the more 'determined' it is to stay as a compound once it has reacted. This means that the most reactive metals are the ones that are most difficult to extract from their ores. The less reactive metals are easier to extract.

Predicting reactions

By studying materials and their reactions, scientists find rules and patterns that can be used to make predictions.

The Reactivity Series tells you about the patterns and rules of behaviour of metals. It can be used to make predictions about the metals.

Question: What will happen if iron nails are dropped into blue copper sulphate solution?

Answer: Iron is more reactive than copper and so it will displace the copper. The iron nails become covered in red-brown copper and the blue colour fades.

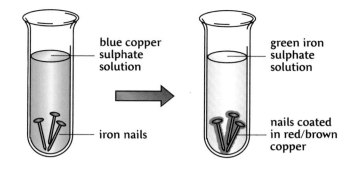

blue copper sulphate solution

green iron sulphate solution

iron nails

nails coated in red/brown copper

| iron + copper sulphate → iron sulphate + copper |

Question: Some dilute hydrochloric acid has been spilled on a gold ring. Will the acid damage the ring?

Answer: The reactivity series shows that gold is very unreactive. Gold does not react with acids and the ring will be unharmed.

- The **Reactivity Series** places metals in order of reactivity.
- The more reactive metals are at the top.
- Reactive metals are never found uncombined in the Earth's crust.
- The more reactive a metal is, the harder it is to extract from its ores.
- The Reactivity Series can be used to make predictions about the reactions of metals.

summary

Questions

A

1 What is the 'Reactivity Series'?

2 Use the Reactivity Series to answer the following questions:

  a) Which is the most reactive metal?

  b) Which is the most unreactive metal?

  c) Name two metals which do not react with dilute acids.

  d) Name a metal which reacts with steam but does not burn in air.

  e) Name a metal which reacts safely with dilute acids and cold water.

  f) Name a metal which does not react with steam but does displace hydrogen from warm dilute acid.

  g) Name a metal which does not react with dilute acids or steam.

B

1 Copy and complete these word equations:

  a) zinc + copper oxide → zinc oxide + ...

  b) magnesium + copper sulphate → .... + copper

  c) .... + ... → magnesium oxide + zinc

  d) iron + ... → iron nitrate + lead

2 For each of the following pairs of materials, write the word equation if you predict they *will* react and 'no reaction' if you predict that they *will not* react:

  a) zinc and lead nitrate

  b) lead and copper sulphate

  c) zinc and magnesium chloride

  d) magnesium and sulphuric acid

  e) copper and hydrochloric acid

  f) copper and silver nitrate

  g) gold and silver nitrate

  h) copper and oxygen

  i) iron oxide and zinc

  j) aluminium and magnesium oxide

C

Beryllium (Be) is less reactive than magnesium and more reactive than iron. Writing a word equation each time a reaction takes place, say how you would expect beryllium to react with:

  a) water

  b) dilute hydrochloric acid

  c) magnesium sulphate solution

  d) oxygen

  e) copper chloride solution

For more information about metals see pages 62–63

Acids and Alkalis

To most people the word 'acid' suggests something that is dangerous and it is true that many acids are dangerous. However, there are acids in the food you eat and these acids are obviously not dangerous. How could you test whether or not a material is an acid and how would you know whether it is dangerous or not?

These pages are about how indicators can be used to test for acids and alkalis, and how the pH scale is used as a measure of acidity.

Indicators

The easiest way to find out whether a solution is **acidic** or not is to add an **indicator** to it. Indicators are solutions of coloured extracts from plants. The indicator always turns the same colour when added to an acidic solution.

A very common indicator is **litmus**. Litmus is a purple dye which can be used either in solution or soaked into paper.

- Litmus solution turns **red** in **acid**.
- Blue litmus paper turns **red** in **acid**.
- Red litmus paper stays **red** in **acid**.

Alkalis

Alkalis are an important group of materials which are the chemical 'opposites' of acids. Alkalis also affect indicators.

- Litmus solution turns **blue** in **alkali**.
- Blue litmus paper stays **blue** in **alkali**.
- Red litmus paper turns **blue** in **alkali**.

Neutral materials

Some materials do not affect indicators at all and are neither acids nor alkalis. They are **neutral**. Pure water is neutral and so are salt in solution and sugar in solution.

The pH scale

Some acids are **strong** acids and need to be handled with care while others are **weak** acids and can be found in foods. The same is true of alkalis. Some are **strong** and some are **weak**.

Scientists measure the strength of an acid or alkali by using the **pH scale**. This scale goes from 0 to 14.

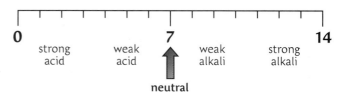

The pH Scale

- Acidic solutions have a pH below 7; the stronger the acid the lower its pH will be.
- Neutral solutions have a pH of exactly 7.
- Alkaline solutions have a pH above 7; the stronger the alkali the higher its pH will be.

Universal indicator

Universal indicator is a mixture of dyes which, like litmus, can be used either as a solution or as universal indicator paper (sometimes called pH paper). You can find the pH of a solution fairly accurately using universal indicator because it turns a different colour at different pH values.

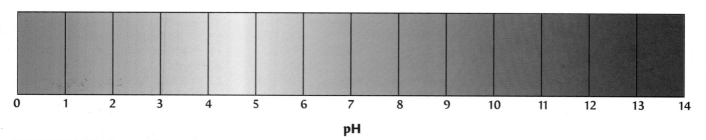

pH

Everyday pH values

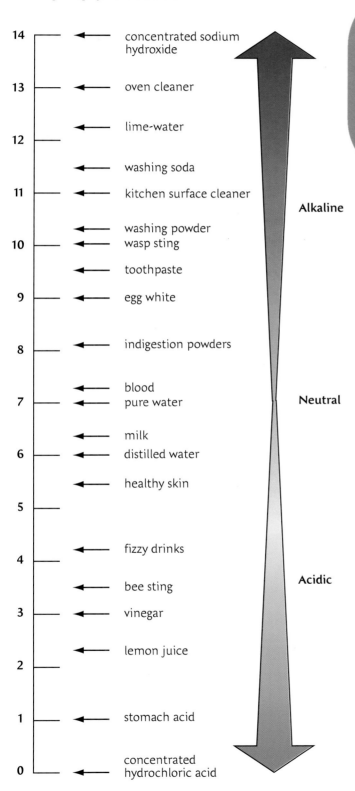

14	← concentrated sodium hydroxide
13	← oven cleaner
	← lime-water
12	
	← washing soda
11	← kitchen surface cleaner
10	← washing powder ← wasp sting
	← toothpaste
9	← egg white
8	← indigestion powders
7	← blood ← pure water
	← milk
6	← distilled water
	← healthy skin
5	
4	← fizzy drinks
	← bee sting
3	← vinegar
2	← lemon juice
1	← stomach acid
0	← concentrated hydrochloric acid

Alkaline

Neutral

Acidic

● Solutions are **acid**, **neutral** or **alkali**.
● Acids and alkalis can be strong or weak.
● You can see whether or not a solution is acidic, neutral or alkaline by using **indicators**.
● You can measure acidity and alkalinity on the **pH scale**.
● The pH scale goes from 0 to 14.
● Solutions of pH less than 7 are acidic, above 7 are alkaline and at 7 are neutral.

summary

Questions

A

1 What do the following words mean?
   a) indicator **b)** neutral **c)** pH scale

2 What colour is:
   a) litmus in acid **b)** litmus in alkali?

3 What is the range of the pH scale?

4 What is the approximate pH range of weak acids?

5 What is the approximate pH range of strong alkalis?

B

1 Nitric acid is very corrosive and dangerous. What do you think its pH will be? Explain your answer.

2 Carbonic acid is found in fizzy drinks. What do you think its pH will be? Explain your answer.

3 Some sugar is dissolved in water and universal indicator is added. What colour will the indicator show? Explain your answer.

4 The solution produced by boiling red cabbage in water can be used as an indicator. It is red in acids and bluish-purple in alkalis. What colour would it go in:
   a) orange juice **b)** washing soda solution
   c) lime-water?

C

1 The information on the back of the container of a material for cleaning kitchen surfaces says that its pH is 11. What does this mean? Describe an investigation you could carry out to check this. Why is it important that you know the pH of a kitchen cleaning material?

2 Using information from the chart of pH values, find the pH of toothpaste and explain why the manufacturers of toothpaste give it this pH.

For more information about acids in everyday life see pages 96–97

The Reactions of Acids

intro

There are many different acids, some strong and some weak. Some of the most common acids, with their formulas, are:

      hydrochloric acid – HCl   sulphuric acid – H_2SO_4
        nitric acid – HNO_3 carbonic acid – H_2CO_3

All acids have similar **patterns of behaviour**. These patterns can be used to predict what will happen in reactions involving acids.

These pages are about the chemical reactions of acids and the patterns found in those reactions.

Acids affect indicators

Acids are soluble in water and acidic solutions give recognisable colours with indicators. The colour shown by universal indicator depends upon the pH of the acid (see page 92).

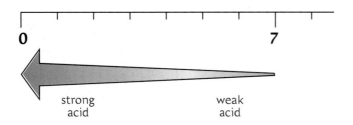

  0   7

      strong   weak
       acid   acid

Acids react with metals

When dilute acids are added to metals, a salt is formed and hydrogen is given off (see page 88).

> zinc + hydrochloric acid → zinc chloride + hydrogen

This is a general reaction for all acids and all metals above copper in the Reactivity Series:

> **acid + metal → salt + hydrogen**

Acids react with carbonates

When dilute acids are added to carbonates, a salt is formed and the other products are water and carbon dioxide.

> sodium carbonate + hydrochloric acid →
>   sodium chloride + water + carbon dioxide

This is a general reaction for all acids and all carbonates:

> **acid + carbonate → salt + water + carbon dioxide**

Acids react with bases

When dilute acids are added to bases, a salt is formed and the other product is water.

Bases are the oxides and hydroxides of metals, for example, copper oxide and calcium hydroxide.

> magnesium oxide + sulphuric acid →
>   magnesium sulphate + water

This is a general reaction for all acids and all bases:

> **acid + base → salt + water**

Neutralisation

As you saw above, the oxides and hydroxides of metals are **bases**. They are all solids and the vast majority do not dissolve in water. The few that do dissolve are called **alkalis**.

An alkali is a soluble base.

Four common alkalis are:

- sodium hydroxide, NaOH
- potassium hydroxide, KOH
- calcium hydroxide, $Ca(OH)_2$ (lime-water)
- ammonium hydroxide, NH_4OH

Because the alkalis can be made into solutions in water they are much more useful than the other bases. They are, however, still bases and they still react with acids:

$$acid + alkali \rightarrow salt + water$$

hydrochloric acid + sodium hydroxide →
sodium chloride + water

This reaction between an acid and an alkali results in a solution of a salt being formed. The solution will have a pH of 7 so it is neutral. For this reason, the reaction between an acid and an alkali is called a **neutralisation** reaction.

Salts

All the general reactions discussed above have a salt as one of the products (see page 88). The table lists some acids, including some not mentioned already, and the names of the salts formed from them.

Acid	Salt
hydrochloric acid	chlorides
sulphuric acid	sulphates
nitric acid	nitrates
carbonic acid	carbonates
phosphoric acid	phosphates
hydrobromic acid	bromides

- Acids react with metals, carbonates and **bases**.
- Oxides and **hydroxides** of metals are bases.
- A few bases dissolve in water. These are called alkalis.
- When an acid reacts with an alkali a neutral solution of a salt is formed. This is **neutralisation**.

summary

Questions

1 What do the following words mean? **a)** acid **b)** base **c)** alkali **d)** neutralisation

2 The salts formed from hydrochloric acid are chlorides. Which salts are formed from:
a) nitric acid
b) phosphoric acid
c) sulphuric acid
d) carbonic acid?

1 Write word equations for each of the following reactions:

a) magnesium and dilute sulphuric acid
b) dilute nitric acid and zinc carbonate
c) copper oxide and dilute hydrochloric acid

2 Write acid + metal word equations to make the following salts:
a) zinc sulphate
b) magnesium chloride.

3 Write acid + carbonate word equations to make the following salts:
a) calcium nitrate
b) potassium sulphate.

4 Write acid + base word equations to make the following salts:
a) aluminium nitrate
b) calcium chloride.

5 Explain the statement 'All alkalis are bases but not all bases are alkalis.'

When dilute carbonic acid is used to neutralise dilute sodium hydroxide exactly, the volume of carbonic acid needed is much greater than the volume of sodium hydroxide. Explain this.

For more information about acid reactions see pages 88–89

Acids in Everyday Life

intro

Acids can be found in air, food, soil and our bodies. If changes occur which cause the amount of acid to increase or decrease then problems may arise. These can often be dealt with by doing chemical reactions to reverse the change.

These pages are about neutralisation and its use in soil treatment and indigestion remedies, and also about acid rain and the problems caused by it.

Acids in soil

Most soils are approximately neutral and have pH levels of between 6.5 and 7.5. This is the pH in which most plants have adapted to grow best. If the soil becomes too acid or too alkaline then plants will either not grow properly or will not grow at all. Gardeners add **peat** (which is acidic) to soil which is alkaline:

$$
\begin{array}{ccc}
\text{peat} + \text{soil} & \xrightarrow{\text{neutralisation}} & \text{neutral soil} \\
\text{(acid)} \quad \text{(alkaline)} &
\end{array}
$$

They add lime (an alkali) to soil which is acidic:

$$
\begin{array}{ccc}
\text{lime} + \text{soil} & \xrightarrow{\text{neutralisation}} & \text{neutral soil} \\
\text{(an alkali)} \quad \text{(acidic)} &
\end{array}
$$

Stomach acid and food

Food arriving in your stomach needs to be broken down so that it can be digested (see page 10). To do this your stomach produces hydrochloric acid with a pH of about 2. The acid is dilute but strong enough to do its job. If the amount of acid in the stomach becomes too high – either naturally or from foods such as fizzy drink, sauce or pickles, which all contain acid – then painful **indigestion** can result.

This extra acid is removed by swallowing indigestion tablets. These usually contain sodium hydrogen carbonate (sodium bicarbonate or bicarbonate of soda). This is mildly alkaline and neutralises the extra acid in the stomach.

$$
\begin{array}{ccc}
\text{stomach} + \text{bicarbonate} & \xrightarrow{\text{neutralisation}} & \text{salt solution} \\
\text{acid} \quad\quad \text{of soda} & & \text{(neutral)} \\
\text{(acid)} \quad\quad \text{(alkali)} & & + \text{water} \\
& & + \text{carbon dioxide}
\end{array}
$$

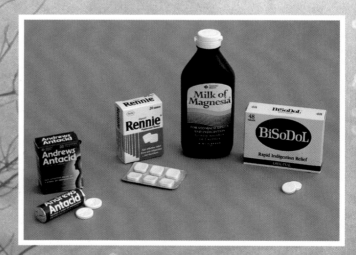

Acid rain

When fossil fuels burn (see page 85), carbon dioxide, sulphur dioxide and nitrogen oxide are among the materials produced. Each of these is a gas which passes into the atmosphere. Unfortunately, they all dissolve in water to form an acid:

- carbon dioxide + water → carbonic acid
- sulphur dioxide + water → sulphurous acid
- nitrogen oxide + water → nitrous acid.

Bee stings contain acid. This can be neutralised by putting an alkali on the sting. Calamine lotion or sodium bicarbonate are both mildly alkaline and will ease the pain by neutralising the acid in the sting.

Wasp stings are alkaline and must be neutralised with acid. Vinegar or lemon juice will help here.

This means that rainfall can sometimes be quite acidic, particularly in industrial areas where there are lots of factories and vehicles burning fossil fuels. We cannot neutralise the rain and so the only way to solve the problem is to prevent the **emission** of acid gases into the atmosphere.

Acid rain causes damage to plants, wildlife (particularly pond life because the pond water becomes acidic), buildings and cars.

The effects of acid rain

It has caused whole areas of forest to be killed or stunted in growth.

It has eliminated whole **food chains** from lakes which have become acidic.

It causes the **chemical weathering** of buildings. It has corroded metal structures because, as you have seen, acids react with metals.

- Acids are present in many of the materials around you.
- If the amount of acid in a material changes, serious problems can result.
- pH changes can often be reversed by adding a neutralising material.
- Acid rain can only be prevented by stopping acid gases entering the atmosphere.

summary

Questions

A

1. What are the following?
   a) neutral soil
   b) stomach acid
   c) chemical weathering
2. What material would you add to soil to make it:
   a) more acidic
   b) more alkaline?
3. Name two gases which produce acid rain.

B

1. Explain why indigestion treatments contain an alkali.
2. Explain why rain can sometimes cause metals to corrode.
3. Hair shampoos are sometimes advertised as 'containing lemon'. Why do you think lemon is used?
4. How would you treat:
   a) a bee sting
   b) a wasp sting?
   Explain your answers.
5. A hundred years ago acid rain was not regarded as a problem. Explain this.

C

1. Write a newspaper article explaining the causes of acid rain and what can be done about it.
2. 'Acid rain is only a problem in industrial areas and not in the open countryside.'

   Describe experiments you could do to see if this statement is correct.

Static Electricity

Have you ever heard your jumper crackle when you pull it over your head? The crackles are caused by **static electricity**.

These pages are about how static electricity is made and what it can do.

Making static electricity

People knew how to make static electricity more than 2500 years ago. The Ancient Greeks rubbed pieces of amber with fur and found that the amber would then pick up pieces of straw.

You can give an **insulating material** (such as plastic) a **charge** of static electricity by rubbing it.

The comb is charged with static electricity. It will **attract** small objects. This means the comb will pull the objects towards it.

There are two kinds of charge. We call them **positive** (+) and **negative** (−) charges. The kind of charge you get depends on the material you are rubbing and the kind of cloth you use. Both kinds of charge will attract things.

Cling film sticks to things because it gets a charge of static electricity when it is pulled off the roll. It is attracted to insulating materials such as plates.

Attracting and repelling

When two charged objects are close together they affect each other.

Opposite charges attract each other.

If two charges are the same (both positive, or both negative) we say they are **like** charges. Like charges **repel** each other. This means the charges push each other away.

This machine makes static electricity. All the strands of the girl's hair have the same charge, and they are standing up because they are all repelling each other.

What causes static electricity?

Everything is made of **atoms**. An atom has a central **nucleus** which contains protons and neutrons. **Electrons** orbit (move in a circle) around the nucleus. Every proton has a positive charge. Electrons have a negative charge, and neutrons do not have a charge at all. Atoms usually have the same number of protons and electrons, so their positive and negative charges balance each other.

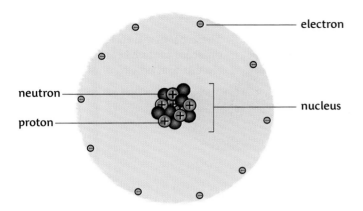

neutron
proton
electron
nucleus

When you rub an object some of the electrons get transferred from one thing to the other. The object that has gained electrons will have a negative charge, because now it has more electrons than protons. The object that has lost its electrons does not have enough negative charges to balance out the positive charges on the protons, so it has a positive charge overall.

The more electrons that are transferred, the bigger the charge.

Moving charges

It is difficult for electrons to move through **insulating** materials. Charges on insulating materials are called static electricity because the charges cannot move around easily. It is easy for electrons to move through **conducting** materials such as metals. An **electric current** is a flow of electrons moving through a conductor.

Sparks and lightning

Static electricity can move if something has a big enough charge. When your jumper crackles you are hearing the noise made by tiny sparks jumping between you and your jumper.

Clouds can build up a charge of static electricity. When the charge is big enough the static electricity can jump from cloud to cloud, or from a cloud to the Earth. This kind of spark is called **lightning.**

> - **Static electricity** can be made by rubbing an **insulating material.**
> - There are two kinds of charge, **positive** and **negative.**
> - An object has a negative charge if it has gained extra **electrons.**
> - An object has a positive charge if it has lost some electrons.
> - **Opposite charges attract, like charges repel.**
> - An **electric current** is a flow of charges.

summary

Questions

A

1 What do these words mean?
   a) static electricity b) nucleus
   c) proton d) electron
   e) electric current f) repel

2 Describe how to give a plastic ruler a charge of static electricity.

3 What happens if you put the charged ruler near some pieces of tissue paper?

B

1 a) These two objects are attracted to each other. What kind of charge is on object B?

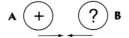

A (+)   (?) B

b) These two objects are repelling each other. What kind of charge is on object D?

C (—)   (?) D

2 Sally's hair sometimes stands away from her head just after she has combed it. Explain why this happens.

3 a) Explain how a rod becomes negatively charged when it is rubbed with a cloth. Use a diagram as part of your explanation.

   b) What kind of charge will the cloth have?

c) How big will the charge on the cloth be compared to the charge on the rod?

C

1 When an aeroplane is being refuelled, a wire is used to connect the aeroplane to the fuel tanker before any fuel is pumped into the tanks. Why is this done?

2 Static electricity is used in factories where paint is sprayed on to metal objects such as chairs. Find out how static electricity is used to prevent wasting paint.

For more information about atoms see pages 56–57

Electrical Circuits

These pages are about different kinds of electrical circuits and how to draw them.

intro

Electricity is very important in everyday life. People use electricity to light their homes, shops and factories. Electricity is needed to make TVs, telephones, radios and computers work. Electricity is needed to control traffic and to make railway signals work.

Circuit symbols

When you work with electrical circuits you need to use **symbols** to show how you have arranged your equipment.

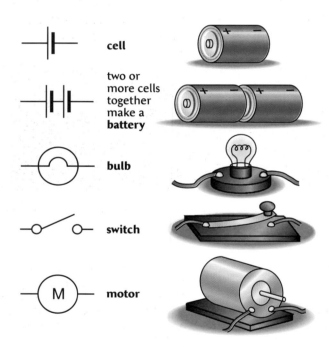

—┤├—	cell
—┤├┤├—	two or more cells together make a **battery**
—○—	bulb
—○⁄○—	switch
—(M)—	motor

Bulbs, switches and motors are all electrical **components**.

Conductors and insulators

A **conductor** is a material which lets electrons move through it easily. All metals conduct electricity, and so does graphite (a form of carbon).

An **insulator** is a material which does not let electrons move through it. **Non-metals** are insulators, and so are materials like wood or plastic, which are mainly made from non-metals.

Circuits

There has to be a complete **circuit** before electricity can flow.

Switches can be used to control electricity.

In this circuit the motor will only work if the switch is pressed. When the switch is not being pressed there is a gap in the circuit so the electricity cannot flow.

f

Electrons were discovered in 1897 by a scientist called Sir Joseph Thomson. Before then people had imagined that electricity was an invisible fluid which flowed through wires. To make it easier to talk about electricity, they decided that this fluid flowed out of the + end of a cell and went back into the - end.

Now that we know about electrons, we also know that the electrons come out of the - end of the battery and go back into the + end.

Series and parallel circuits

If you have two or more components there are two different ways of arranging them.

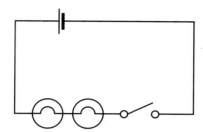

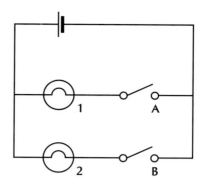

These bulbs are arranged **in series**. The switch turns on all the bulbs at once. If one of the bulbs breaks there will be a gap in the circuit and no electricity can flow. The other bulb will go off.

These bulbs are arranged **in parallel**. Switch A turns on bulb 1, and switch B turns on bulb 2. If one of the bulbs breaks, the other stays on because there are two different paths for the electrons to move along.

- **Conductors** are materials which allow electrons to move through them.
- **Insulators** are materials which do not allow electrons to move through them.
- A complete **circuit** is needed for an electric current to flow.
- **Series circuits** have components arranged one after the other.
- **Parallel circuits** have components arranged in separate branches of the circuit.

summary

Questions

1 What do the following words mean?
a) cell b) battery c) component
d) conductor e) insulator

2 a) Name an insulating material.
b) Name a conducting material.

1 a) Why are electrical wires made of metal?
b) Why do they usually have a plastic coating on the outside?

2 a) Draw two bulbs and a cell in a series circuit.
b) Draw two bulbs and a cell in a parallel circuit.

3 a) Which switches have to be pressed to make bulb 2 come on?
b) Which bulbs will come on if you press switch B?
c) Which bulbs will come on if you press switches A and C?

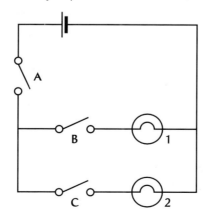

4 Mr Smith has some Christmas tree lights. One bulb is missing and the other lights will not come on until he has replaced the bulb.
a) Are the lights on a series or a parallel circuit?
b) Explain how you worked out your answer.

5 a) Are the lights in your house on a series circuit or a parallel circuit?
b) Explain how you worked out your answer.

C

Two-way switches are used on staircases so that the light can be switched on or off from upstairs or downstairs. Find out what a circuit with a two-way switch would look like and explain how it works. Draw a diagram of the circuit to help you explain.

Changing the Current

The electricity flowing around a circuit is the **electric current**.
The size of the current flowing around a circuit has to be
controlled if the circuit is to work properly.

intro

These pages are about electrical current and how to change it.

Measuring the current

The size of the current is a way of measuring how
many electrons are flowing around the circuit.
If a lot of electricity is flowing, the current is said to
be large. If only a little electricity is flowing the current
is small. A large current would make a bulb light up
brightly, and a small current would make the bulb dim.

You can measure the size of the current flowing in
a circuit with an **ammeter**.

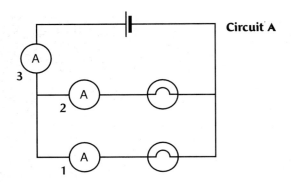

Circuit A

Ammeter 1 is measuring the current flowing through
the bottom branch of the parallel circuit and ammeter
2 is measuring the current flowing through the top
branch. Ammeter 3 is measuring the current coming
out of the **battery**.

A current of one amp (1 A) means that
about 6 250 000 000 000 000 000
electrons are going through the ammeter
every second.

Changing the current

There are two ways of changing the current.

1 The voltage can be increased by using more cells
   (or by changing the setting of the power supply).
   If you use a higher voltage you will get a higher
   current flowing in the circuit.
2 The number of components in the circuit can
   be changed. For instance, if you add more bulbs
   to a series circuit the current will get smaller.
   It is more difficult for electricity to get through
   lots of bulbs, so not as much gets through.

Units

The units used for measuring current are called
amps (or A).

Resistors

Resistors are special components made to control
the current in the circuit.

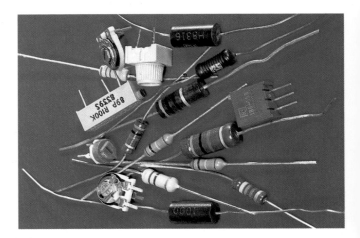

A resistor with a large resistance will let only a small
current through. A resistor with a small resistance will
let a larger current through.

The current around a circuit

Does it matter where in the circuit you put an ammeter? All the ammeters in this series circuit are showing the same reading. The current is the same everywhere in a series circuit. The bulbs do not 'use up' the current.

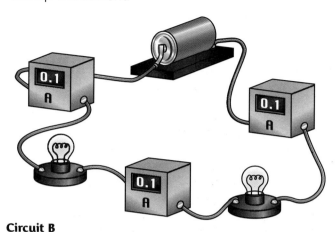

Circuit B

What happens in parallel circuits?

The current splits up when it comes to a junction. The currents through the two branches add up to the total current in the main part of the circuit.

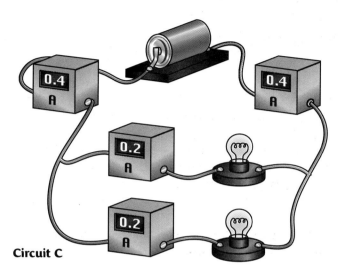

Circuit C

- The size of the current can be measured using an **ammeter**.
- The units for current are **amps** (A).
- The size of the current depends on the **voltage** of the battery or power supply.
- The size of the current also depends on the number of components in the circuit, and on what kind of components they are.
- Current does not get used up by bulbs or other components. The current is the same everywhere in a series circuit.

summary

Questions

A

1. What do these words mean?
   a) current **b)** ammeter **c)** resistor

2. What are the units for measuring electric current?

B

1. Describe two different ways of changing the current in a circuit.

2. You have two cells, two bulbs and some connecting wires.
   a) Draw a circuit diagram to show how you would make a circuit to give the brightest bulb.
   b) Draw a circuit diagram to show how you would get the dimmest bulbs.

3. In circuit A both bulbs are the same and ammeter 1 reads 0.1 A.
   a) What does ammeter 2 read?
   b) What does ammeter 3 read?

4. If there were four bulbs in circuit B, what would the ammeters read?

5. If there were two cells in circuit C, what would the ammeters read?

C

What is a variable resistor? Explain how it works.

Magnetism

Magnets are all around you. You have probably used fridge magnets to stick messages to doors, but loudspeakers, electric motors, computer disks and cassette tapes also use magnetism.

These pages are about magnets and magnetic fields, and how to make magnets using electricity.

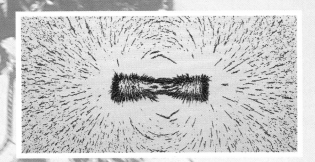

▶ Scrap iron and steel can be picked up using an electromagnet

Magnetic materials

Magnetic materials are materials that can be picked up using a magnet. Iron, nickel and cobalt are magnetic materials. Materials which contain one of these metals are also magnetic. Steel, for instance, is made from iron and carbon, so steel is attracted to a magnet. Other metals, like aluminium, are not magnetic and will not be attracted to a magnet.

Attracting and repelling

The two ends of the magnet are called the **north pole** and the **south pole**.

If you put two magnets down with their north poles together or their south poles together they will push each other away. **Like poles repel.**

If a north pole and a south pole are put near each other they attract. **Opposite poles attract.**

Compasses

A **compass** is a small magnet that can move around on a **pivot**. The red end of a compass needle (or the end with an arrow on it) is a north pole. It will point away from the north pole of a magnet.

The Earth behaves as if it had a massive magnet inside it. The south pole of this imaginary magnet is in the Earth's northern hemisphere, which is why the north end of a compass needle points towards it.

This is why the two ends of the magnet are named north and south. Originally the north pole of a magnet was called a 'north-seeking pole' because it was the end of the magnet that pointed north.

Magnetic fields

Magnetism is a **non-contact** force. Magnets can make pieces of metal move even when the magnet is not touching the metal. The space around the magnet where it has this effect is called the **magnetic field**. You can find the shape of a magnetic field using **iron filings** (very small pieces of iron).

This is the shape of the magnetic field around a bar magnet. A bar magnet is a **permanent magnet** because it is always magnetic.

Electromagnets

You can make a magnet using electricity, like this.

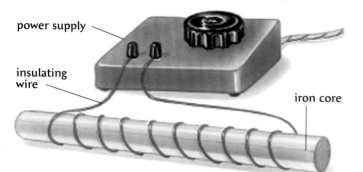

power supply

insulating wire

iron core

The **iron core** concentrates the magnetic field. This is called an **electromagnet**.

An electromagnet has a magnetic field similar to the magnetic field of a bar magnet.

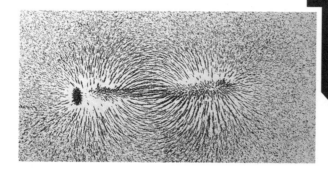

An electromagnet is useful because it is only magnetic when electricity is flowing through the wire. The strength of the magnetic field of an electromagnet depends on the current. A large current makes a strong electromagnet. An electromagnet can also be made stronger by having more turns of wire in the coil.

- **Magnets** will attract materials containing iron, nickel or cobalt.
- The two ends of a magnet are called the **north pole** and the **south pole**.
- **Like poles repel** and **opposite poles attract**.
- The space around a magnet, where it can attract magnetic materials, is called the **magnetic field**.
- Magnets can be made using electricity. An **electromagnet** is only magnetic while the electricity is flowing in the wires.

summary

Questions

1 What do these words mean?
   a) magnet **b)** magnetic material
   c) magnetic field
   d) permanent magnet
   e) electromagnet **f)** core

2 Which materials can be attracted to magnets?

1 **a)** Why are magnets often fitted to the doors of cupboards or refrigerators?
   b) Are permanent magnets or electromagnets used on doors?

2 These magnets are repelling each other.

| N | S | | |

   a) Copy the diagram and mark the poles on the second magnet.
   b) What would happen if you turned one of the magnets around?

3 Why do cranes in scrapyards or steelworks have electromagnets fitted instead of permanent magnets?

4 How could you use a magnet to separate a pile of aluminium drinks cans and steel food cans for recycling?

5 You need to have a coil of insulated wire to make an electromagnet. Why do you need the insulation? (*Hint* – think how the current would flow if the wire was not insulated.)

How can a magnet be used to measure the thickness of paint on a steel ship?

For more information about forces see pages 108-109

Using Electromagnets

People use electromagnets every day to start their cars or to ring door and alarm bells. If you look around you will see many electromagnets at work.

These pages are about how electromagnets can be used in relays and electric bells.

Relays

A **relay** is an electrical switch which works by remote control. It is switched on and off with an electromagnet.

The coil of wire on the electromagnet is sometimes called a **solenoid**. The piece of magnetic material that is attracted to the electromagnet is called the **armature**.

Starter motors

A relay is used to start a car engine. The starter motor needs a large current, and the wires must be thick to carry this current without overheating. It would cost a lot of money if these thick wires had to run all the way from the battery to the starter motor and to the ignition switch inside the car, so a relay is used to switch on the starter motor. This also makes it safer, as the driver does not have to touch the part of the circuit carrying a high current.

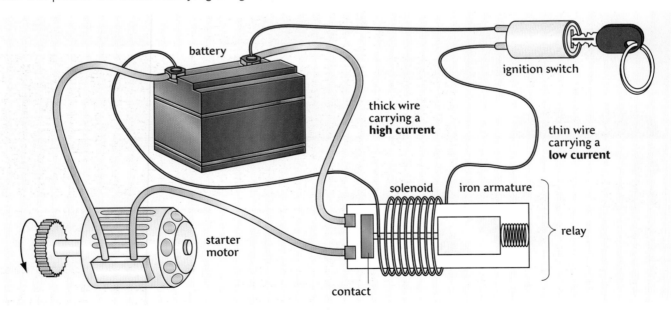

battery

ignition switch

thick wire carrying a **high current**

thin wire carrying a **low current**

solenoid   iron armature

relay

starter motor

contact

When you turn the ignition switch it switches on the low current part of the circuit. This current turns the solenoid into an electromagnet. This attracts the iron armature in the relay. When the iron moves it completes the high current circuit, and the starter motor turns.

As soon as the engine has started the driver lets go of the ignition switch. The solenoid stops being an electromagnet. The iron armature springs back and the high current circuit is broken and the starter motor stops turning.

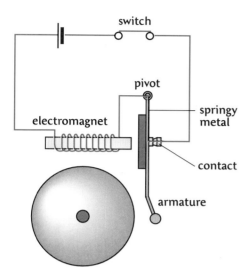

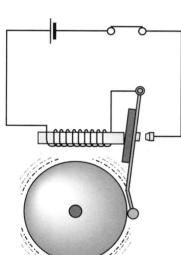

Electric bells

An electric bell has an electromagnet inside it.

The red line shows where the electric current flows when the bell is switched on. When electricity is flowing around the circuit the solenoid is magnetised and attracts the armature. The hammer fastened to the end of the armature hits the gong, so it rings.

As soon as the armature is attracted to the solenoid it moves away from the contact and breaks the circuit. The solenoid stops attracting the armature, and the armature springs back.

When the armature touches the contacts again, current flows through the circuit and magnetises the solenoid, which attracts the armature. The hammer hits the gong again, and so on. The circuit keeps 'making and breaking' as long as the bell is switched on.

- A **relay** is an electrical switch that works by **remote control**.
- Relays use an electromagnet to attract an **armature**.
- The movement of the armature can be used to switch on another circuit.
- Electromagnets can also be used to work electric bells.

summary

Questions

A

1 What do these words mean?
   a) relay **b)** armature **c)** solenoid

B

1 Why is a relay used to switch on a starter motor? (There are two reasons.)

2 **a)** Explain in your own words how an electric bell works.
   b) Why is a spring attached to the armature?

3 Some kinds of metal can be magnetised very easily, and they also lose their magnetism quickly when the current is switched off. Other metals are harder to magnetise, but they keep their magnetism longer after the electricity has been switched off. Which kind of metal should be used for the core of electro-magnets in relays and bells? Explain your answer.

C

1 Explain how a loudspeaker works.

2 How can trains use electromagnets instead of wheels? (You may need to look up the word 'maglev'.)

Forces and Friction

Forces can be pushes or pulls, or they can be twisting or turning forces.

> These pages are about what forces can do, and about friction and air resistance.

Units

Forces are measured in newtons (N).
Forces can be **balanced** or **unbalanced**.

Balanced forces can change the shape of things but they cannot change the speed or direction of moving things.

table pushing up on cat

cat pushing down on table

Balanced forces are often present even though nothing seems to be happening.

Unbalanced forces can make things start or stop moving, speed up or slow down, or change direction. When there are unequal forces pulling or pushing in opposite directions, the smaller force cancels out part of the bigger force.

These forces ...

200 N

400 N

200 N

... have the same effect as this force.

Gravity, magnetism & static electricity

Some forces can push or pull at a distance. The Earth's **gravity** pulls things downwards even if they are not touching the Earth.

Magnets can attract and repel each other without touching, and so can objects charged with static electricity. These three forces are sometimes called **non-contact forces**.

Friction

Friction is a force which slows down moving things. There is a force of friction whenever two things are moving against each other.

A heavy box is difficult to push along the floor because there is a large force of friction between the box and the floor.

Friction between the air and the parachute is slowing the car down. This kind of friction is sometimes called **air resistance**.

Friction can be a useful force, or it can be a force that people want to make as small as possible.

When you ride a bicycle you need friction between the tyres and the road to stop you skidding. You need friction between the brake blocks and the wheels to slow you down. You do not need friction in the axles. This friction makes it more difficult to pedal the bicycle.

Changing friction

Friction can be increased by making the surfaces rougher. Trainers have a good grip when their tread is deep. In the winter, grit is put on the roads to make the road's surface rougher so that car tyres will not slip.

Friction can be reduced by having very smooth surfaces, by using wheels, or by using oil or other liquids to **lubricate** moving parts. Air resistance can be reduced by giving things a smoother, streamlined shape.

When a space shuttle is flying back to Earth, friction between its wings and the air heats up the front edges of the wings to 1600°C. Engineers have to use special heat-resistant materials when they build the wings so that they will not melt in the heat.

Friction and heat

When friction slows things down the **kinetic energy** that is lost is converted to heat energy. You can feel this yourself when you rub your hands together. Friction between the palms of your hands will warm them up.

Arrows are used to show forces in diagrams. The direction of the arrow shows the direction of the force. The size of the arrow shows the size of the force.

- **Balanced** forces can change the shape of things, but not their speed or direction of movement.
- **Unbalanced** forces can change the speed or the direction of moving things, or start or stop things moving.
- **Friction** is a force which slows down moving things.
- **Friction** usually heats things up.
- **Air resistance** is caused by friction between the air and a moving object.

summary

Questions

1 What do these words mean?
a) force b) gravity
c) non-contact force d) friction
e) air resistance f) lubrication
2 What can balanced forces do?
3 What can unbalanced forces do?

1 Why is a bicycle difficult to ride if its parts need oiling?
2 Why is it very dangerous to drive a car with smooth tyres?
3 Why should drivers slow down if the road is wet or icy?
4 This bag of apples has stretched the spring. The apples are not moving.

Copy the diagram and add arrows to show the force the apples are putting on the spring, and the force the spring is putting on the apples.

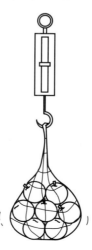

5 A car's engine produces a forwards force, and friction tries to slow the car down.
What will happen to the speed of a moving car if:
a) the force from the engine is smaller than the force of friction
b) the two forces are the same size?

Rock climbers use ropes to stop themselves hitting the ground if they fall off a rock face.
a) Find out how friction is used to control the ropes.
b) Why are climbing ropes stretchy?

Levers and Turning Forces

Levers are simple machines which can magnify forces.

> These pages are about how levers can be used to magnify forces, and how to calculate the size of a turning force.

Levers and loads

A lever is a piece of stiff material, like a metal bar, which has a **pivot**.

In this case, the **load** is the weight the girl is trying to lift. The **effort** is the force she is putting on the end of the lever.

The size of the load force, compared to the size of the effort force, depends on how far the load and the effort are from the pivot.

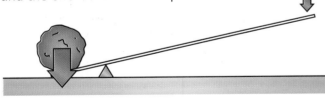

If the effort distance is bigger than the load distance, the force will be magnified.

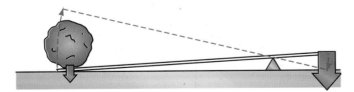

If the effort distance is smaller than the load distance, the load force will be smaller than the effort, but it will move further.

When the girl pushes on the lever she is producing a **turning force** about the pivot. The size of the turning force depends on the size of the force and on how far it is from the pivot. A turning force is sometimes called a **moment**.

moment (Nm) = force (N) × distance (m)

Units

The units for moments are newton-metres (Nm).

How much weight can Samir lift using this lever?

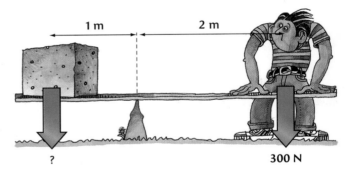

The turning force Samir is putting on the lever is

300 N × 2 m = 600 Nm

Because the lever is stiff there is the same turning force on the other side of the pivot, so:

600 Nm = load × 1 m
load = 600 N

He can lift 600 N using the lever.

Everyday levers

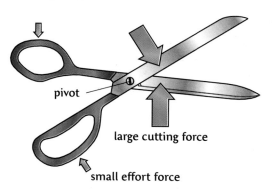

pivot

large cutting force

small effort force

If you need to cut something very stiff, you will put it right next to the pivot. This keeps the load distance small, so you get a big magnification of the force.

Balancing

Sometimes it is important that turning forces are balanced.

1 m

?

600 N

200 N

How far from the pivot is the boy sitting to balance the seesaw?

If the seesaw is balanced than the anti-clockwise moment is equal to the clockwise moment:

$$200 \text{ N} \times \text{distance} = 600 \text{ N} \times 1 \text{ m}$$
$$\text{distance} = \frac{600 \text{ N} \times 1 \text{ m}}{200 \text{ N}}$$
$$\text{distance} = 3 \text{ m}$$

The boy is sitting 3 metres from the pivot.

- A **lever** is a simple machine which can magnify forces.
- The change in the force depends on the load distance and the effort distance.
- A turning force is called a **moment**.
- **Moment (Nm) = force (N) x distance (m).**
- When something is balanced, the clockwise and anti-clockwise moments are the same.

Questions

A

1 What do these words mean?
   a) lever **b)** load **c)** effort **d)** load distance
   e) effort distance **f)** moment

2 Write down the formula for calculating a moment.

3 What are the units for moments?

B

1 If you are trying to undo a rusty nut, why do you need a spanner with a long handle?

2 How much weight will this lever lift?

3 m

400 N

? 1 m

3 How far from the pivot should the 2 N weight be to balance the seesaw?

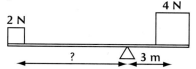

4 N

2 N

? 3 m

4 Wire cutters are tools with short handles. They are used for cutting thin pieces of wire. Bolt cutters have much longer handles, and they are used for cutting through thick metal bars. Explain as fully as you can why the tools have handles of different lengths.

C

1 How many levers are there on a bicycle? You should be able to find at least four different ones. Describe what each lever does.

2 There are levers in your own body. Find out where these levers are.

Pressure

These pages are about pressure, what it means and how to calculate it.

Pressure is a way of describing how **concentrated** a force is. For instance, you cannot make a hole in a wooden table by pressing your thumb on it. But you can easily make a hole if you push a drawing pin into the table with the same force. All the force from your thumb is concentrated at the point of the pin.

Your thumb on its own had **low pressure** underneath it because the force was spread out. The point of the pin had **high pressure** underneath it.

High pressure

To get a high pressure you need either a very big force or a very small area. Knives cut things easily because their blades are sharp. All the force that you put on the knife is concentrated on the very small area of the edge of the blade. There is a high pressure under the blade.

Low pressure

To get a low pressure you must have a small force or a big area.

If you try walking in soft snow in ordinary boots you will sink. The pressure under your feet is too high. To make the pressure under your feet lower you must make the area of your boot soles bigger. You can do this by putting on snowshoes. The snowshoes spread your weight out over a bigger area so that there is lower pressure underneath them.

Calculating pressure

The pressure caused by a force is calculated using this formula:

$$\text{pressure} = \frac{\text{force}}{\text{area}}$$

Units

The units for pressure depend on the units being used for measuring the area.

If the units for area are cm^2 then the units for pressure are 'newtons per centimetre squared' (N/cm^2).

If the area is measured in square metres, then the units for pressure are N/m^2.

A girl weighs 500 N. The area of the soles of her shoes is 250 cm^2. What is the pressure under her shoes? First write the formula:

$$\text{pressure} = \frac{\text{force}}{\text{area}}$$

then put the numbers in:

$$\text{pressure} = \frac{500 \text{ N}}{250 \text{ cm}^2}$$

then work out the answer:

$$\text{pressure} = 2 \text{ N/cm}^2$$

The air around you is pressing on you with a force of just over 10 N on every square centimetre. This is like having a 1 kg mass standing on each square centimetre of your skin!

Calculating force or area

Sometimes you need to calculate the force or area instead of the pressure. You would need to use one of these formulae:

$$area = \frac{force}{pressure}$$

$$force = pressure \times area$$

Some people find it easier to remember the three equations by remembering this triangle.

To use it, cover up the letter you need to calculate and you will see the formula.
So if you need to calculate the force causing a pressure, cover up the F like this,

and you can see
P × A, so
force = pressure × area.

A girl weighing 500 N is wearing a pair of skis. If the pressure under her skis is 0.2 N/cm², what is the area of her skis?

You have to calculate an area, so choose the formula that starts with 'area ='

$$area = \frac{force}{pressure}$$

then put the numbers in:

$$area = \frac{500 \text{ N}}{0.2 \text{ N/cm}^2}$$

then work out the answer:

$$area = 2500 \text{ cm}^2$$

Questions

1. What do these terms mean?
   a) low pressure b) high pressure
2. Write down the formula for calculating pressure.
3. Write down two different units for pressure.

1. Explain why an armoured tank can move over muddy ground when a normal truck with wheels would sink.
2. Why is it easier to make a hole in a piece of paper with a pin than with the end of a pen?

3. A woman weighs 600 N. She is wearing shoes with stiletto heels, and each heel has an area of 0.5 cm². What pressure does she put on the floor if she stands on one heel?

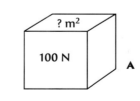

4. a) Box A is putting a pressure of 50 N/m² on the floor. What is the area of the base of the box?
   b) How much must box B weigh to have the same pressure underneath it as box A?

How much pressure do *you* put on the floor? You will need to work out the area of your feet by drawing around them on squared paper and counting the number of centimetre squares, and you will need to know your weight in newtons. (Convert kilograms to newtons by multiplying by 10, so if your mass is 50 kg your weight is 500 N.)

Measuring Speed

These pages are about how to use a formula to calculate speed from measurements of distance and time.

Some things are easy to measure. The length of a box can be measured with a ruler, or the time you can hold your breath can be measured with a stopwatch. If you want to measure speed, you need to measure a distance and a time. Then you calculate the speed.

intro

A car travels 50 miles in one hour. Its speed is 50 miles per hour. This is the formula used to calculate speed:

$$\text{speed} = \frac{\text{distance}}{\text{time}}$$

Units

The scientific unit for speed is metres per second (m/s). In everyday life people also use miles per hour (mph) or kilometres per hour (km/h or kph).

A woman walked 22 km in 4 hours. How fast was she walking?

First, write the formula:

$$\text{speed} = \frac{\text{distance}}{\text{time}}$$

then put the numbers in:

$$\text{speed} = \frac{22 \text{ km}}{4 \text{ hours}}$$

then work out the answer:

$$\text{speed} = 5.5 \text{ km/h}$$

If you have to calculate the speed of something, the units for your answer depend on the units used in the question.

For instance, if the question says a girl ran 2 metres in one second, her speed was 2 metres per second (2 m/s).

Bicycle speedometer

Some bicycle speedometers use small computers to work out the speed of the bicycle. Before the speedometer will work properly, you have to tell it the size of your front wheel.

A small magnet is attached to the wheel, and a **detector** is attached to the front fork of the bicycle. The detector sends a signal to the computer every time the magnet goes past it. The computer has a clock inside it and this counts how many signals arrive each second. The computer uses this information to work out the speed.

For instance, if your wheel has a circumference of 1.5 metres, and the computer receives 6 signals in one second, then you have moved 6×1.5 m in one second, so your speed is 9 m/s.

Average speed

A bus takes half an hour to travel 5 miles through town. You could say that its speed is 5 miles/0.5 hours = 10 mph. But this does not mean that the bus was going at 10 mph all the time. It had to stop to let people on or off, and it may also have stopped at junctions or traffic lights. At other times during the journey it may have been travelling at 30 mph.

The **average speed** of the bus only takes into account the total distance it travels and the overall time it takes.

Calculating time or distance

Sometimes you need to calculate a time or a distance instead of a speed. The formula needs to be rearranged:

$$\text{time} = \frac{\text{distance}}{\text{speed}}$$

$$\text{distance} = \text{speed} \times \text{time}$$

Mr Jones has to drive 210 miles on the motorway. If he can travel at 70 mph all the way, how long will it take him?

You have to calculate a time, so choose the formula that starts with 'time ='

$$\text{time} = \frac{\text{distance}}{\text{speed}}$$

then put the numbers in:

$$\text{time} = \frac{210 \text{ miles}}{70 \text{ mph}}$$

then work out the answer:

$$\text{time} = 3 \text{ hours.}$$

Some people find it easier to remember the three equations by remembering this triangle.

To use it, cover up the letter you need to calculate and you will see the formula. So if you need to calculate how long a journey will take (time), cover up the T and you can see $\frac{D}{S}$, so

$$\text{time} = \frac{\text{distance}}{\text{speed}}$$

▶ *This is ThrustSSC, the first land vehicle to travel faster than sound.*

● Speed is calculated from measurements of distance and time.
● The formula is **speed = distance/time**.
● The units for speed are **m/s, mph or km/h**.

summary

Questions

A

1 What does average speed mean?
2 Write down the formula for calculating speed.
3 Write down three different units for speed.

B

1 A man runs 100 m in 15 seconds. What is his speed?
2 A cyclist takes 3 hours to cycle 60 km. How fast is she going?

3 A woman can walk at 3 mph.

a) How far can she walk in 3 hours?
b) How long will it take her to walk 18 miles?

4 If you put the wrong wheel size into your bicycle speedometer it will not give the correct speed. If the size you put in is too small, will the speed it tells you be too fast or too slow? Explain your answer.

C

1 a) *ThrustSSC* first broke the sound barrier on 13 October 1997, but it could not claim the official record until two days later when the team made two supersonic runs in opposite directions within one hour. Why are two runs necessary before a record can be given?

b) *ThrustSSC* reached a speed of Mach 1.020. What does the 'Mach number' mean?

2 Ships use 'knots' as a unit for speed instead of miles or kilometres per hour.

a) What is a knot?
b) Why is the unit called a knot? (*Hint* – you will have to find out how ships used to measure speed, using a device called a 'log'.)

Light

These pages are about light and how it travels.

Light is a kind of energy which your eyes can detect. You need light to see things. During the day light comes from the Sun. At night or indoors you need to use electric lights to help you to see things.

intro

Making light

The Sun is **luminous**, which means that it makes its own light. Electric lights, fires and television screens all make their own light. Luminous things are **sources of light**. You can see luminous things when the light from them goes into your eyes.

Light travels in straight lines. You can sometimes see where the light is travelling in a cinema if the air is dusty.

light cannot travel through **opaque** materials

light can travel through **transparent** materials, such as glass

light cannot go through your body, so your body makes a **shadow**

Light and shadows

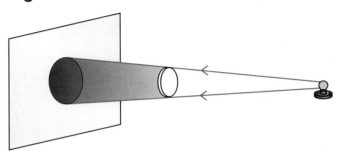

You get a shadow with sharp edges if you use a light source smaller than the object.

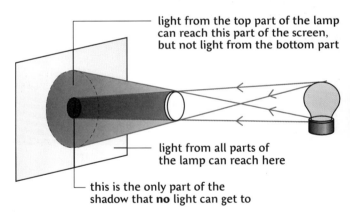

light from the top part of the lamp can reach this part of the screen, but not light from the bottom part

light from all parts of the lamp can reach here

this is the only part of the shadow that **no** light can get to

You get a shadow with blurred edges if you use a light source larger than the object.

Light takes time to travel, but it travels very fast. Light moves at 300 million metres per second, which is nearly 650 million miles per hour! Light travels about a million times faster than an aeroplane.

116

Seeing things

You can see luminous things when the light from them goes into your eyes. But how can you see things that do not make their own light?

You see **non-luminous** objects when light is **reflected** from them and this light enters your eyes.

When you think about reflections you probably imagine looking at yourself in a mirror. Mirrors have very smooth surfaces which reflect light in a special way. If you look into a mirror you can see an **image** of your face.

If you look at them really closely, most things have rough surfaces. When light is reflected by rough surfaces it is scattered in all directions. Because the light is scattered you cannot see an image. You can see this page because it is rough and is reflecting light.

Always use a ruler when you draw diagrams showing the way light travels. Put arrows on your lines to show which way the light is going.

- Light travels in straight lines, and it travels very fast.
- Light can travel through transparent materials.
- Light cannot travel through opaque materials.
- Opaque materials can form shadows when light hits them.
- Luminous things make their own light.
- You see luminous things when light from them enters your eyes.
- You see non-luminous things when light is reflected from them and then enters your eyes.

summary

Questions

1 What do these words mean?
a) transparent **b)** opaque
c) shadow **d)** luminous **e)** reflect

1 Make a list of as many luminous things as you can think of.

2 Make a list of as many transparent materials or objects as you can think of.

3 How fast does light travel?

4 Copy this diagram, and draw arrows on it to show how light from the Sun helps the boys to see the football.

5 This diagram shows an object making a shadow on a screen.

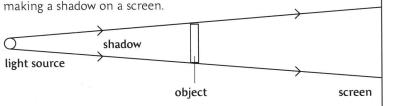

Draw similar diagrams to show:
a) why the shadow gets smaller if the object is moved nearer to the screen.
b) why the shadow gets bigger if the object is moved nearer to the source of light.

6 Explain why you can only see the light travelling from the projector to the screen if the air in the cinema is dusty. Use a diagram if it helps.

1 **a)** What is an eclipse?
b) Draw a diagram to show what happens when there is an eclipse of the Sun.

For more information about how we see things see pages 120–121
For more information about different kinds of energy see pages 136–137

Mirrors

Mirrors **reflect** light in a special way.
When you look in a mirror you can see an **image** of yourself.

These pages are about mirrors
and how they reflect light.

Images in mirrors

A flat mirror is called a **plane mirror**. If you look at
your image in a plane mirror carefully you should
notice these things:

- your image is upright (the right way up)
- the image of your face looks the same size as your face
- it looks as though the image is behind the mirror
- left and right are the wrong way round (your image
  is **laterally inverted**).

How do mirrors reflect light?

You can investigate what happens to light when it
is reflected by a mirror by marking the **rays** of light.
This is called **ray tracing**.

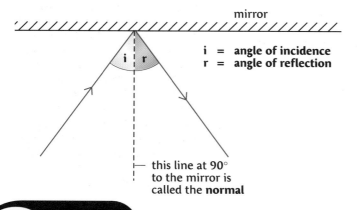

The **angle of incidence** is always equal to the **angle
of reflection**.

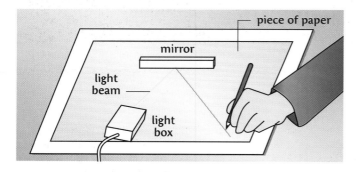

i = angle of incidence
r = angle of reflection

this line at 90°
to the mirror is
called the **normal**

This diagram shows how an image is formed by
a plane mirror.

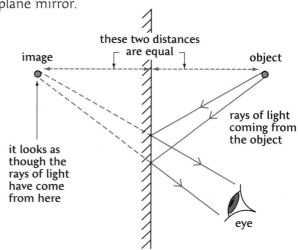

these two distances
are equal

image

object

rays of light
coming from
the object

it looks as
though the
rays of light
have come
from here

eye

If you have to draw a diagram like this it is easiest
to draw it in this order.

1   Draw the mirror and the object.
2   Draw the image behind the mirror. Make sure
    the object and the image are both the same
    distance from the mirror.
3   Draw the eye on the same side of the mirror
    as the object.
4   Draw the two lines from the image to the eye.
    Make the lines dotted where they are behind
    the mirror.
5   Draw lines joining the object with the places
    where the other two lines cross the mirror.
6   Draw the arrows to show which way the light
    is travelling.

When you look at the image of something in a mirror
it looks as though the rays of light have come from
a point behind the mirror. The image seems to be
behind the mirror. The image is called a **virtual
image** because even though it looks as if it is behind
the mirror, there is nothing there.

Using mirrors

People use mirrors every day. Drivers use mirrors in cars so that they can see behind their cars without having to turn around, and dentists use mirrors so that they can see right into the back of your mouth. Can you think of any other uses for mirrors?

Submarines use **periscopes** to look around the surface of the sea without having to come up out of the water. A periscope has two mirrors.

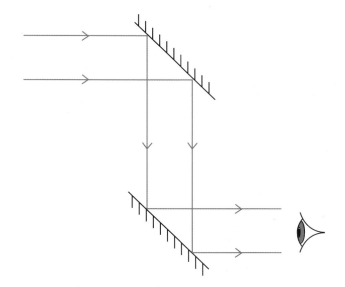

The ancient Greeks and Romans used metal mirrors made out of pieces of polished bronze. The mirrors people use today have metal in them too. The part of the mirror that reflects light is a thin layer of silver on the back of the glass. The glass provides a very smooth surface for the silver, and also protects it.

- Flat mirrors are called **plane mirrors**.
- The image in a plane mirror is the right way up but left and right are the wrong way round.
- The image in a plane mirror looks as though it is behind the mirror.
- When light is reflected by a mirror the **angle of incidence** and **angle of reflection** are equal.

summary

Questions

1 What do these words mean?
a) image b) plane
c) ray d) virtual image

2 Draw a diagram to show how one ray of light is reflected by a mirror. Make sure the angles of incidence and reflection are equal. Label your diagram.

1 Write a list of all the different ways that mirrors can be used. There are four ideas on this page to start you off.

2 The front of an ambulance often has this written on it:

AMBULANCE

Explain why the word is written back to front.

3 Copy the diagram on the opposite page showing why an image appears to be behind a mirror. Make sure you draw the different parts of the diagram in the right order.

4 Copy this diagram showing two mirrors and a ray of light. Draw the path the light will take when it is reflected by the mirrors. Make sure the angles between the light rays and the mirror are accurate.

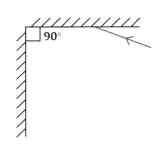

5 When sunlight is reflected off the sea it often sparkles. Why does this happen? Explain in as much detail as you can.

1 **Convex** mirrors are mirrors which bulge outwards in the middle. Find out where mirrors like this are used, and why they can be better than plane mirrors for some purposes. (*Hint* – the back of the curved bowl of a polished metal spoon will act like a convex mirror.)

2 A **concave** mirror curves away from you in the middle. Find out how concave mirrors reflect light, and how they are used in reflecting telescopes.

Refraction

Light normally travels in straight lines.
You can make light bend by using a piece of glass.

These pages are about bending light and making coloured light.

Refraction

When light bends like this it is called **refraction**.

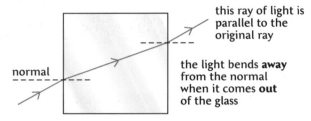

this ray of light is parallel to the original ray

the light bends **away** from the normal when it comes **out** of the glass

normal

the light bends **towards** the normal when it goes **into** the glass

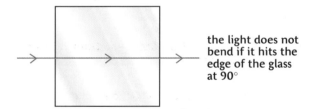

the light does not bend if it hits the edge of the glass at 90°

The same thing happens when light goes into clear plastic or into water. You can see this for yourself.

Using refraction

Lenses are pieces of glass or plastic which have been shaped so that they will bend light in a particular way.

Converging lenses make a beam of light converge to a point. Converging lenses are used in telescopes and binoculars to make distant things look bigger. They are also used in microscopes which make small things look bigger.

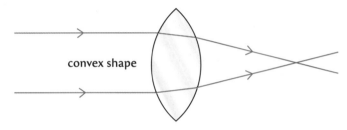

convex shape

Diverging lenses make a beam of light spread out.

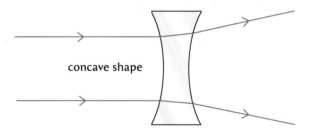

concave shape

Many people need spectacles or contact lenses to help them to see clearly. Some people need diverging lenses and other people need converging lenses. The kind of lens they need depends on what is wrong with their eyes.

Making coloured light

The normal light that comes from the Sun or from light bulbs is called **white light**. White light is really a mixture of different colours of light. When all the colours of light go into your eyes at once your brain tells you that the colour is white.

There are seven colours in the **spectrum** that makes up white light. The colours are red, orange, yellow, green, blue, indigo and violet.

Prisms are triangular blocks of glass. A prism can be used to help you to see the colours in white light.

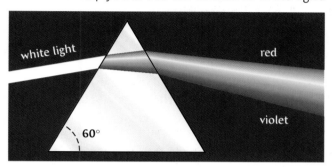

white light

red

violet

60°

This 60 degree prism is being used to split a beam of light so you can see the colours of the spectrum. This happens because the prism bends the different colours by different amounts.

You can also see the spectrum by looking at the playing side of a CD.

Rainbows are formed when there are tiny droplets of water in the air. Sunlight is split up into different colours by the drops of water.

You can remember lists of things by making their initial letters into a sentence. The first letters of the words in this sentence are the same as the first letters of the colours in the spectrum:

Richard Of York Gave Battle In Vain. Some people prefer to remember the colours using the name ROY G BIV.

For more information about colour see pages 122–123

- When light travels from one material into another its direction may change.
- This bending is called **refraction**.
- When light goes from air to glass it bends towards the normal.
- When light goes from glass to air it bends away from the normal.
- **Lenses** are pieces of glass shaped to refract light in a particular way.
- A **prism** can be used to split up white light into the colours of the **spectrum**.

summary

Questions

 A

1 What do these words mean?
   a) refraction **b)** prism **c)** white light **d)** spectrum

 B

1 Write down the colours of the spectrum in order, starting with red.

2 What is a rainbow?

3 Make a list of things that use lenses. Write down as many things as you can think of.

4 Write down three different ways of turning white light into a spectrum of colours.

5 Look carefully at the diagram of the prism being used to split up white light.

   a) How many times is the light bent as it goes through the prism?

   b) Does the red or the blue part of the light bend more?

6 Copy these diagrams and finish drawing the rays of light.

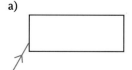

   a)   b)

 C

Why do some cameras use lots of lenses next to each other instead of just one lens? (You might need to look up the words 'chromatic aberration'.)

Colour

These pages are about coloured objects and coloured light.

Why do leaves look green? Why does blood look red?
When you see **non-luminous** things you are seeing the light that has been reflected by them. When things reflect light they do not always reflect all the colours in the light. Sometimes some of the colours are absorbed.

White things reflect all the colours in white light.

A blue thing reflects the blue light but it absorbs all the other colours.

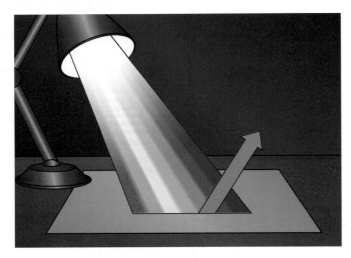

Black things absorb all the light that hits them.

So, leaves look green because they absorb all the colours in light except for the green. The green light is reflected. And blood is red because it reflects red light and absorbs the other colours.

Primary colours in light are different from primary colours in paints. Red, green and blue are primary colours when you are thinking about coloured light.

Making coloured light

Disco spotlights often produce coloured light, but they use ordinary light bulbs to do it. The white light from the light bulb is made into coloured light using a filter. Filters are made from materials which let some colours go through but absorb other colours.

The filter absorbs all the colours except green. It lets the green light through.

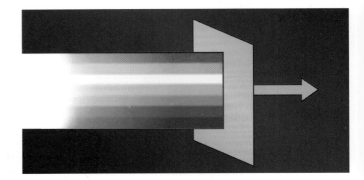

If you use two different filters you can stop all the light getting through. This happens because the blue filter lets the blue light through and absorbs all the other colours. The red filter would let red light through, but there is no red light hitting it. It absorbs all the other colours so it absorbs the blue light that is hitting it.

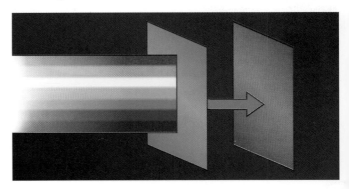

Mixing coloured light

Colours can be mixed again to give white light. The diagram on the right shows what happens when you use red, green and blue light. Red, green and blue are called the **primary colours.**

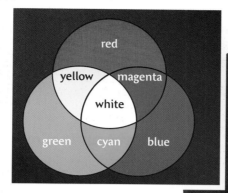

Disco lights!

Have you ever noticed that your clothes look different when you are in a disco with coloured lights?

her jacket only reflects red light

her shirt reflects all 7 colours, so it looks white

her jeans only reflect blue light

▶ *This is what Jenna's clothes look like in normal white light.*

her jacket reflects red light

her shirt can reflect all 7 colours, but only red light is hitting it so it can only reflect red light

her jeans absorb red, so they do not reflect any light at all

▶ *This is what Jenna looks like in red light.*

▶ *This is what she looks like in a blue spotlight.*

summary

- Coloured objects reflect only some of the colours in **white light**.
- If an object reflects only yellow light it looks yellow.
- **Filters** can be used to make coloured light.
- Filters absorb some of the colours in white light and let others through.
- Coloured objects look different if you look at them in coloured light.

Questions

A

1 What do these words mean?
   a) reflect **b)** absorb **c)** filter
   d) primary colours

2 Explain why grass looks green.
   Use a diagram if it helps you to explain.

B

1 Why does a daffodil look yellow?

2 **a)** Explain why Jenna's white shirt looks blue when she stands in a blue light.

   b) Explain why Jenna's red jacket looks black when she stands in a blue light.

3 What would a red rose look like in blue light? Explain your answer.

4 A TV screen is made up of red, green and blue dots which light up to make the picture.
   a) Which dots on the TV screen would have to be lit up to make the screen look white?
   b) Which ones would be needed to make it look yellow?
   c) Which ones would be lit up if it looked black?

C

Why can't you see colours very well at night or in dim light? (*Hint* – you might need to look up 'rods and cones' in a biology book or a book about the human senses.)

Sound

Sound is as important to us as light. Sound helps people and animals to communicate with each other.

These pages are about sound, how it is made and how it travels.

Making sound

Sound is made when things **vibrate**. If you put your fingers gently on your throat when you talk, you can feel vibrations.

Musical instruments also make vibrations.

Guitars, violins and cellos make sounds when their strings vibrate. The player has to pluck the strings or use a bow to make the strings vibrate. Pianos also have strings which vibrate when they are hit by wooden hammers at the end of the keys.

When you blow into a trumpet the air inside the tubes vibrates. Church organs, recorders and whistles also make sounds when air inside them vibrates. Electronic instruments, radios and CD players make sounds with a vibrating loudspeaker. If you touch a loudspeaker when music is playing, you will feel the vibrations.

Sound on the move

You hear things when the vibrations travel to your ears. The vibrations must have a substance to travel through. You usually hear sounds that have travelled through the air around you, but you can also hear sounds through solid things and through liquids.

▶ *You can hear sound through something solid.*

You can also hear things when you are under water.

A **vacuum** is a completely empty space. There is nothing there, not even air! Sound cannot travel through a vacuum because there is nothing to pass on the vibrations.

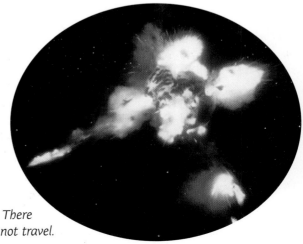

▶ *This explosion would be silent! There is no air in space so sound cannot travel.*

Light and sound

You see things when light travels to your eyes, and you hear things when sound travels to your ears. Light and sound travel in different ways.

Light travels at 300 000 000 metres per second but sound travels at only about 330 metres per second (when it is travelling through air).

Light can travel through space, but sound must have something to travel through (a solid, a liquid or a gas).

Thunder and lightning

Lightning and thunder happen together at the same time. The thunder is the sound made as the lightning suddenly strikes through the air.

During a thunderstorm you usually see the lightning before you hear the thunder. This happens because the light travels to your eyes very quickly. The sound of the thunder takes longer to reach your ears.

Light travels so quickly that you see the lightning almost as soon as it happens.

How far away is the thunderstorm?

Thunder takes about 3 seconds to travel 1 kilometre. If you count the number of seconds between seeing the lightning and hearing the thunder, you can work out how far away the storm is.

The distance of the storm (in kilometres) is the time between the lightning and the thunder divided by three.

If you hear thunder 6 seconds after you see the lightning,

$$\frac{6}{3} = 2,\text{ the storm is 2 km away.}$$

Questions

A

1 What do these words mean?
   a) vibration **b)** vacuum **c)** thunder

2 What vibrates in these instruments?
   a) guitar **b)** trumpet **c)** flute
   d) drum **e)** piano

B

1 Make a list of all the things you could not do if there was no such thing as sound.

2 You see a flash of lightning, and you hear thunder 12 seconds later. How far away is the storm?

3 Why do astronauts in space have to use radios to talk to each other?

4 Two astronauts could talk without using a radio if they touched their helmets together.

   Explain how the sound could travel from the person talking to her friend's ears.

5 If you used a powerful telescope you could see explosions on the surface of the Sun. Why could you see these explosions but not hear them?

C

How do bats use sound to find their way around?

For more information on different kinds of energy see pages 136–137

Loudness and Pitch

intro

How can you describe sounds?
If you sing, you can make your voice loud or quiet, and you can also make high or low sounds. Why are these sounds different?

Loud and quiet sounds

If you bang a drum gently, you get a quiet sound. If you bang a drum hard, you get a much louder sound.

The loudness of a sound depends on the size of the vibrations. Big vibrations make a loud sound. If you hit a drum hard, the skin vibrates up and down further than when you hit it gently.

The size of the vibrations is called the **amplitude**.

You can use a microphone and a machine called an **oscilloscope** to see the differences between different sounds.

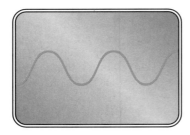

This oscilloscope is showing a quiet sound. This sound has a small amplitude.

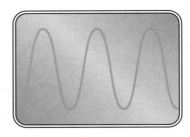

This oscilloscope is showing a loud sound. This sound has a large amplitude.

High and low sounds

You can play a tune on a recorder and each note sounds different. High notes have a **high pitch**, and low notes have a **low pitch**.

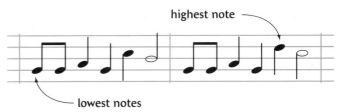

highest note

lowest notes

This music is the first line of the tune for 'Happy Birthday to You'.

The amplitude of a wave like this is the distance from the middle to the top, not the whole distance from top to bottom.

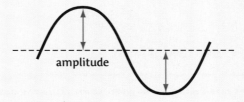

amplitude

High-pitched notes have more vibrations every second than low-pitched notes. The number of vibrations every second is called the **frequency**.

Units

The units for frequency are **hertz** (Hz).
　　　1 Hz = 1 vibration per second.

This oscilloscope is showing a low-pitched sound. There is only one vibration every second.

This is showing a high-pitched sound. It is just as loud as before but it has more vibrations every second so it sounds higher.

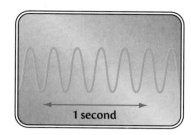
1 second

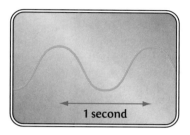
1 second

● Loud sounds have a large **amplitude**, and quiet sounds have a small amplitude.
● Large amplitude sounds have large **vibrations**.
● Sounds with a **high pitch** have a **high frequency**.
● High frequency sounds have a lot of vibrations every second.
● Frequencies are measured in **hertz** (Hz). **1 Hz = 1 vibration every second.**

summary

Questions

1 What do these words mean?
a) amplitude **b)** oscilloscope
c) pitch **d)** frequency **e)** hertz

2 What are the units for measuring frequency?

1 **a)** Are loud sounds made by large or small vibrations?
b) Do loud sounds have large or small amplitudes?

2 **a)** Which of these oscilloscopes is showing the loudest note?

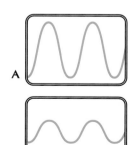

b) Explain how you worked out your answer.

3 **a)** Do high-pitched sounds have a lot of vibrations per second, or not very many?
b) Do high-pitched sounds have a high or low frequency?

4 **a)** Which of these oscilloscopes is showing the lowest note?

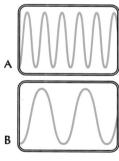

b) Explain how you worked out your answer.

5 What is the frequency of the sound shown on this oscilloscope?

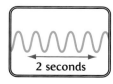
2 seconds

6 Draw two oscilloscope screens. Screen A should show a quiet, high-pitched sound and screen B should show a loud, low-pitched sound.

7 Jane is playing a guitar.
a) How does she change the amplitude of the notes she is playing?
b) How are the vibrations of the strings different when she plays loud and quiet notes?
c) How are the vibrations of the strings different when she plays high and low notes?

a) Why do the different strings on a guitar or violin sound different?
b) How can you change the note that a particular string makes? (*Hint* – there are two different ways.)

Hearing Sounds

intro

You hear sounds with your ears.
The flaps of skin on the sides of your head are just part of your ears.
The parts of your ears that detect sounds are inside your head.

These pages are about how you hear things, and how your ears can be damaged.

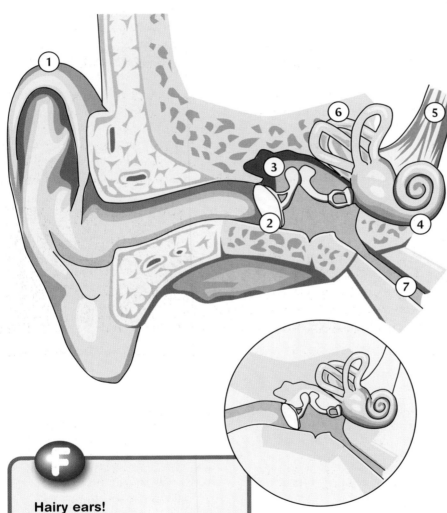

1 The **outer ear** helps to collect sound waves and channel them down the **ear canal** towards the ear drum.

2 The **ear drum** is a piece of skin that stretches across the ear canal. Vibrations in the air make the ear drum vibrate.

3 The **middle ear** contains some tiny bones, called the **hammer**, **anvil** and **stirrup** because of their shapes. The hammer touches the ear drum, so it vibrates when the ear drum vibrates. The bones pass the vibrations on to the inner ear.

4 The inner ear contains a long, curled tube full of liquid called the **cochlea**. Nerves in the cochlea detect vibrations in the liquid and send signals to the brain.

5 The **auditory nerve** carries signals from the cochlea to the brain. You 'hear' the sound when these signals reach your brain.

6 The ear also contains three **semicircular canals**, which help us to keep our balance.

7 The Eustachian tubes connect your ears to your throat, and help to keep the air pressure the same on both sides of the ear drum.

F

Hairy ears!
Your cochlea contains over 15 000 microscopic hairs which pick up the vibrations caused by sound.

This sketch shows the true size of the parts of your ears that are inside your head.

Which sounds can you hear?

When you are young, you can hear sounds as low as 20 hertz and as high as 20 000 hertz. This range of frequencies is called your **audible range**. As you get older your audible range will get smaller. This means that a child may be able to hear very high and very low notes that an older person cannot hear.

Animals have different audible ranges. Dog whistles make a very high-pitched noise which dogs can hear but which is too high for humans to hear.

Seals have better hearing than humans. When they are in the sea, seals can hear sounds up to 160 000 Hz. This is eight times higher than you can hear!

What can go wrong with your ears?

Wax is made by the lining of the ear passage. Sometimes too much wax collects and blocks the passage. This prevents vibrations in the air from reaching the **eardrum** and stops you hearing things clearly. If your ears get blocked, the wax must be removed by a doctor or nurse. If you try to remove the wax yourself, you may damage your eardrum.

Some children have a condition called 'glue ear', when a liquid collects behind the eardrum. Sometimes these children have a **grommet** put into their eardrum to allow the fluid to drain out. A grommet is a small tube made of plastic.

Very loud sounds can also damage your ears. You may sometimes feel slightly deaf after listening to very loud music, but this feeling usually goes away. If you listen to loud music too often, however, the nerve endings in your **cochlea** will be damaged. This damage is permanent and cannot be cured by doctors.

- Vibrations in the air make your eardrums vibrate.
- The vibrations are passed on to the inner ear where they are detected by nerve endings.
- Young people usually have a greater **audible range** than older people.
- Loud sounds can permanently damage your ears.

summary

Questions

1 What do these words mean?
a) outer ear **b)** ear canal
c) eardrum **d)** middle ear
e) cochlea **f)** auditory nerve

2 What does 'audible range' mean?

1 Would you expect an old person or a young person to have the greater audible range?

2 Write down two things that could go wrong with your ears but which can be cured.

3 What can cause permanent damage to your hearing?

4 Write a list of all the parts of the ear that help to pass on vibrations, starting with the eardrum.

5 Factories often display posters like this in rooms which contain machinery. Why are these signs important?

Wear ear protectors

6 Some personal stereos have a switch marked AVLS. When this is switched on, it limits the loudness of the music. Why do the manufacturers put this switch on their machines?

7 Sometimes people with ear infections feel dizzy or cannot balance properly. Which part of the ear is being affected?

a) What does the word 'ultrasound' mean?

b) How is ultrasound used to make a picture of an unborn baby?

The Earth and the Sun

Long ago people thought the Earth was flat with a dome fixed over it which held the stars and stopped the oceans from running over the edge. The Sun travelled across the dome each day. If you never travelled very far, this idea would seem quite sensible.

These pages are about how people's ideas about the Earth have changed, and why there is day and night and the seasons.

The shape of the Earth

As people began to travel further, they noticed that as they went further north or south they could see different patterns of stars in the sky. This would not happen if the Earth was flat. Also, people who lived near the sea noticed that as ships sailed away the bottom part of the ship disappeared first, as if it was going over a hill. These things could be explained if the Earth was **spherical** (round, like a ball).

The idea that the Earth was shaped like a sphere was proved in 1522 when a ship called the *Victoria* sailed back into port in Portugal after having travelled right around the world.

Day and night

We have day and night because the Earth spins on its axis.

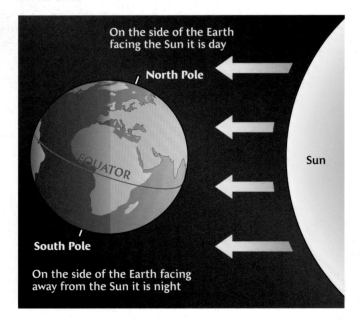

On the side of the Earth facing the Sun it is day

North Pole

EQUATOR

Sun

South Pole

On the side of the Earth facing away from the Sun it is night

Because the Earth is spinning, the Sun seems to move across the sky each day and the stars and the Moon seem to move across the sky each night.

When people talk about a day being 24 hours long, they mean that it takes 24 hours for the Earth to spin around once.

Models of the Solar System

Until about 500 years ago most people thought that the Earth was the centre of everything, and that the Sun and the other **planets** moved around the Earth. **Astronomers** had been making careful measurements of the positions of the stars and the planets for hundreds of years, but their measurements did not always agree with the idea that the Sun moved around the Earth.

Today we know that the Sun is in the centre of the **Solar System**, and the Earth and the other planets move around the Sun in **elliptical orbits** (oval-shaped orbits). The Moon orbits around the Earth.

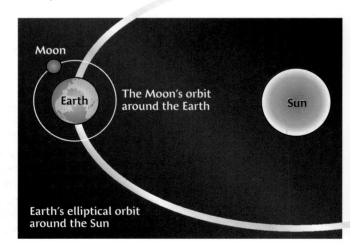

Moon

Earth

The Moon's orbit around the Earth

Sun

Earth's elliptical orbit around the Sun

intro

Seasons

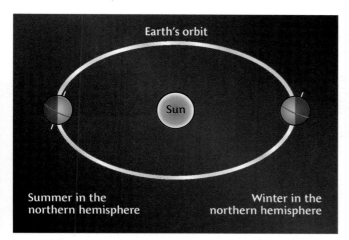

Earth's orbit

Sun

Summer in the
northern hemisphere

Winter in the
northern hemisphere

How does this model explain the seasons? We live
in the Northern hemisphere. The Earth's **axis** is tilted.
It points towards the Sun in the summer. This means
that the Sun is high in the sky in the summer, and
the days are longer. In the winter the axis is tilted
away from the Sun, giving us a lower Sun and
shorter days.

Phases of the Moon

The Moon does not always appear to be the same
shape. You see these different shapes (called the
phases of the Moon) because you can see only
the part of the Moon that is lit up by the Sun.

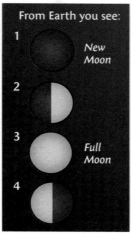
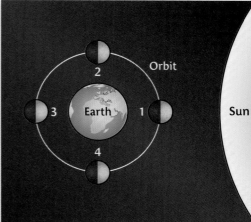

From Earth you see:

1 New Moon

2

3 Full Moon

4

Orbit

2

3 Earth 1

4

Sun

The time from one full Moon to the next full Moon
is 28 days.

Questions

1 What do these words mean?
 a) spherical **b)** day **c)** night
 d) elliptical orbit **e)** seasons

2 Which season has the longest days?

1 In which season is the midday
 sun lowest?

2 Write down two observations
 that led people to believe that
 the Earth was not flat.

3 When you look at the Moon
 it does not always look round.
 Why is this?

4 It is summer in Britain when the
 North Pole is tilted towards the Sun.
 Explain why it is winter in Australia
 when it is summer in Britain.

Use a diagram to help you to
explain. (*Hint* – Australia is south
of the Equator.)

Explain why the Sun feels hotter
in the summer than in the winter.
(*Hint* – it is not because the Earth is
closer to the Sun in the summer.)

**For more information about
the Earth see pages 72–73**

The Solar System and the Stars

The Earth is part of the **Solar System**.
The Earth and eight other **planets** travel in orbits around the Sun.

These pages are about the Sun, the planets and the stars.

Pluto

Neptune

Saturn

Jupiter

Mars

Merc

Earth

Venus

Uranus

Sun

The Sun and the stars

The Sun is a huge sphere of gas. **Nuclear reactions** happening inside the Sun make this gas so hot that the surface of the Sun has a temperature of about 6000°C. The Sun gives off so much light and heat that you can feel and see it here on Earth, 93 million miles away.

The stars you see at night are like the Sun, although some of them are much bigger than the Sun. The stars make their own light. They look so small because they are so far away.

The planets

The planets are much smaller than the Sun. Mercury, Venus, Earth, Mars and Pluto are made of rocks. The other planets are larger, and are made of gas.

Planets do not give off light. We can see the other planets in the Solar System because they reflect light from the Sun. The Moon also reflects light from the Sun.

You can see some of the planets with a pair of binoculars if you know where to look. The planets look brighter and larger than the stars, but this is only because they are much closer to us than the stars.

Other stars may have planets orbiting around them, but they are very difficult to see because they are so small and far away.

You can remember the order of the planets by remembering this sentence: **My Very Excellent Mother Just Sent Us Nine Pizzas.**

The first letters of the words in the sentence are the same as the first letters of the names of the planets (Mercury, Venus, Earth, Mars, Jupiter, Saturn, Uranus, Neptune, Pluto).

The nearest star to the Earth (apart from the Sun) is Proxima Centauri. It is 24 792 500 000 000 miles away. It takes light 4.22 years to travel from Proxima Centauri to the Earth. It takes light only about 8 minutes to travel from the Sun to the Earth!

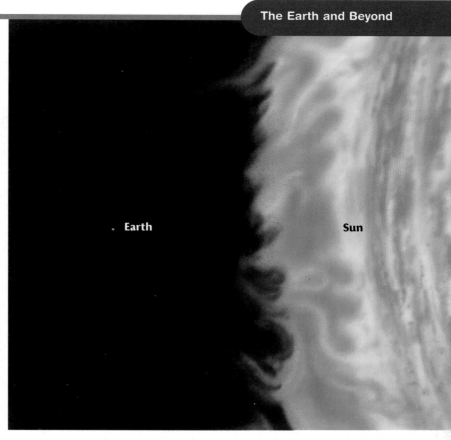

. Earth   Sun

▶ *The Earth and Sun drawn at the same scale*

- The Sun is a star.
- All stars make their own light.
- Planets do not make their own light.
- We can see planets because they reflect light from the Sun.
- The Earth and eight other planets orbit the Sun.
- A 'year' is the length of time it takes a planet to go around the Sun.
- A 'day' is the length of time it takes a planet to spin around once.

summary

Questions

 A

1 What do these words mean?
   a) star
   b) planet
   c) day
   d) year
   e) Solar System
   f) orbit
   g) constellation

2 Write down the names of all the planets in our Solar System in order, starting with Mercury.

 B

1 How long does it take for:
   a) the Earth to go around the Sun
   b) the Earth to spin around once?

2 Which is the closest star to the Earth?

3 Stars make their own light and planets do not. Why do planets look brighter than stars?

4 Which planet has the shortest year? Explain how you worked out your answer.

5 Which planet would you expect to be the coldest? Why?

 C

1 What does a 'light year' measure?

2 Which planet has the hottest surface? Why? (*Hint* – it isn't Mercury!)

For more information about light see pages 116–117

Gravity and Orbits

You can feel the force of **gravity**. Gravity is the force that keeps you on the ground. Gravity is also the force that keeps all the planets orbiting around the Sun. Gravity always pulls you towards the centre of the Earth.

These pages are about the force of gravity and how it affects planets and satellites, and why satellites are useful.

How strong is gravity?

The strength of the force of gravity between two things depends on how much mass the things have and how far apart they are.

Every object has gravity, and pulls other things towards it. You have a force of gravity, but your gravity is so weak compared to the Earth's gravity that you never notice it.

Units

Mass is measured in **grams** (g) or **kilograms** (kg). Weight is a force, and is measured in **newtons** (N). On the Earth, 1 kilogram weighs about 10 newtons.

Mass and weight

Mass is a way of saying how much stuff there is in something. The **weight** of something is the size of the force of gravity pulling on it. For instance, you might have a mass of 40 kg.

Gravity and orbits

An **orbit** is the path that a **satellite** follows around the Earth, or the path a planet follows around the Sun.

A satellite in orbit around the Earth does not need a force to keep it going because there is nothing in space to cause **friction** and slow it down.

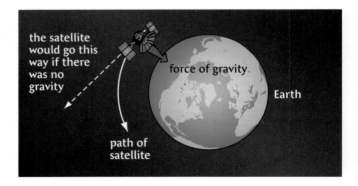

the satellite would go this way if there was no gravity

force of gravity

Earth

path of satellite

If there was no gravity, the satellite would just move in a straight line. The force of the Earth's gravity bends the path of the satellite, and makes it move in an **elliptical** (oval-shaped) orbit around the Earth.

On Earth, gravity pulls on every kilogram with a force of approximately 10 N, so you would weigh 400 N.

If you went to the Moon your mass would still be 40 kg but, because gravity is not as strong on the Moon as on the Earth, your weight would be only about 66 N.

If you went into space, far away from any stars or planets, you would have no weight, but your mass would still be 40 kg.

Satellites

A **satellite** is anything that is in orbit around something else. The Moon is a natural satellite of the Earth.

Artificial satellites are satellites that have been launched into space by rockets to do a particular job.

Communications satellites broadcast television pictures, or pass on telephone or radio messages. Earth observation satellites take pictures of the Earth from space. These pictures can be used for making maps, for weather forecasting, or to find out how well crops are growing in remote areas.

Satellites can be used to look into space. The Hubble space telescope takes very good pictures because there is no air between the telescope and the planets or stars it is pointing at.

Satellites can be put into orbit around other planets to explore them.

This picture of the surface of Venus was made from information sent back by a satellite orbiting the planet. A computer was used to produce and colour the picture.

Even while you are sitting still you are moving at many thousands of kilometres per hour. The Earth is spinning on its axis at nearly 1700 km/h and it is moving around the Sun at over 100 000 km/h.

summary

- **Mass** is measured in kilograms.
- **Weight** is a force and is measured in **newtons**.
- Everything that has mass attracts other things with the force of **gravity**.
- Gravity makes the planets move in elliptical orbits around the Sun.
- **Artificial satellites** can be used to take pictures of the Earth or to look into space.
- Satellites can be put into orbit around other planets to find out about them.

Questions

A

1 What do these words mean?
   a) gravity **b)** mass
   c) weight **d)** satellite

2 **a)** What are the units for weight?
   b) What are the units for mass?

B

1 Write down three things that artificial satellites can be used for.

2 Why is the Moon called a 'natural satellite'?

3 What prevents satellites flying off into space?

4 The diagram shows bottles standing at different places on the surface of the Earth.

Copy the diagram and show what would happen if a little water was poured into each bottle (one has been done for you).

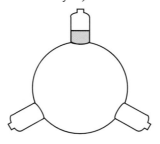

5 Sam's doctor says, 'You weigh 50 kg.'
   a) What should the doctor have said?
   b) What is Sam's weight?

6 The force of gravity on the Moon is much less than the force of gravity on the Earth. What does this tell you about the mass of the Moon?

7 Mars has a very thin atmosphere. The mass of Mars is about one tenth of the mass of the Earth. Why do you think Mars does not have much atmosphere?

C

a) What is a geostationary orbit, and what kinds of satellites are put into geostationary orbits?

b) What is a polar orbit, and why is it useful?

For more information about forces see pages 108–109

Energy and Machines

Energy can be a difficult idea to grasp. You cannot touch or see most kinds of energy, but everything that changes needs energy to do so. Plants use energy from the Sun to make the food they need. You eat food to get energy to keep yourself alive. People use energy to heat and light their homes and schools, and to make cars and buses move.

These pages are about different kinds of energy, and how energy can be changed from one kind to another.

Things in high places have **gravitational potential energy**

Most things have **thermal energy** (sometimes called **heat energy**). Hot things have more thermal energy than cold things

We can see **light energy** and hear **sound energy**

Electrical energy is being used by the television

Chemical energy is stored in food, in batteries, and also in fuels such as coal, oil and gas

Stretched things have **strain energy** (or **elastic potential energy**)

Moving things have **kinetic energy**

Energy is also stored inside **atoms**. **Nuclear energy** is used by some power stations.

Using energy

Energy can be changed from one kind of energy to another. Machines change energy and help us to do things.

For example, a light bulb changes electrical energy into light energy. A gas fire changes chemical energy stored in the gas into heat energy. A toy car changes chemical energy stored in the batteries into kinetic energy.

Describing energy changes

You can describe energy changes like this:

Gas fire		
chemical energy (stored in the gas)	→	thermal energy

The chemical energy stored in the gas is released when the gas combines with **oxygen** in the air. Energy stored in the food you eat is released when it is combined with oxygen in the **cells** of your body.

This skier has gravitational potential energy

This skier has changed all her gravitational potential energy to kinetic energy

Skier
gravitational potential energy → kinetic energy

Sometimes energy is changed into more than one kind of energy. Light bulbs get hot when they are switched on. However, the important energy is the **light energy** because that is the kind of energy you want the light bulb to give out.

Light bulb
electrical energy → light energy and heat energy

A television produces two kinds of important energy.

Television
electrical energy → light energy and sound energy and heat energy

Toy car
chemical → electrical → kinetic and sound
energy   energy   energy   energy
(in the   (in the
batteries) wires inside
                the car)

Units

Energy is measured in **joules** (J)

1 J is about the amount of energy it takes to lift an apple from the floor on to a table. If the amounts are very big, you can also use

kilojoules (kJ), 1 kJ = 1000 J

Questions

1 What do these words mean?
  a) kinetic energy
  b) thermal energy
  c) electrical energy
  d) chemical energy
  e) gravitational potential energy
  f) strain energy
  g) nuclear energy

2 Write down an example of something that gives out:
  a) thermal energy
  b) sound energy
  c) light energy.

3 Write down an example of something which has:

  a) chemical energy

  b) gravitational potential energy
  c) strain energy.

1 Describe the energy changes in the following things:
  a) a torch
  b) a catapult
  c) an electric kettle
  d) a battery powered cassette player

2 Write down the names of machines that produce the following energy changes:

  a) electrical energy → thermal energy

  b) chemical energy → kinetic energy
  c) electrical energy → kinetic energy.

Find out how much energy each of these people need each day:
  a) a toddler
  b) an eight-year-old child
  c) a teenager
  d) an adult office worker
  e) an adult building site worker
  f) a mother who is breast feeding a baby.

Explain why these people need different amounts of energy.

For more information on energy see pages 20–21 and 84–85

Conservation of Energy and Energy Resources

When a fire is burning, **chemical energy** stored in the wood is changed into **heat energy**. But what happens to this energy when the fire has gone out?

These pages are about what happens to energy when it has made things work, and where your energy comes from.

Heat energy

The heat energy released from the burning fuel is useful because it is concentrated. Heat from the fire can be used to cook food or to boil water for making tea or coffee.

When the fire has gone out the air around the fire is warmer than it was before, and the water is still hot. Gradually the heat energy in the water will spread out into the air around it. All the energy that was stored up in the wood is still there, but it has been **dissipated** (spread out) and is not very useful any more.

This is the idea that scientists call '**conservation of energy**'.

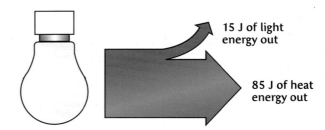

15 J of light energy out

85 J of heat energy out

100 J of **electrical energy** is going into this light bulb every second. Only 15 J of light energy comes out. The other 85 J comes out as heat energy. The light energy is useful energy, because you want the light bulb to light up the room. The heat energy is **wasted energy.**

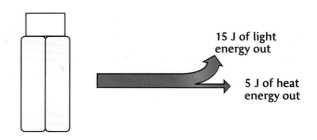

15 J of light energy out

5 J of heat energy out

This is a new kind of light bulb. It uses only 20 J of energy every second but produces as much light as a normal light bulb which uses 100 J of energy per second. Much less energy is wasted as heat.

Energy is never created or destroyed. You always end up with the same amount of energy that you started with, but some of this energy may not be in a useful form any more.

This plate had **gravitational potential energy** when it was on the table. The potential energy is changed to **kinetic energy** as the plate falls, but what happens when it hits the floor?

Some of the kinetic energy is converted to **sound energy**, and the broken pieces still have some kinetic energy (until they lie still on the floor). Most of the energy is changed to heat energy. This heat energy is spread out so you do not notice it, and it is not useful energy.

Where does your own energy come from?

The energy you need every day comes from lots of different sources.

Oil, gas and coal are **sources** of energy. Electricity is not an energy source, because it has to be **generated** using other kinds of energy. Power stations use energy to turn generators, and the generators produce electricity. Power stations can use coal, gas or **nuclear fuel**. Electricity can also be generated using falling water (**hydroelectricity**) or by **solar cells** or windmills.

Some of these sources of energy will run out one day. Oil and nuclear fuel are **non-renewable** resources. Other resources, like wind or solar power, will not run out. They are called **renewable resources**.

summary

- The total amount of energy always stays the same.
- Energy may become spread out.
- Spread out energy is not as useful as concentrated energy.
- There are many different energy resources.
- Resources that will run out one day are called **non-renewable resources**.
- Resources that will not run out are called **renewable resources**.
- Electricity is not a source of energy, It is a way of transferring energy from one place to another.

Questions

1 What do these words mean?
a) renewable resource
b) non-renewable resource
2 What is the idea behind 'conservation of energy'?
3 Name two non-renewable energy resources.
4 Name two renewable energy resources.

B

1 Is electricity a fuel? Explain your answer.

2 A cooker uses 400 kJ of energy to boil a pan of water. The water gets only 300 kJ of extra energy.
a) How much energy has been wasted?
b) Where has this wasted energy gone?

3 Your body uses 7500 joules of energy when you walk up a flight of stairs, but you have only 1500 joules of extra potential energy when you reach the top.
a) How much energy has your body wasted?

b) What has happened to the wasted energy?
4 A car goes on a 20 mile journey and uses 2 litres of petrol. What has happened to all the energy that was originally stored up in the petrol?

C

a) Find out the name of your nearest power station.
b) What kind of fuel does it use?

Non-renewable Energy Resources

These pages are about different non-renewable energy resources.

Non-renewable energy resources will run out one day. Coal, oil and gas are the most important non-renewable resources used in Britain. These fuels are known as **fossil fuels**. The other important non-renewable resource is **nuclear energy**.

Fossil fuels

Coal, oil and gas are called fossil fuels because they are formed from the remains of dead animals and plants. Most of the coal in Britain was formed around 300 million years ago. At that time much of Britain was covered by swamps or river deltas, with lots of trees and other plants. Every so often the swamps would flood, and the trees and plants would be buried under layers of mud and other sediments. The mud kept oxygen away from the dead trees so they did not rot away. Over millions of years these layers of dead plant material became buried under thick layers of rock, and pressure and heat changed them into coal.

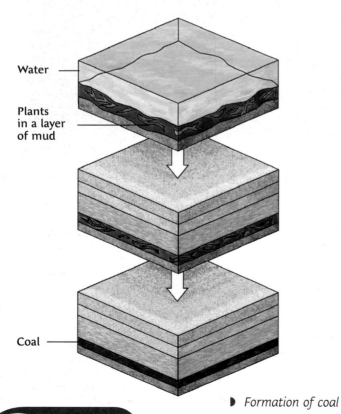

Water

Plants in a layer of mud

Coal

▶ *Formation of coal*

The coal reserves in Britain took millions of years to form. People have only been using coal for a few hundred years but there is now only enough left to last another few hundred years.

Oil and gas are often found together, trapped beneath layers of rock. They formed from the remains of tiny sea animals and plants that fell to the bottom of the sea and became buried in sand and mud. Layers of rock eventually formed above them, and pressure and heat gradually changed the remains into oil and gas.

Where did the energy come from?

The energy stored in fossil fuels is the energy that was in the living things that were changed into coal, oil and gas. Plants get their energy by converting the energy in sunlight into food, in a process called photosynthesis. Animals get their energy from eating plants or from eating other animals which eat plants, so the energy in the bodies of animals originally came from the Sun. So you can see that the energy stored in fossil fuels originally came from the Sun.

Using fossil fuels

Crude oil from oil wells is a mixture of chemicals. Oil refineries produce gas, petrol, diesel and other chemicals from crude oil. These fuels can be used to run vehicles, to heat homes and factories, or to generate electricity.

Coal and gas can be burned to provide heat for buildings, or they can be used to fuel power stations.

Fossil fuels cause **pollution** when they are burned, causing **acid rain** and contributing to **global warming**. Many people think that we should try to reduce the amount of fossil fuels we use to prevent this pollution.

Chemicals made from fossil fuels are also important as raw materials for making things like **plastics**, so that is another good reason for trying to cut down on their use as fuels.

Nuclear energy

Atoms have energy locked up inside them. Some **elements**, like **uranium**, give out some of this energy as heat in nuclear reactions. This heat can be used in power stations to drive the generators that make electricity.

When the Earth was formed there was only a certain amount of uranium in the rocks. When we have used up this uranium we will no longer have **nuclear power**.

Nuclear energy is a non-renewable resource, but the uranium will last a very long time. Nuclear energy does not contribute to global warming or acid rain, but it can cause other kinds of pollution.

Nuclear fuels produce dangerous **radiation** as well as heat. Nuclear power stations have to be carefully designed to prevent this radiation escaping. Many people think that nuclear energy is too dangerous to make it worth using.

How long will fossil fuels last?

These figures are only estimates. More oil and coal may be discovered, or we might change the amount of fossil fuels that we use each year.

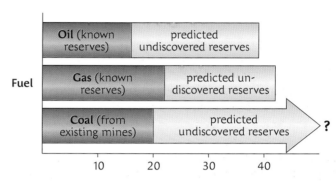

▶ *Length of time fuel reserves will last*

▶ *A nuclear power station*

- Coal, oil and gas are **fossil fuels**.
- Fossil fuels were formed millions of years ago from the remains of dead plants and animals.
- We will run out of fossil fuels one day.
- Burning fossil fuels causes **acid rain** and **global warming**.
- Nuclear energy can be used to generate electricity.
- Nuclear energy does not cause acid rain or global warming, but can cause other kinds of dangerous **pollution**.

summary

Questions

A

1 What do these words mean?
 a) fossil fuel **b)** non-renewable fuels

2 Name four non-renewable fuels.

3 Which non-renewable fuels cause acid rain and global warming?

B

1 Give two reasons why we should reduce the amount of fossil fuels we use.

2 **a)** Which non-renewable resource is only used for generating electricity?

 b) Which non-renewable resource did not originally get its energy from the Sun?

3 We do not know exactly how long fossil fuels will last. Give two reasons why our estimates might have to be changed.

4 Coal and oil are probably being formed somewhere in the world today. If more of these fuels are being formed, why do we refer to them as 'non-renewable'?

C

The non-renewable resources discussed on this page are coal, oil, gas and nuclear energy. Find out when each source of energy was first used, and what it was used for.

For more information about pollution and global warming see pages 30–31, 84–85 and 96–97

Renewable Energy Resources

Renewable energy resources will never run out. The energy is free, but money has to be spent on building machinery that can use the energy.

There is no single renewable resource that could supply all the world's energy needs, but a combination of different renewable resources could be used.

These pages are about different renewable energy resources, and their advantages and disadvantages.

Biomass

Biomass means any fuel that comes from living things. You could think of the food you eat as biomass, but the word usually refers to fuels that can be burnt to supply heat. Wood has been used as a fuel for thousands of years. It is only a renewable resource if you are careful about how many trees you cut down in a forest. New trees have to be given time to grow.

Animal droppings and vegetable waste can be fermented to produce methane gas which can be burnt. Sugar can be grown to produce alcohol for burning, and some plants produce oil which can be used as a fuel.

Wind

Wind has been used to provide energy for over a thousand years. Windmills were used for grinding corn, pumping water or working machinery, and sailing ships used to be driven by the wind. Today the wind can be used to generate electricity.

Winds blow because the Sun heats up different parts of the Earth and its atmosphere by different amounts, so the energy we get from the wind originally came from the Sun.

Resource	Advantage	Disadvantages
Biomass	● You can always grow more plants.	● The plants may need lots of fertiliser. ● It may not be possible to grow enough plants to meet the demand for energy. ● The plants may take up land needed for growing food.
Wind	● There is no pollution. ● This resource will never run out.	● It only works when the wind blows. ● Lots of generators are needed in hilly areas to produce large amounts of electrical energy.
Waves	● There is no pollution. ● This resource will never run out	● It only works on coastlines which get lots of waves. ● Lots of generators would be needed to produce large amounts of energy.
Solar power	● This resource will never run out.	● It only works when the Sun shines. ● Collector panels can produce only small increases in temperature. ● Solar cells are expensive to produce. ● In Britain we get most solar energy in the summer, which is when we need the least energy.
Hydro-electricity	● Rain will always fill up the reservoirs again.	● It only works in wet, hilly regions. ● Dams and reservoirs may disturb wildlife.
Geo-thermal energy	● This resource will never run out.	● It only works in certain parts of the world where there are hot rocks near the Earth's surface.

Waves

When the wind blows across the sea it causes waves. The energy in waves can be used to generate electricity by building **wave stations** on the coast.

Solar power

Energy from the Sun can be used in two ways. **Collector panels** can be used to heat water for washing or heating houses, or **solar panels** can be used to convert the energy into electricity.

Geothermal energy

The inside of the Earth is hot. In some places, like Iceland, the hot water comes to the surface naturally and can be used for heating homes and providing hot water for washing. In other countries cold water can be pumped down into the ground where it absorbs energy from the hot rocks. This hot water can then be used for heating.

Hydroelectricity

Rain falling in the mountains can be trapped behind a dam and led in pipes to a power station at the bottom of the mountain. The water is falling quite fast by the time it reaches the bottom and it can be used to drive generators for producing electricity.

- **Biomass** refers to animal or plant material that can be used as fuel.
- **Wind energy** can be used to drive machinery or to generate electricity.
- **Waves** can be used to generate electricity.
- **Solar power** can be used for heating or to generate electricity.
- **Hydroelectricity** is generated using the energy in falling water.
- Hot rocks beneath the surface of the Earth can provide **geothermal energy**.

summary

Questions

A

1 What do these words mean?
a) biomass b) solar power
c) hydroelectricity d) geothermal energy e) renewable resource

B

1 a) Where did the energy in biomass fuels come from originally?
b) Where did the energy in the waves come from originally? (*Hint* – the answer is not 'wind'.)
c) The energy transferred by hydroelectricity originally came from the Sun. Explain how the

Sun's energy is transferred to the electricity. (*Hint* – how did the water get up into the mountains?)
d) Which energy resource on these pages does not provide energy that originally came from the Sun?

2 a) Write a list of the renewable resources that can be used for generating electricity.
b) Write another list of the renewable resources that can be used directly for heating.
c) Which resources are on both lists?

3 Burning wood releases carbon dioxide into the atmosphere, but this does not contribute to global warming. Why not?

4 What source of energy do satellites use? Explain the advantages of this source of energy for satellites.

C

Reservoirs can be used to store energy. Find out about pumped storage power stations and why they are useful. (*Hint* – there are pumped storage power stations at Dinorwic, in Wales, and at Ben Cruachan in Scotland.)

For more information about photosynthesis see pages 28–29

Temperature and Energy

Sparklers are fireworks which throw off sparks of white-hot burning iron, but if one of the sparks accidentally lands on your hand it will not usually burn you. A pan full of boiling water is at a much lower temperature than the sparks from the sparkler, but it can give you a nasty burn. This is because the boiling water has a lot more **energy** than the sparks.

These pages are about the difference between the energy contained in something and its temperature.

Is temperature different from energy?

You know that if you switch a kettle on it uses electrical energy and the water inside it gets hotter. The temperature of the water goes up, and if you leave the kettle on for longer the temperature goes up even more.

For most substances the more energy you put in, the hotter they get, but this is not always true.

When you heat a beaker of ice over a Bunsen burner you are putting energy into the ice. But if you measure the **temperature** of the melting ice the thermometer stays at 0°C. You are putting energy in but the temperature is not going up. This happens because the energy is being used to melt the ice. A similar thing happens when you boil water. The temperature stops going up at 100°C because the energy is being used to change the water into steam.

So what is temperature?

Temperature is a way of measuring how fast the **particles** in a substance are moving. The higher the temperature the faster the particles are moving.

How much energy do you need to make something hotter?

A kettle boils far quicker if you put only a little water into it. The amount of energy needed to heat the water in a kettle depends on how much water there is in it. In the same way, the amount of energy in a hot object depends on the **mass** of the object. A cannon ball heated to 300°C contains a lot more energy than a tiny piece of iron at the same temperature.

This is why a pan full of boiling water will burn you when a spark from a sparkler will not, because even though the spark is hotter, its mass is so small that it contains only a very small amount of energy. The boiling water is not as hot but there is more of it, so there is more energy there. The mass of the sparkler itself is much bigger than the mass of a single spark, so it contains a lot of energy. If you touch a sparkler you will burn your hand badly.

Nothing can be colder than -273°C. Temperature is a way of measuring how fast particles are moving, and at -273°C particles have slowed down so much that they are not moving at all. You can't get any colder than that! -273°C is called absolute zero.

Sand and concrete become much hotter than water when the Sun is shining on all three with the same energy. This is because the amount of energy needed to heat something depends on the substance it is made of. It takes only 800 joules to heat up 1 kg of sand by 1°C, but it takes 4200 joules to heat the same amount of water by 1°C!

John's soup is much hotter than Jane's. John's soup contains more energy because it is at a higher temperature. We can't say whether John's soup has more energy than Jane's cup of tea, because the tea and soup are different substances and may have needed different amounts of energy to heat them up.

- **Temperature** is a way of measuring how fast the **particles** in a substance are moving.
- The amount of **energy** needed to heat something depends on its **mass**, on the material it is made from and on how hot it needs to be.

summary

Questions

1 What do these words mean?
a) temperature b) mass

1 You have two identical buckets of hot water. Bucket A has a temperature of 60°C, and bucket B has a temperature of 80°C. Which one has more energy? Explain your answer.

2 You have a large mug of tea and a small cup of tea. The tea in both containers is at the same temperature. Which one contains the most energy? Explain your answer.

3 You have one bucket which contains 5 kg of sand, and another bucket which holds 5 kg of water. If they are at the same temperature, which one contains more energy? Explain your answer.

4 The swimming pool in the picture was at the same temperature as the paddling pool at the beginning of the day. Which one will be hotter now? Explain your answer.

5 How much energy would it take to heat:
a) 2 kg of sand from 24°C to 26°C
b) 1 kg of sand from 24°C to 35°C
c) 5 kg of sand from 24°C to 30°C?

a) What is the Kelvin temperature scale?
b) What are the melting and boiling points of water on the Kelvin scale?

For more information on particles see pages 50–55

Answers

**Answers for biology questions
pages 2 to 49**

Cells in Animals and Plants (page 3)

A 1 a) Living thing **b)** Smallest living thing **c)** Unit inside a cell that does a particular job **d)** Group of similar cells **e)** Part of a living thing made up of different tissues that does a particular job **f)** Set of organs that work together **2** Nucleus, membrane, cytoplasm **3** Cell wall, vacuole, chloroplasts
B 1 a) Controls the cell **b)** Holds the cytoplasm together, and controls chemicals going in and out **c)** Where chemical reactions happen **2 a)** Protects and supports the cell **b)** Make food for the cell **c)** Stores chemicals and keeps plants stiff **3** There is not enough water in the vacuoles to support the cells
C Nerve cells have branched surfaces that form many connections with other cells. Some nerve cells have one long thin fibre that carries signals to other parts of the body.

Leaves and their Cells (page 5)

A 1 a) Cells inside the leaf **b)** Protective waterproof layer on the outside of the leaf **c)** Holes protected by guard cells found mainly on the underside of leaves **d)** Green colour in leaves which traps light **e)** Long thin leaf that wraps round objects **f)** Outside layer of cells on a leaf **g)** When light bounces off something
B 1 Carry water to the leaf and food away **2** Chlorophyll is the green colour, while chloroplasts are organelles containing the colour **3** Gases diffuse through the stomatal pores **4** In the palisade mesophyll cells
C b) Scientists use words like notched, lobed, dentate (toothed)

Chemicals in Living Things (page 7)

A 1 a) Animal that only eats plants **b)** Animal that only eats other animals **c)** Animal that eats plants and other animals **2** Water, proteins, carbohydrates, lipids, minerals, vitamins, nucleic acids **3** Fats, oils, waxes
B 1 a) Growth and repair of cells **b)** Energy **c)** Storing energy, waterproof coatings, keeping warm **d)** To control body processes **2 a)** Their food **b)** They can make vitamins, and get minerals from the soil **3** To make food for humans and animals
C Weigh about ten slices, note the weight (initial weight), then leave in a warm place to dry out. Weigh again and repeat until the weight doesn't change (final weight), then subtract the final weight from the initial weight to give the weight of water. Divide the weight of water by the initial weight and multiply by 100 to give the percentage weight of water in the cucumber.

Nutrients, Vitamins and Minerals (page 9)

A 1 a) Getting the right food for health and growth **b)** Animal with diet of animal flesh and plants **c)** Food eaten by an animal **d)** What happens if an organism is lacking something in its diet **e)** Chemicals which are needed by animals in tiny amounts **f)** Flesh of animals and plants that make up the diet **g)** Animal or person having too little food **h)** Inorganic chemicals needed by animals and plants in tiny amounts **i)** Overweight person
B 1 a) Night blindness, skin sores **b)** Weak or brittle bones **c)** Anaemia **2 a)** Green vegetables **b)** Vegetables **3 a)** Calcium, iron, phosphorous, potassium, sodium, sulphur, vitamin A, vitamin B6 **b)** Calcium, iodine, potassium, sodium, sulphur, vitamin D3 **4** Vitamin D is formed beneath the skin in sunlight
C a) Protein is for the growth and repair of cells. Carbohydrates and fats are sources of energy. **b)** If the diet contains very little protein, a person is malnourished and will not grow properly.

Guts and Food (page 11)

A 1 a) Proteins which break up molecules **b)** Large nutrient molecules are broken down **c)** Group of cells which produce and release a liquid **d)** Tube leading from a gland **e)** Chemical on which an enzyme works **f)** Substance formed when an enzyme works on a substrate **g)** Temperature at which an enzyme works best **2 a)** Food is chopped up and mixed with saliva **b)** Churns up food with acid and enzymes **c)** Absorbs small, soluble molecules **d)** Absorbs water
B 1 They are already soluble **2** Food goes through the gut too quickly for water to be absorbed **3** Mix starch with amylase and keep at a range of temperatures. Remove a small sample from each temperature at known intervals and test with iodine. When the solution remains brown, the starch has been digested.
C a) Salivary glands, pancreas and small intestine **b)** Pancreas **c)** Stomach, pancreas, duodenum

The Skeleton, Muscles and Movement (page 13)

A 1 a) Collection of muscle fibres which can shorten **b)** Gets shorter **c)** Bones inside your body **d)** Place where bones meet **e)** Tissue that connects muscle to bone **f)** Muscle pairs that contract in turn to make joints work **2** Raised, contracts, relaxes, an antagonistic pair
B 1 a) Tendon **b)** Connective tissue **2** Respiration **3 a)** Elbow moves like a hinge, shoulder can rotate **b)** Both have hinge joints, so they can only move in one direction
C 1 a) Humerus, radius, ulna **b)** Femur, tibia, fibula **c)** Ribs, sternum (chest bone), clavicle (collar bone), scapula (shoulder blade), spine (made of 33 vertebrae), pelvis **d)** Spine (neck vertebrae), skull, jaw **2** Fixed joints are found in the skull, where the bones are joined together and cannot move. Ball and socket joints are found at the shoulders and hips; the limbs can rotate and move in many directions.

Blood and Circulation (page 15)

A 1 a) Tube taking blood away from heart **b)** Tube returning blood to heart **c)** Fine blood vessels which link arteries to veins **d)** Pump which forces blood around the body **e)** Top chamber on right and left side of heart **f)** Bottom chamber on right and left side of heart **g)** Fluid part of blood **2** Carries oxygen, carbon dioxide, food and all other chemicals around the body and protects body from disease
B 1 Thick – Thin – Very thin, Away from heart – Towards heart **2** From artery to vein **2** Right atrium – right ventricle – artery – capillaries in the lungs – vein – left atrium – left ventricle **3** 70 times
C 1 You would expect different numbers of pulse beats **2 a)** The valves between the atrium and the ventricle are the atrio-ventricular valves; those on the right are the triaspid valves and on the left the bicuspid. They stop blood going backwards from the ventricles into the atria. The valves between the left ventricle and the aorta are the semi-lunar valves. These stop blood going backwards from the aorta into the ventricle. **b)** The sounds made by the heart are LUB, DUP. LUB is when the atrio-ventricular valve slam shut; DUP when the semi-lunar close. **c)** Force at which blood is pumped out from the heart **d)** They help to return blood to the heart by stopping blood flowing in the wrong direction

Growing Up and Puberty (page 17)

A 1 a) Sex cells, sperm or egg **b)** Time when the human body becomes sexually mature **c)** Male sex hormone **d)** Female sex hormone **e)** Organ inside the woman's body that will hold a developing baby **f)** When blood and dead cells pass out through the vagina **g)** Male sex organs **h)** Female sex organs

2 a) The penis grows, voice deepens, hair appears on the face, around sex organs and in armpits and body becomes more muscular **b)** Hips widen, breasts develop, menstruation begins and hair appears around sex organs and in armpits
B 1 Changing levels of hormones **2** Lining of the uterus breaks up and passes out through the vagina, and a new lining thickens in preparation for the next ovulation
C a) Endocrine glands including the pituitary (brain), thyroid (throat), adrenal glands (kidneys) pancreas (abdomen) and the ovaries or testes, produce hormones **b)** Endocrine glands do not deliver their hormones through ducts

Pregnancy (page 19)

A 1 a) Sperm containing fluid **b)** When sperm and egg cells meet and their nuclei fuse **c)** When fertilised egg is embedded into womb lining **d)** First stage in development of a baby **e)** Organ formed from the mother's and baby's tissues, which nourishes the baby **f)** Time taken for baby to develop and be ready for birth **g)** Contractions of uterus or womb wall, which force the baby out at birth **h)** Placenta pushed out of the mother's body after the baby has been born
B 1 Single fertilised egg divides many times to form a hollow ball of cells, which arrives at womb wall about 4 days after egg has been released from ovary **2** Fetus contains bone in its skeleton, an embryo does not **3** Amniotic fluid protects it from knocks and insulates it from temperature changes and the placenta acts a barrier between the two blood supplies. **4** Lighter, cooler, noisier
C Smoking and drinking can affect the development of the baby

Breathing and Respiration (page 21)

A 1 a) Organ in the chest where gas exchange takes place **b)** Sheet of muscle separating chest from lower body **c)** Using oxygen to release energy from glucose in living cells **d)** Movement of air into and out of the lungs **e)** Fine blood vessel
B 1 a) Increases **b)** Decreases **2 a)** Decreases **b)** Increases **3** Contract – Relax, Contract – Relax, Moves downwards – Moves upwards, Inflate/Expand – Deflate/Reduce **4** When you breathe through your nose the air if filtered, warmed and moistened **5** Good blood supply and air sac walls are very thin
C You would expect that the size and number of breaths to get bigger because the body needs more oxygen

Health and Disease (page 23)

A a) Organism that causes disease **b)** Signs or symptoms showing that the body is not working properly **c)** Identifying a disease from its symptoms **d)** Signs shown by a disease **e)** Poison produced by pathogens **f)** Small cells found in warm, damp places, which may cause disease **g)** Tiny structures that come alive inside other living cells **h)** Substance which makes the body more active **i)** Substance which makes the body less active
B 1 a) 'Trapping' sneezes by using a handkerchief **b)** Supplying clean food and water **2** Nicotine stops the cleaning cells in the breathing tubes working and affects the nervous system; tar irritates the breathing tubes **3 a)** The driver's reactions may be slow and she may have an accident **b)** The liver will be damaged
C 1 Nicotine is addictive and can affect the heart; carbon monoxide attaches itself to red blood cells and stops them carrying oxygen; other chemicals can cause cancer, blood clots, strokes, heart attacks, bronchitis, emphysema, miscarriages and still-births **2** Different amounts affect people in different ways e.g. slurring of speech, loss of body control, inability to focus eyes, etc.

Protection from Disease (page 25)

A **a)** Stops microbes multiplying **b)** Tiny hairs on the cells lining the breathing passages **c)** Sticky fluid which traps dust and microbes in the breathing passages **d)** Dried plug of protein fibres and blood cells at a wound **e)** Blood cell which destroys microbes

B **1** Cells are working and therefore releasing energy **2** Blood proteins form a sticky net at an open wound; blood cells are trapped and dry out to form a scab **3** Hydrochloric acid and digestive juices in the stomach kill the microbes swallowed in food **4** It surrounds the microbe and digests it

C **1** Surgeons scrub their hands and arms with antiseptic soaps and wear sterilised clothing **2** Surgical instruments are sterilised by heating them to very high temperatures

Immunity (page 27)

A **1 a)** Protein that enters the blood stream, normally on the outside of a microbial cell **b)** Defence protein made by the body **c)** Chemical made by the body which destroys toxins or poisons **d)** Protecting the body from disease **2** Injecting it with antibodies, or with weakened pathogens

B **1** A child is given a weak dose of the polio virus. This multiplies and the child's body makes antibodies. Second and third doses of the virus are given later to boost the level of antibodies. **2** It kills bacteria

C Weak dose of the tuberculosis (TB) bacterium is scratched into the skin surface, depending on the reaction a child is given a BCG injection: TB is a disease of the lungs, affecting breathing.

Photosynthesis (page 29)

A **1 a)** Green colour of plants **b)** Process in cells which uses light energy trapped by chlorophyll to form glucose (food) from carbon dioxide and water **c)** Plant kept in darkness for 24 hours so the leaves do not contain starch **2** Carbon dioxide + water → glucose + oxygen **3** To get the materials and energy they need for life

B **1** So that you know that any starch in the leaves has been made during the experiment **2** It produces bubbles of gas from its stem, and lives in water so the gas can be collected easily

C **1** The rate of photosynthesis will increase as a factor like light increases until a certain point is reached, then, no matter how much brighter it gets the rate of photosynthesis stays the same. The rate is limited by something else

Gas Exchange and Respiration in Plants (page 31)

A **1 a)** Hole surrounded by two guard cells on the underside of leaves, which allows gases in and out **b)** Opening in a stem which allows gases in and out **c)** Release of energy from glucose using oxygen **d)** Process in cells in which light energy trapped by chlorophyll is used to make glucose (food) from carbon dioxide and water **e)** Gradual increase in the temperature of the Earth **2 a)** glucose + oxygen → carbon dioxide + water + energy **b)** carbon dioxide + water → glucose + oxygen

B **1** The soil particles are very closely packed so there is hardly any air or oxygen in the soil. The roots do not get the oxygen they need for respiration and so do not grow well. **2** Photosynthesis occurs during the day, this is when carbon dioxide needs to get into the leaves and oxygen needs to get out. The plant also loses water through the stomata, so they are closed at night to prevent water loss.

C **1** Global warming is an increase in the average temperature of the Earth caused by an increase in carbon dioxide in the air. The carbon dioxide reflects some of the heat radiated by the Earth. **2** The plants in the bottle garden respire and photosynthesise, balancing the oxygen and carbon dioxide levels in the bottle.

Plants, Water and Minerals (page 33)

A **1 a)** Very thin tube growing from a cell near the tip of a root **b)** Mineral needed in very tiny amounts by plants **c)** Solution with known ingredients used for growing plants or cuttings **d)** Effect on a plant if a certain mineral is missing from the soil **e)** Chemicals added to the soil which make plants grow better **f)** Amount of material in a plant

B **1** It is the waste of animals **2** To improve the texture and drainage of the soil and add minerals **3** Plants need nitrogen to make proteins and so grow

C It could drain off into rivers and affect many other organisms

Pollination in flowering plants (page 35)

A **1 a)** Male gamete or sex cell of a flower **b)** Female gamete or sex cell of a flower **c)** Part of flower containing the ovules **d)** Transfer of pollen to the stigma **e)** Sweet fluid made by flowers to attract insects

B **1** To catch pollen being blown past **2** To stick to the insect's body **3 a)** Brightly coloured to attract insects **b)** Protects the flower when it is in bud **c)** Produces pollen at its tip

Fertilisation in Flowering Plants (page 37)

A **1 a)** Hard outer covering of a fertilised ovule **b)** Ripened ovary of a flower containing a seed **c)** Pollen fertilising the ovum in the same flower **d)** Pollen fertilising the ovum in a different flower of the same type **e)** Spreading of seeds away from the plant that made them

B **1** Pollination is the movement of pollen from the anther/stamen to the stigma. Fertilisation is when the male pollen nucleus and the female ovum nucleus fuse. **2 a)** Shrivels **b)** Shrivels **c)** Develops into a fruit

Animal and Plant Breeding (page 39)

A **1 a)** Feature that helps an animal to survive in the wild **b)** Survival of animals best suited to their surroundings **c)** Humans choosing the animals that will breed **d)** Wild animals changing to become part of the human community **2** It makes animals hard to see, so that animals that hunt (predators) can creep up on their prey more easily, or animals that get eaten (prey) may be more difficult for predators to see

B **1** It is easy to see, so will be easy prey. It will be killed and so not survive. **2 a)** Giraffes with longer necks would be able to get more food from the tops of trees, and so would be more likely to survive and breed. **b)** Striped tigers would be camouflaged and able to catch more food, and so would be more likely to survive and breed.

Sorting out Living Things (page 41)

A **1 a)** Classifying living things **b)** Single celled organisms without a nucleus **c)** Single celled organisms with a nucleus **d)** Number of clues used to identify something **e)** Living thing that makes food by photosynthesis **g)** Lives by eating food **2** Breathing, feeding, excreting, reproducing, sensitivity, growth and movement

B **1** It does not grow, reproduce or react to its surroundings **2 a)** Conifer does not have flowers, a buttercup does **b)** Vertebrates have backbones and invertebrates do not
3

Group	Warm/Cold Blood	Limbs	Covering
Mammals	Warm	Four	Hair/Fur
Birds	Warm	Four	Feathers
Fish	Cold	None (Fins)	Slimy Scales
Reptiles	Cold	Four	Dry Scales
Amphibians	Cold	Four	Damp Skin

C **1 a)** Mammal - Most mammals do not fly **b)** Bird – It cannot fly but it can swim **c)** Mammal – It lives in the sea, most mammals live on land **d)** Reptile – It lives in the sea, most reptiles live on land **e)** Reptile – It has no legs, most reptiles have four

The Environments of Living Things (page 43)

A **a)** Feature that helps an organism survive **b)** Number of one kind of organism in a particular place **c)** All the living and non-living things in a particular place **d)** Organisms that live in seawater **e)** Organisms that live in brackish water **f)** Organisms that live on land or in the air

B **1** Rocks, sand, water, light **2** All the living things **3** It is colder and has less oxygen

Food Chains, Webs and Pyramids (page 45)

A **1 a)** Green plant **b)** Animal (something that eats food) **c)** Shows how energy is passed from one organism to another **d)** Animal that eats both plants and other animals **e)** Shows the numbers of different organisms at each stage in a food chain **f)** Mass of living things

B **1** It means it can survive if there is a shortage of either plants or animals **2** Over 90% of the energy is lost at each transfer, so there is less energy to pass on **3** If the producer is an oak tree, the pyramid of number doesn't make much sense. If you use biomass, the size of each 'block' in the pyramid gets less as you go along the food chain. **4** plankton → herring → human, plankton → mussels → human, plankton → seaworm, plankton → mussels → starfish

Food Chains and Pollution (page 47)

A **1 a)** Chemicals added to the soil which make plants grow better **b)** Chemicals which kill pests which feed on crops **c)** Animals or other organisms that feed on crops

B **1** Because the chemicals enter the bodies of living things in the food chain **2** If it gets into water supplies it can damage blood cells in babies **3** DDT does not break down in the soil or air, and remains active for a long time

Death and Decay (page 49)

A **1 a)** Organism that feeds on dead remains and helps them decay **b)** Keeping the number of animals and plants in a community steady **c)** Using animals, plants, bacteria or viruses to control or kill pests **d)** Usually a carnivore feeding on prey **e)** Animal hunted by a carnivorous predator

B **1** They help to decompose leaves and dead wood **2** The disease killed rabbits, which foxes used for food. However, when the rabbits were killed the foxes needed to find other food. Chickens on chicken farms were easy for foxes to find and kill. **3** When the population of the prey increases then the predator's population increases shortly after. However, as more predators eat more prey, the population of prey drops. Therefore, the two populations have a pattern of peaks and troughs.

C **a)** It has blocked rivers and streams **b)** It has become a garden pest **c)** They grow rapidly and stop native plants from growing

Answers for chemistry questions
pages 50 to 97

Solids, liquids, gases (page 51)

A **1 a)** Moves about **b)** Can be squeezed into smaller volume **c)** Amount of matter packed into a space **d)** Amount of space taken up **2 a)** Solid **b)** Liquid **c)** Solid **d)** Gas **e)** Gas **f)** Gas **g)** Solid **h)** Solid, liquid

B **1 a)** Solid **b)** Liquid **c)** Solid **d)** Solid **e)** Gas **f)** Liquid **g)** Solid **h)** Gas **i)** Gas **j)** Liquid **2** Fixed volume **3** Flow; no fixed shape; compressible **4** Solids do not flow, have fixed volume and shape and are not compressible **5** Solids cannot be squeezed into smaller volume; gases are easily squeezed into smaller volume **6** Lead; because it has the higher density

C **1** Mud could be solid because it can keep its shape, liquid because it can flow when a force acts on it and it can take the shape of a container, neither solid nor liquid (or both) because it is made up of a solid dirt in liquid water. **2** Butter/spread is solid because it keeps its shape and does not flow and when it is heated it melts. Butter/spread is liquid because it changes shape and flows when it is spread, can be transferred from container to container and can be made to take the shape of the container.

The particles of matter (page 53)

A **1 a)** Temperature at which a solid becomes a liquid **b)** Temperature at which a liquid becomes a gas **c)** Gas becoming liquid **d)** Liquid becoming solid **2 a)** Solid **b)** Gas **c)** Solid **d)** Liquid **e)** Liquid **f)** Solid **g)** Gas

B 1 Particles moving from side to side in a fixed place; particles not moving from place to place **2** Solid changing to liquid; the particles in the solid gain enough heat energy to break out of the structure/overcome the forces holding them together; the particles now move from place to place **3** Gas becoming liquid; the particles lose energy as gas is cooled; the forces between particles come into play; the particles are pulled together into the much smaller volume of the liquid **4** Solid has particles very close together and no space to compress them closer; gas has particles spread well apart and therefore lots of room to be compressed together **5** At the boiling point of the water the particles have enough energy to overcome the forces holding them together; they spread to become a gas

Properties and particles (page 55)
A 1 Movement of particles **2** Particles hitting container walls **3** Increases **4** Increases
B 1 Hot cooked cheese; the heat means the particles leave the cheese more quickly and travel faster **2** Particles lose energy; exert less pressure on balloon from inside; balloon contracts **3** As balloon gets smaller, particles inside hit it more often; eventually this increases the total pressure enough to burst balloon
C Particles slowly leave the block and diffuse across the room; they can then be detected by smell; as particles keep leaving, the block gets smaller and smaller until it is gone completely

Elements and atoms (page 57)
A 1 a) Single material; cannot be broken down into simpler materials; consists of one type of atom **b)** Smallest part of an element that can exist **2 a)** Cu **b)** H **c)** Na **d)** Zn **e)** Fe **3 a)** Lead **b)** Nitrogen **c)** Magnesium **d)** Sulphur
B 1 Small, heavy, central part of the atom; contains protons and neutrons **2** Same elements both contain same number of (6) protons **3 a)** Lithium Li or potassium K **b)** Silicon Si **c)** Fluorine F **d)** Beryllium Be or magnesium Mg **e)** Helium He or neon Ne

Compounds (page 59)
A 1 Pure material of two or more elements chemically combined **2** Smallest part of a compound, two or more atoms joined/combined together **3 a)** H_2O **b)** NaCl **c)** CO_2 **d)** $CaCO_3$
B 1 Iron oxide; potassium, chlorine, zinc, sulphur **2** Magnesium sulphide; magnesium, sulphur; ZnO, zinc, oxygen. **3** Aluminium oxide, 2 aluminium, 3 oxygen; magnesium chloride; 1 magnesium, 2 chlorine; Fe_2O_3; iron oxide
C a) SO_2; 32 g of sulphur is the equivalent of 1 atom, 32 g of oxygen is the equivalent of 2 atoms **b)** 16 g

Mixtures (page 61)
A 1 a) Liquid becoming gas/vapour **b)** Separate a mixture of coloured materials by using a solvent **c)** Vapour becoming a liquid **d)** Solid left in filter paper after filtration **e)** Clear liquid passing through filter paper during filtration **2** Material containing a number of other materials jumbled together but not combined with each other **3** Pure compounds: steam, sugar, copper, oxygen Mixtures: air, fizzy drink, potato, sea water, pizza, petrol **4** See text
B 1 a) Distillation **b)** Filtration **2** Chromatography **3** Solution and evaporation
C Describe solution and evaporation; evaporate the ethanol by methods not involving direct heat

Metals and non-metals (page 63)
A 1 a) Can be beaten into shapes **b)** Easily broken into pieces **c)** Makes a sound when struck **d)** Can be stretched into wires **3** Mercury; bromine **4** Graphite (carbon) **5** Diamond (carbon) **6 a)** Copper **b)** Copper, aluminium, iron **c)** Iron
B 1 Appearance, strength, malleability, ductility, sonority, conduction of heat/electricity, melting/boiling point, density, etc. **2** A: metal; high m.pt., conducts electricity, shiny B: non-metal; low m.pt., non-conductor C: non-metal; low m.pt., non-conductor D: metal; conducts electricity, shiny

3 a) Ductile, good conductor of electricity **b)** Malleable, good conductor of heat, light, non-corrosive **c)** Malleable, strong, cheap **d)** Shiny, non-corrosive, malleable, **e)** Good conductor of heat, malleable, strong, cheap
C Answers would be expected to refer to physical properties noted in the text that are exceptions to rules, e.g. carbon – it is very hard (diamond) like metals and it conducts electricity (graphite) like metals

Physical changes (page 65)
A 1 Reversible; no new substance formed **2** Changes of state, dissolving, etc. **3** New structure formed; change not reversible **4** Iron rusting; metals corroding; food rotting, etc.
B 1 a) Chemical **b)** Physical **c)** Chemical **d)** Physical **e)** Chemical **f)** Chemical **g)** Chemical **h)** Physical **i)** Chemical **j)** Physical **2** 15 g: Ice to steam is a physical change and mass does not change **3** Add 110 g of water and stir
C Mixture can be separated because mixing is a physical change; after heating a chemical change has taken place and new, non magnetic, substance is produced; change not reversible

Solutions and solubility (page 67)
A 1 a) Material that dissolves **b)** Material in which solute dissolves **c)** Formed when a solute dissolves in a solvent **d)** When a material will dissolve in a particular solvent **e)** When a material will not dissolve in a particular solvent **f)** Solution that cannot contain any more solute at that temperature **g)** Maximum weight of a solute that will dissolve in 100 g of water at a particular temperature **2** Three solvents taken from the table in the text **3** Cleaning without water
B 1 Evaporate it to remove water/solvent **2** Add more water/solvent **3** Cheap; safe; available; versatile **4** Solute would separate out
C Grease insoluble in water

Change of state (page 69)
A 1 a) gains energy **b)** loses energy **c)** loses energy **d)** gains energy
B 1 Heat energy used to give particles energy to escape and not to raise temperature **2** Lose heat; energy given out as particles cease to move **3** Gain heat; energy needed by particles to overcome forces and begin to move about **4** Has greater inter-particle forces **5** Material absorbs energy from hand; energy used for vaporisation **6** Body keeping cool by using energy to vaporise body liquid as sweat
C

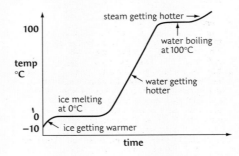

Expansion and contraction (page 71)
A 1 Gets bigger **2** Heating **3** Gets smaller **4** Cooling
B 1 a) Heat gives energy to particles; particles vibrate more; this pushes them apart **b)** Cooling removes energy from the particles; particles now less able to overcome forces of attraction; particles pulled closer together **c)** Heat needed to break strong bonds in solid, which liquid does not have; therefore liquid expands more **2** Gap is left so that the metal can expand in hot weather, without the gap the line buckles **3** Metal expands more than glass; hot water causes metal to expand away from glass; metal top is loosened **4** Gas expands; syringe pushed outwards; diagram as appropriate

C 1 Mercury in fixed volume; as temperature increases mercury particles move about more; volume increases and mercury moves up column in proportion to temperature increase; therefore can be used to measure temperature increase. Reverse process to measure fall in temperature.
2 Explanation centres on the contraction of the metal when it cools; this causes it to become very tight on the wooden wheel

The rock cycle (page 73)
A 1 a) Formed from cooling molten lava **b)** Formed by action of heat and pressure on igneous or sedimentary rocks **c)** Formed when pressure compacts the lower layers of sediment **2 a)** Rocks broken up/changed by attack from their surroundings **b)** Broken pieces of weathered rock; collects at bottom of cliffs **c)** Molten rock ejected from volcanoes during eruption **d)** Molten rock deep under the earth's crust
B 1 Wind, sea, rivers, streams, glacier movement, gravity, etc. **2** Physical beating, chemical attack, wearing down and smoothing, depositing, plant life, etc. **3** Lava → igneous → weathering → sediment → pressure → metamorphic → magma → lava, etc. **4** Igneous; all other rock types come from igneous
C a) Quartz (silicon dioxide) and feldspar (sodium aluminium silicate) **b)** Quartz, mica (silicates from silicon and oxygen), feldspar **c)** Quartz, carbonates such as sodium carbonate and calcium carbonate, various oxides of iron **d)** calcium carbonate

Chemical changes (page 75)
A 1 a) Material(s) that react together/take part in a chemical reaction **b)** Material(s) produced as a result of a chemical reaction **c)** Change that produces new materials/products and is difficult to reverse **d)** Activity undergone by atoms/molecules to bring about chemical change **e)** Total mass of products in a reaction is equal to total mass of reactants
B 1 Mass of marble chips = mass of lime and mass of carbon dioxide 50 g = x g + 22 g :x = 28 **2** Mass of magnesium + mass of oxygen = mass of magnesium oxide 24 g + x g = 40 g :x = 16 **3** New substances produced; change very difficult to reverse **4** Carbon dioxide lost to the atmosphere; this has mass which is unaccounted for **5** New substances (carbon dioxide, water, energy) produced; change not reversible **6** New substances (for instance, starch becomes sugar) produced; change not reversible
C 1 Answers should centre on not allowing any material used or produced to escape into the atmosphere **2** Most glass is made by heating together silicon dioxide (silica, sand), calcium carbonate and sodium carbonate at 1300–1400°C. Carbon dioxide gas is given off leaving a mixture of sodium silicate, calcium silicate and excess silica. This mixture is glass.

Word equations (page 77)
A 1 a) Material(s) that react together/take part in a chemical reaction **b)** Material(s) produced as a result of a chemical reaction **c)** Shortened way of saying what the reactants and products are in a chemical reaction **2 a)** Magnesium oxide **b)** Sodium chloride **c)** Copper sulphate, iron sulphate (nitrate or chloride could be used instead of sulphate) **d)** Zinc chloride, hydrogen
B 1 Names of reactant(s) and product(s) **2 a)** Magnesium hydroxide **b)** Sodium hydroxide **c)** Magnesium sulphate **3** Calcium oxide + water → calcium hydroxide (or water + calcium oxide) **4 a)** Calcium, water **b)** Hydrogen, calcium hydroxide **c)** Calcium + water → hydrogen + calcium hydroxide (or water + calcium) (or calcium hydroxide + hydrogen)
C 1 Food + oxygen → carbon dioxide + water + energy **2** Copper carbonate → copper oxide + carbon dioxide: (green powder) → (black powder) + (colourless gas lost to the atmosphere)

Types of reaction (page 79)
A 1 a) Gain of oxygen in a chemical change **b)** Chemical reaction in which a material burns in air/oxygen **c)** Breaking down of a material in a chemical reaction **2** Breaking down a material by heat

3 Chemical reaction in which two compounds break into halves and recombine with new 'partners'

B **1 a)** Magnesium carbonate → magnesium oxide + carbon dioxide **b)** Calcium + oxygen → calcium oxide **c)** Magnesium + steam → magnesium oxide + hydrogen **d)** Calcium chloride + sodium sulphate → calcium sulphate + sodium chloride **2** Because the food chain gains oxygen **3** Students will give the answer 'yes' or 'no' and support this with evidence and reasoning

C **1** Blue copper sulphate crystals become white copper sulphate powder because water is lost from within the crystal by heating; the crystal becomes anhydrous powder and the reaction is thermal decomposition **2** Synthesis is the making of a compound from its elements, e.g. sodium + chlorine → sodium chloride

Useful products (page 81)

A **1 a)** Rocks in the earth's crust **b)** Obtaining a metal from its ore by means of chemical reaction **c)** Long molecules; made from the joining of small molecules into chains **d)** Small molecule(s) joined together in chains to make polymers **2** Metals, fibres, plastics, glass, ceramics **3** See table in the text; there are other plastics not listed that would be acceptable

B **1** Roasting copper pyrites in air; see text **2** Haematite; see text **3** Sodium is a very reactive metal and therefore very difficult to extract from its ores; electrolysis must be used; see text

C **1** Ore: bauxite (aluminium oxide), method: electrolysis of a solution of bauxite dissolved in molten crystal (sodium aluminium fluoride) at about 900°C, word equation: aluminium oxide → aluminium + oxygen **2** PVC in polyvinyl chloride and is produced from the monomer vinyl chloride (now called chloroethene)

Not so useful products (page 83)

A **1 a)** Attack of a metal by chemicals in the air/atmosphere **b)** Corrosion of iron **c)** Mixing metals together **d)** Coating iron with zinc **e)** Wrapping food and then removing air from inside the sealed wrapping **f)** Keeping food cold **2** Exclude air and water from the metal **3** Exclude air and water from the metal

B **1** Alloying; expense **2** See text **3** See text **4** Lack of peel exposes flesh of apple to air; decay begins **5** More damp at the bottom where post enters ground

C **1** Experiment in the text using tap water will be done with distilled water and sea water and timings taken **2** Anodising is an electrolytic method of strengthening the oxide film that coats aluminium; to give extra protection

Energy from chemical reactions (page 85)

A **1 a)** Material that gives out energy when burned in air/oxygen **b)** Fuels formed from decaying plant and animal remains **c)** Production of gases in the atmosphere which cause the earth to retain heat **d)** Gas that contributes to the greenhouse effect

B **1** Rain that is acidic caused by the rain dissolving gases from the atmosphere as it falls; these gases form acids when in water **2** Fewer plants to take up carbon dioxide from the atmosphere; thus the amount of carbon dioxide in the atmosphere increases **3** Answers should centre on the increasing amount of waste and sewage in our present society **4** Electric vehicles, plants trees, ban coal fires, etc.

C **2** CFC: chlorofluorocarbon, use: coolant in fridges and freezers, effect on atmosphere: CFCs react with and remove ozone in the earth's upper atmosphere. This removal of ozone allows more ultra-violet radiation from the sun to reach the earth. This damages plants and produces a greater risk of skin cancer in human beings. CFCs are heavy gases and remain in the earth's atmosphere thus helping to keep heat in. This is called the greenhouse effect.

Metals in oxygen and water (page 87)

A **1 a)** Metal + oxygen → metal oxide **b)** Metal + water (steam) → metal oxide + hydrogen **c)** Metal + water → metal hydroxide + hydrogen **d)** Zinc + oxygen → zinc oxide **e)** Sodium + water → sodium hydroxide + hydrogen **f)** Magnesium + water (steam) → magnesium oxide + hydrogen

B **1** Potassium is more vigorous in its reactions than sodium **2** Zinc; evidence from text **3** Copper; evidence from text **4** Students will support their answers with evidence from the text; essentially X will react very slowly indeed, if at all, with cold water but quite well, not dangerously, with steam **5 a)** Copper oxide; by surface reaction of copper with oxygen from the air; copper + oxygen → copper oxide **b)** More black copper oxide will form; when the original black powder was scrapped off fresh copper was exposed which can react with oxygen

C **1** The experiments should include: burning both in air, zinc + oxygen → zinc oxide, heating both in steam, zinc + steam → zinc oxide + hydrogen, adding dilute acid to both, zinc + sulphuric acid → zinc sulphate + hydrogen The student should predict that in each case the powdered zinc will react quicker and more easily than the zinc block beacuse of the increased surface area **2 a)** Reacts easily with cold water with the reaction being treated with care as it could be violent, lithium + water → lithium hydroxide + hydrogen **b)** no reaction at all in either cold water or steam **c)** no reaction at all in either cold water or steam **d)** no reaction in cold water but reacts if heated in steam, aluminium + steam → aluminium oxide + hydrogen

Metals in acids and salts (page 89)

A **1 a)** Compound formed when hydrogen in acid replaced by metal **b)** When an element takes the place of another element in a compound **c)** Quick, instantaneous reaction **2 a)** Zinc (iron acceptable) **b)** Copper (silver, gold acceptable) **c)** Metals above copper, up to and including magnesium, in the reactivity series **d)** Metals below iron in the reactivity series

B **1 a)** Magnesium + sulphuric acid → magnesium sulphate + hydrogen **b)** Zinc + sulphuric acid → zinc sulphide + hydrogen **c)** Magnesium + zinc sulphate → magnesium sulphate + zinc **d)** Lead + copper chloride → lead chloride + copper **2 a)** Zinc sulphate **b)** Iron nitrate **c)** Magnesium chloride **3** Bubbles of a gas rising from the lead; solution remains clear; lead + nitric acid → lead nitrate + hydrogen

C The series of experiments could be one of: burning in air, reaction with water or steam, reaction with dilute acids. Students would be expected to describe how X, Y and Z could be investigated by one of these and then describe one of the others to back up their results. Better students may realise and explain that a series of reactions with dilute acids should not be performed first as some idea of the reactivity/danger of the metals needs to be obtained by reaction with either air or water.

The reactivity series (page 91)

A **1** Metals arranged in order of the ease with which they react; the most reactive are at the top **2 a)** Potassium **b)** Gold **c)** Copper, silver, gold **d)** Iron **e)** Magnesium **f)** Lead **g)** Copper, silver, gold

B **1 a)** Copper **b)** Magnesium sulphate **c)** Magnesium, zinc oxide **d)** Lead nitrate **2 a)** Zinc + lead nitrate → zinc nitrate + lead **b)** Lead + copper sulphate → lead sulphate + copper **c)** No reaction **d)** Magnesium + sulphuric acid → magnesium sulphate + hydrogen **e)** No reaction **f)** Copper + silver nitrate → copper nitrate + silver **g)** No reaction **h)** Copper + oxygen → copper oxide **i)** Iron oxide + zinc → zinc oxide + iron **j)** No reaction

C **1 a)** No reaction with water; beryllium + steam → beryllium oxide + hydrogen **b)** Beryllium + hydrochloric acid → beryllium chloride + hydrogen **c)** No reaction **d)** Beryllium + oxygen → beryllium oxide **e)** Beryllium + copper chloride → beryllium chloride + copper

Acids and alkalis (page 93)

A **1 a)** Indicators tell you, by changing colour, whether a solution is acidic or alkaline **b)** Solution which is neither acidic or alkaline **c)** Numerical measure of acidity and alkalinity; goes from 0 to 14 **2 a)** Red **b)** Blue **3** 0–14 **4** 4 to 6 **5** 11 to 14

B **1** 0 or 1; a strong acid as it is corrosive and dangerous **2** 4 to 6; it must be a weak acid if it is found in consumable food **3** Green; sugar solution is neutral; pH7 **4 a)** Red **b)** Purple **c)** Purple

C **1** pH II shows that the material is moderately alkaline. This can be tested with universal indicator. The information indicates how dangerous the material is and how much care needs to be exercised when using it. **2** Toothpaste is weakly alkaline to remove slightly acidic deposits on teeth.

Reactions of acids (page 95)

A **1 a)** Solution of pH less than 7 **b)** Oxides and hydroxides of metals **c)** Soluble base; solution of pH greater than 7 **d)** Reacting an acid with an alkali to make a solution that is neutral, i.e. pH exactly 7 **2 a)** Nitrates **b)** Phosphates **c)** Sulphates **d)** Carbonates

B **1 a)** Magnesium + sulphuric acid → magnesium sulphate + hydrogen **b)** Nitric acid + zinc carbonate → zinc nitrate + water + carbon dioxide **c)** Copper oxide + hydrochloric acid → copper chloride + water **2 a)** Zinc + sulphuric acid → zinc sulphate + hydrogen **b)** Magnesium + hydrochloric acid → magnesium chloride + hydrogen **3 a)** Calcium carbonate + nitric acid → calcium nitrate + water + carbon dioxide **b)** Potassium carbonate + sulphuric acid → potassium sulphate + water + carbon dioxide **4 a)** Aluminium oxide (or hydroxide) + nitric acid → aluminium nitrate + water **b)** calcium oxide (or hydroxide) + hydrochloric acid → calcium chloride + water **5** Alkalis are soluble bases and so all alkalis must be bases; not all bases dissolve in water and so not all bases can be alkalis

C If the solutions are of approximately equal strength, the volume of carbonic acid needed will be much greater because it is a weak acid whilst sodium hydroxide is a strong alkali.

Acids in everyday life (page 97)

A **1 a)** Soil with pH7 **b)** Acids produced by the body to react with food in the stomach **c)** Weathering of rocks by chemical reaction **2 a)** Peat; which is acidic **b)** Lime, which is alkaline **3** Carbon dioxide, sulphur dioxide, nitrogen oxide

B **1** To neutralise stomach acid **2** Because rain is acidic **3** Hair shampoos are usually slightly acidic; one way of making them so is to add dilute lemon juice preparation **4 a)** Bee stings are acidic; treat with mild alkali; calamine or bicarbonate **b)** Wasp stings are alkaline; treat with mild acid; vinegar, lemon juice **5** Acid gases are produced by emissions from various industrial processes; 100 years ago these processes and the resultant acidic gases were much less prevalent.

Answers for physics questions
pages 98 to 145

Static Electricity (page 99)

A **1 a)** Electricity made by rubbing things **b)** Centre of an atom **c)** Particle in the nucleus with a positive charge **d)** Tiny particle with a negative charge that orbits the nucleus **e)** Electrons flowing through a conductor **f)** Pushing away **2** Rub it with a cloth **3** It will pick them up

B **1 a)** Negative **b)** Negative **2** She gives her hair a charge when she combs it. All the pieces of hair have the same charge, so they repel each other. **3 a)** Electrons are transferred to the rod from the cloth **b)** Positive **c)** The same

C **1** Static electricity built up on the aeroplane might cause a spark which would make the fuel explode. The static can run along the wire without making a spark. **2** The object being sprayed is given a charge of static electricity, so the paint is attracted to it.

Electrical circuits (page 101)

A **1 a)** Something that produces electricity **b)** Two or more cells together **c)** Any part of a circuit except the wire **d)** Something that lets electricity go through it **e)** Something that does not let electricity go through it **2 a)** Plastic or wood or glass, etc **b)** Metal

B **1 a)** So they conduct electricity **b)** To stop people getting an electric shock **2 a)** See diagram on top left of page 101

b) See diagram on top right of page 101 **3 a)** A and C **b)** None **c)** Bulb 2 **4 a)** Series **b)** The broken bulb has made a gap in the circuit, so the electricity cannot flow **5 a)** Parallel **b)** If one breaks the other lights stay on

C

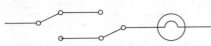

The light is on if both switches are up or both switches are down. If either switch is moved the light will go off

Changing the current (page 103)
A 1 a) Amount of electricity flowing **b)** Something that measures the current **c)** Component that makes it more difficult for electricity to flow **2** Amps
B 1 Change the voltage or number of components in the circuit **2 a)** Circuit diagram contains 2 cells and 1 bulb **b)** Circuit diagram contains 1 cell and 2 bulbs **3a)** 0.1A **b)** 0.2A **4** 0.1A **5** 0.8A and 0.4A
C It is a component whose resistance can be adjusted. It composes a coil of wire, a slider and a thick bar. When the slider is at one end of the coil the resistance is low as the electricity goes up through the slider and flows along the thick bar. When the slider is at the other end the electricity has to go all the way along the coiled wire, so the resistance is higher.

Magnetism (page 105)
A 1 a) Something that attracts iron **b)** Material attracted by a magnet **c)** Space around a magnet where it has an effect **d)** Magnet that is always magnetic **e)** Magnet made using electricity **f)** Iron bar inside an electromagnet **2** Anything made from iron, nickel or cobalt
B 1 a) To hold them closed **b)** Permanent magnets **2 a)** South pole on the left, north pole on the right **b)** They would attract each other **3** So the magnet can be turned off to drop the metal **4** Magnet will only attract the steel cans **5** So the electricity has to go along all the wire, and not jump from one coil to another
C The strength of a magnetic field decreases as you get further away from a magnet. If you can measure the force between a magnet and the steel of a ship, you can work out the thickness of paint between the magnet and the steel. The force is smaller if the paint is thick.

Using electromagnets (page 107)
A 1 a) Electrical switch that works by remote control **b)** Piece of magnetic material that is attracted by an electromagnet **c)** Coil of wire that acts as an electromagnet
B 1 So the driver does not have to touch the high current part of the circuit, and to reduce the amount of thick wire needed **2 a)** When the switch is pressed the electromagnet attracts the armature which moves and rings the bell **b)** To pull the armature back when the switch is released **3** Metal that can be magnetised easily and loses magnetism easily, because it has to become magnetic as soon as the electricity is switched on, and it must stop being magnetic as soon as the electricity is switched off
C 1 A coil of wire is attached to the loudspeaker cone. When the current in the wire changes it makes the cone move, which passes vibrations through air as sound waves. **2** The track has magnets in it, and the train has magnets arranged so that they repel the track. The train 'floats' above the track without touching it.

Forces (page 109)
A 1 a) A push or a pull **b)** Non-contact force that pulls down on things **c)** Force that can push or pull without touching **d)** Force that slows down moving things **e)** Friction between air and moving things **f)** Oil that reduces friction **2** Change the shape of things **3** Change the speed or direction of movement, or make things start or stop moving

B 1 Because some of the force from the pedals would be wasted pushing against friction in the axles **2** Tyres would not grip the road, and the car might skid and could not stop quickly **3** Because there will not be as much friction between their tyres and the road so they are more likely to skid and will take longer to stop
4

5 a) It will slow down **b)** Its speed will stay the same
C a) The rope is fed through a piece of metal attached to the person holding the rope. If the climber falls off there is a lot of friction between the rope and the metal, which slows the movement of the rope enough so that the person can hold it. **b)** If the rope was not stretchy a climber falling would stop suddenly if she fell. The stretch in the rope absorbs some of the force of the fall.

Levers and turning forces (page 111)
A 1 a) Piece of stiff material with a pivot, that can magnify forces **b)** Weight you are trying to move **c)** Force you put on a lever **d)** Distance the load moves **e)** Distance you have to move the lever **f)** Turning force **2** Moment = force x distance **3** Newton metres (Nm)
B 1 To give a bigger turning force **2** 1200 N **3** 6 m **4** Bolt cutters need to exert bigger forces, so they need longer handles to magnify the force.
C 1 Brake levers pull on the wires leading to the brakes. Brake callipers transfer this pull to the brake blocks and push them against the wheel rims. The handlebars are levers which help you to turn the front wheel. The pedals are on the ends of levers. **2** Your arms, legs and jaw are levers Most of the levers in your body magnify the distance moved, not the force.

Pressure (page 113)
A 1 a) Small force on a big area **b)** Big force on a small area **2** Pressure = force/area **3** N/m^2 or N/cm^2
B 1 Its weight is spread out over its tracks, so the pressure underneath it is low **2** There is high pressure under the point of the pin because all the force is concentrated **3** 1200 N/cm^2 **4 a)** $2m^2$ **b)** 250 N

Measuring speed (page 115)
A 1 Speed worked out from the total distance travelled and the total time taken **2** Speed = distance/time **3** Metres per second (m/s), miles per hour (mph), kilometres per hour (km/h)
B 1 6.7 m/s **2** 20 km/h **3 a)** 9 miles **b)** 6 hours **4** Too slow, because it will think you have not moved as far each second
C 1 a) If a wind is blowing, it will help the car in one direction but will be blowing against it when the car goes in the other direction. Making two runs cancels out the effect of the wind. **b)** Mach Number is the speed of something divided by the speed of sound Mach 1 is the speed of sound, Mach 2 is twice the speed of sound, etc. **2 a)** One knot is one nautical mile per hour. **b)** Ships used to measure speed by throwing a piece of wood over the side (a 'log'). The log would float on the water, and as the ship sailed away the log would pull a rope out. The sailors tied knots in regular intervals on the rope, and counted how many 'knots' were pulled out in a certain time.

Light (page 117)
A 1 a) Something that light can go through **b)** Something that light cannot go through **c)** Place where light cannot get to **d)** Something that produces light **e)** Light bouncing off something

B 1 Candle, fire, light bulb, etc. **2** Glass, perspex, water, windows etc. **3** 300 million m/s **4** Arrows should come from Sun and reflect off ball towards boys eyes
5 a)

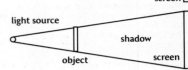

b)

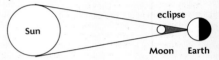

6 You cannot see the light itself. You can only see the light when some of it is reflected towards you by bouncing off a dust particle.
C a) A solar eclipse (an eclipse of the Sun) happens when the Earth goes into the shadow of the Moon. If you are watching from Earth the Sun will be blocked out by the Moon. A lunar eclipse happens when the Moon goes into the shadow of the Earth.
b)

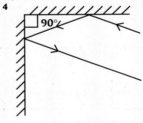

Mirrors (page 119)
A 1 a) Thing you see in a mirror **b)** Flat **c)** Beam of light **d)** Image that you cannot touch **2** See diagram on page 118
B 1 Doing your hair, looking behind in a car, dentists looking at teeth, submarines looking above the water, etc. **2** It looks the right way round when drivers see it in their mirrors **3** See diagram on page 118
4

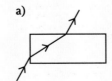

5 Only the parts of the waves that are exactly the right angle reflect the light into your eyes, and as the waves are moving all the time the reflections 'sparkle'
C 1 They are used in buses so the driver can see the top deck, and in shops to spot shoplifters **2** Concave mirrors make light beams converge to a point. In a reflecting telescope a plane mirror is used to send the converging rays to the eye lens.

Refraction (page 121)
A 1 a) Light bending **b)** Triangular piece of glass **c)** Mixture of 7 colours of light **d)** 7 colours of the rainbow
B 1 Red, orange, yellow, green, blue, indigo, violet **2** Thing we see when sunlight is split into its colours by drops of water in the air **3** Spectacles, binoculars, telescopes, microscopes, cameras, etc. **4** Prisms, CDs, water droplets, etc. **5 a)** Twice **b)** Blue
6

a)   b)

C A lens bends the blue light more than the red light, so if just one lens was used the colours in the photograph would not be correct. The effects of this 'chromatic aberration' can be removed by using lenses of different shapes next to each other.

Colour (page 123)
A 1 a) Light bouncing off something **b)** Light not reflecting **c)** Something that lets only one colour of light through **d)** Red, green and blue light **2** It reflects green light and absorbs all the other colours
B 1 It absorbs blue light and reflects green and red **2 a)** Only blue light is hitting it, so it can only reflect blue **b)** It can only reflect red light, but there is no red light hitting it so it does not reflect anything **3** It would look black, because there is no red light hitting it so it cannot reflect anything **4 a)** All three **b)** Red and green **c)** None of them
C There are two kinds of light 'detectors' at the back of our eyes. The 'cones' detect colours, but they only work when the light is fairly bright. The 'rods' work in dim light, but they do not detect colours.

Sound (page 125)
A 1 a) Backwards and forwards movement **b)** Completely empty place **c)** Noise made as lightning strikes through the air **2 a)** Strings **b)** Air inside the trumpet **c)** Air **d)** Top of the drum (the 'skin') **e)** Strings inside the piano
B 1 Talking, listening to music, etc. **2** 4 km **3** Because there is no air in space to pass on the sound waves **4** The air in one helmet makes the helmet itself vibrate, and the vibrations are passed on to the other helmet, and then to the air inside the helmet and to the astronaut's ears. **5** Light can travel through a vacuum but sound cannot
C They send out sounds and listen for the echoes

Loudness and pitch (page 127)
A 1 a) The size of the vibrations **b)** Electronic machine that converts sound waves into a wave on a screen **c)** Whether a sound is high or low **d)** Number of waves per second **e)** Units for frequency **2** Hertz
B 1 a) Large **b)** Large **2 a)** B **b)** It has the largest amplitude **3 a)** A lot **b)** High **4 a)** B **b)** It has the longest wavelength **5** 2 Hz
6

a)   b)

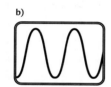

7 a) By plucking the strings harder **b)** They vibrate further for loud notes **c)** They vibrate faster for high notes
C a) They are different thicknesses **b)** Make it tighter or slacker, or make it shorter by putting your finger on it

Hearing sounds (page 129)
A 1 a) Flap of skin on the outside of your head **b)** Tube that leads to your eardrum **c)** Piece of skin that vibrates when sound waves hit it **d)** Where the ear bones are located **e)** Curled tube full of liquid that contains tiny hairs which detect vibrations **f)** Nerve that carries signals to the brain **2** Range of frequencies of sound that your ears can detect
B 1 A young person **2** Too much wax, glue ear **3** Very loud noises **4** Ear drum, ear bones, liquid in the cochlea **5** They warn people to protect their ears against loud noises **6** To protect people against playing the personal stereo too loudly and damaging their hearing **7** Semi-circular canals
C a) Sound that is too high for us to hear **b)** Machine sends ultrasound waves into the pregnant woman, and detects the sound reflected by the baby. The machine converts these echoes into a picture.

The Earth and the Sun (page 131)
A 1 a) Shaped like a football **b)** When it is light outside **c)** When it is dark outside **d)** Oval oath of planet around Sun **e)** Spring, summer, autumn and winter **2** Summer

B 1 Winter **2** Different stars in the sky if they travelled north or south; the bottom parts of ships disappeared first as they sailed away; people could sail around the Earth without falling off **3** Because we can't see all of the part of the Moon that is lit up by the Sun **4** When the North Pole is tilted towards the Sun the South Pole is tilted away from the Sun, so it is winter in countries (like Australia) that are near to the South Pole
C The Sun's rays are more spread out in the winter

The Solar System and the stars (page 133)
A 1 a) Sphere of hot gas, like our Sun **b)** Spheres made of rock or gas, that orbit around a star **c)** Length of time it takes a planet to spin once on its axis **d)** Length of time it takes a planet to orbit the Sun **e)** Sun and the nine planets **f)** Path a planet follows as it goes around the Sun **g)** Pattern of stars **2** Mercury, Venus, Earth, Mars, Jupiter, Saturn, Uranus, Neptune, Pluto
B 1 a) 365 days/1 year **b)** 24 hours/1 day **2** The Sun **3** They are much closer than the stars **4** Mercury It is closest to the Sun, so it does not have as far to go to complete one orbit (It also travels faster than the other planets) **5** Pluto: It is furthest from the Sun, so it does not get much heat from the Sun
C 1 Distance: It is the distance that light can travel in one year **2** Venus: It has an atmosphere with lots of carbon dioxide, which traps the Sun's heat (like a very strong 'greenhouse effect')

Gravity and orbits (page 135)
A 1 a) Force that attracts things to each other **b)** Amount of stuff something has **c)** Force of gravity pulling on a mass **d)** Something that orbits around the Earth or another planet **2 a)** Newtons **b)** Kilograms
B 1 Communications, taking pictures of the weather, making maps, or surveying other planets, etc. **2** Because it orbits the Earth but it has not been manufactured **3** The Earth's gravity **4** The other two bottles will be identical to the first **5 a)** 'Your mass is 50 kg' **b)** 500 N **6** It is less than the mass of the Earth **7** 'Mars' gravity is not strong enough to stop the air escaping into space
C a) An orbit that takes 24 hours, so that the satellite is always over the same place on the Earth. TV and communications satellites are put into this kind of orbit. **b)** An orbit that passes over the North and South Poles. A satellite in this kind of orbit can pass over all points of the Earth as the Earth turns, so it is useful for mapping or surveying.

Energy and machines (page 137)
A 1 a) Energy that moving things have **b)** Heat energy **c)** Energy carried by electricity **d)** Energy stored in food, fossil fuels and batteries **e)** Stored energy that things in high places have **f)** Energy stored in stretched things **g)** Energy stored inside atoms **2** e.g. **a)** Fire **b)** Radio **c)** Light bulb **3** e.g. **a)** Food **b)** Stone at the top of a cliff **c)** Stretched rubber band
B 1 a) Chemical → electrical → light **b)** Strain → kinetic **c)** Electrical → heat **d)** Chemical → electrical → kinetic and sound **2** e.g. **a)** Electric fire **b)** Battery powered toy car **c)** Electric fan
C a) 5 000 kJ **b)** 7 000 kJ **c)** 12 000 kJ **d)** 9 600 kJ **e)** 16 000 kJ **f)** 12 000 kJ Growing bodies need energy to grow; larger bodies need more energy than smaller bodies; active people need more energy than inactive ones; a mother who is breast feeding will need energy to produce milk.

Conservation of energy and energy resources (page 139)
A 1 a) Resource that will not run out **b)** Resource that will run out **2** Energy cannot be created or destroyed **3** Coal, oil, gas, nuclear **4** Wind energy and solar power
B 1 No, because it has to be made using other sources of energy **2 a)** 100 kJ **b)** It has heated the pan and the air in the kitchen **3 a)** 6000 J **b)** It has heated your body **4** It has been wasted mainly as heat in the engine, and some of this heat has spread out into the air. Some has been wasted as noise.

Non-renewable energy resources (page 141)
A 1 a) Coal, oil and gas, which are made from the remains of dead plants and animals **b)** Fuels that will run out **2** Coal, oil, gas, nuclear **3** Coal, oil and gas (the fossil fuels)
B 1 To reduce pollution and to make the remaining fuels last longer **2 a)** Nuclear **b)** Nuclear **3** We might find more sources, and we might not carry on using them at the same rate **4** Because we are using them up much faster than they are being formed
C Coal; mid 18th century, for running steam engines and heating houses. Oil; mid 19th century, for running vehicles and used in lamps. Gas; mid 20th century, for cooking and heating, and for generating electricity. Nuclear; mid 20th century, for generating electricity.

Renewable energy resources (page 143)
A 1 a) Any fuel that comes from living things **b)** Energy from the Sun **c)** Electricity generated using energy from falling water **d)** Energy from hot rocks underground **e)** Resource that will not run out
B 1 a) The Sun **b)** The Sun **c)** The Sun's energy evaporated water, which fell as rain. The rain that collected in the hills had potential energy which is used to generate electricity. **d)** Geothermal energy **2 a)** Wind, waves, solar, hydroelectricity **b)** Biomass, solar, geothermal **c)** Solar power **3** The carbon came from the atmosphere when the trees grew **4** Solar power, so they do not have to carry fuel with them
C Power stations fuelled by non-renewable sources of energy cannot easily be switched on and off, so they generate electricity even during the night when it is not needed. A pumped storage power station uses this electricity to pump water up into a lake or loch. When there is a sudden demand for electricity this water is allowed to fall down the hill again, and it drives turbines to generate electricity.

Temperature and energy (page 145)
A 1 a) Way of measuring how fast the particles in a substance are moving **b)** Amount of substance in something
B 1 Bucket B, because it is hotter **2** Mug, because there is more tea in it **3** Water, because it takes more energy to heat up water **4** Paddling pool, because there is less water to heat up so the temperature rises faster **5 a)** 3 200 J **b)** 8 800 J **c)** 24 000 J
C a) Scientists have worked out that all particles would stop moving altogether at a temperature of −273°C. You cannot get any colder than zero movement, so this temperature is called absolute zero, and is called 0°K (zero degrees Kelvin). The Kelvin temperature scale is used to measure temperatures relative to absolute zero. **b)** Melting point = 273°K, boiling point = 373°K

Index